CHICANO COMMUNISTS AND THE
STRUGGLE FOR SOCIAL JUSTICE

CHICANO
COMMUNISTS
AND THE STRUGGLE FOR SOCIAL JUSTICE

ENRIQUE M. BUELNA

THE UNIVERSITY OF
ARIZONA PRESS

TUCSON

The University of Arizona Press
www.uapress.arizona.edu

ISBN-13: 978-0-8165-3866-9 (cloth)
ISBN-13: 978-0-8165-4066-2 (paper)

Cover design by Carrie House, HOUSEdesign llc
Cover art by Enrique M. Buelna

Publication of this book is made possible in part by the proceeds of a permanent endowment created with the assistance of a Challenge Grant from the National Endowment for the Humanities, a federal agency.

Library of Congress Cataloging-in-Publication Data
Names: Buelna, Enrique M., author.
Title: Chicano communists and the struggle for social justice / Enrique M. Buelna.
Description: Tucson : The University of Arizona Press, 2019. | Includes bibliographical references and index.
Identifiers: LCCN 2018037379 | ISBN 9780816538669 (cloth : alk. paper)
Subjects: LCSH: Mexican American political activists—History. | Mexican American communists—History.
Classification: LCC E184.M5 B767 2018 | DDC 322.4068/72073—dc23 LC record available at https://lccn.loc.gov/2018037379

Printed in the United States of America
♾ This paper meets the requirements of ANSI/NISO Z39.48-1992 (Permanence of Paper).

To my parents,
Enrique and Lilia Buelna.
Their sacrifice and determination to succeed in the United States
made it possible for me to write this story.

And in memory of Ralph Cuarón,
1923–2002.

CONTENTS

ILLUSTRATIONS

PREFACE
The Gadflies

A S THE BODY OF Jesús Cruz lay in view at a funeral home in Tijuana, Mexico, two well-dressed men entered the room holding cameras. Before moving forward to observe the body, one of the men approached Celia Rodríguez, Jesús's niece, to confirm the identity of the deceased. What happened next caught many of those present by surprise. "They went up to the coffin and took a couple of pictures," Rodríguez recalled, "and [then] took off." She immediately suspected that these strangers were U.S. law enforcement agents—FBI, most probably. As Rodríguez surmised, these men had come that day in 1953, "I guess, to close the case."[1]

As far back as they could remember, Rodríguez and her sister, Julia, recalled that their uncle had been a radical activist. The miserable working conditions and treatment of the poor, and of Mexican Americans and immigrants in particular, informed his commitment to labor and community organizing. But that commitment meant that authorities would pursue him on a regular basis. And what made him ultimately a special target of the government was his membership in the Communist Party USA (CP). During the Great Depression, Cruz had helped organize the Workers Alliance of America in Los Angeles, a national grassroots effort that mobilized the unemployed to demand public relief, whether this meant employment, cash compensation, food, or an end to evictions. Through direct action—including mass mobilizations in the streets and confrontations with police—the Communists were most successful in wrenching concessions from relief offices.[2]

Rodríguez recalled the first time she and her sister, as young teenagers, joined their uncle in a protest at the local welfare office. The group, as she recalled, was "going to go to the welfare office and ask [administrators], politely, to pay people their rent when it was due." Anticipating intransigent officials, Cruz warned his nieces that the plan was to "stage a sit-in" and remain there until their demands were met. For Rodríguez, her uncle appeared larger than life, seemingly unafraid of the dangers of physical harm and of the legal consequences he could face. Fortunately, no violence occurred at their first protest that day. And in the end, the group managed to gain some actual concessions. The lesson of their experience could not have been clearer for the two siblings: for any change to happen, power had to be confronted head on—and without fear. "When people saw that it could be done," Rodríguez proudly recalled, "if you got together at one time, instead of just one [person] complaining, that sometimes, you could get things done." The courageous effort of this small group of intrepid activists was no small achievement, Rodríguez concluded. "It was a major force in the community."[3]

Almost thirty years after that encounter, another intrepid activist, Ralph Cuarón, was arrested and hauled off to jail in East Los Angeles for demanding that the local schools be accountable to the community they served. Cuarón was the parent of a student at Garfield High School and a longtime resident of the Eastside. And yet he was no ordinary citizen. Cuarón was a veteran of World War II, an activist in the Congress of Industrial Organizations (CIO), and, more significantly, a member of the Communist Party. His arrest, and subsequent trial, occurred in the midst of the largest urban protests by Mexican American students in the history of the United States at that time. The walkouts of 1968, in which close to twenty thousand students took to the streets, shook the community to its core and helped spark similar protest throughout the country.

At the height of the civil rights movement, Mexican American students, and entire communities, rose up to reject inferior schools and discriminatory policies. They had gained the courage to demand an end to segregation and to a system of dual tracking that denied them an opportunity to pursue higher educational goals. In fact, there was no shortage of problems in these schools, including high dropout rates, overcrowding, abysmal test scores, understaffing, belittling treatment by teachers and administrators, and educational materials that did not reflect the realities of Chicana/o students—the majority in these schools. But none of these issues mattered to the prosecuting attorney at the time, Reuben Ortega, who appeared intent on litigating the case against Cuarón on a strict reading of the law. Accordingly, the history of community activism to resolve these long-standing and volatile issues at the high schools mattered little: the prosecutor readily dismissed it as *irrelevant*.

Throughout the trial, Ortega disparaged Cuarón's efforts, portraying them simply as disruptive, disrespectful, and self-serving. Incensed by the direct actions employed by the students, not only did the district attorney attempt to blame "forces outside the school," he was also loath to make any connection in the case to the issue of racial discrimination.[4] In fact, he used his own ethnicity in an attempt to deflect that charge: "I happen to be a Mexican myself," Ortega assured the jury. "I don't think that [racism] makes any difference whatsoever."[5] Ortega was able to convince the jury that the defendants, including student witnesses who had been active in the walkouts, were volatile figures—each with a penchant for defiance of authority. Hence, from the perspective of the government, protest, of any sort, was illegitimate and unnecessary. "Can't we solve these things peacefully?" Ortega pleaded with the court. "Do we have to go into the principal's office, taking over the place, keeping him there for two hours, students out of class, I really don't think so."[6] In the end, the prosecution painted a picture that undermined the sense of urgency in the actions of the defendants. In other words, there was no rational reason to have been present on school grounds that day. Therefore, the tumultuous protests surrounding the schools in 1968 were nothing more than a circus of ungrateful children taking advantage to have a day off from school.

Both Ralph Cuarón and Jesús Cruz were considered public enemies by the state precisely because they dared to question and directly confront the status quo. The charge of disturbing the peace and resisting arrest, so readily dispensed by authorities, was par for the course for these indefatigable radicals. And like Cruz, Cuarón was hounded by authorities for many years as a result of his civic militancy. In fact, Cuarón and his wife, Sylvia, had been under surveillance by the FBI for over two decades for their seemingly dangerous and subversive activities. And contrary to the prosecuting attorney's assertions, the issue of race *was* absolutely critical to the activism of these individuals. Mexican Americans and Mexican immigrants had long been victimized by racist policies and restrictive social norms dating back to the mid-nineteenth century. It was not uncommon for this population to experience extrajudicial killings, illegal property seizures, segregation, voting rights violations (poll taxes, literacy tests, gerrymandering), employment discrimination, dual wage systems, and miscegenation laws, just to name a few. For the Communist Party, capitalism in the United States thrived not only on class exploitation but also on race exclusivity. This explains, in part, why the party invested time and resources in the struggle for civil rights. As was the case for African American activism within the party, Mexican American Communists took leading roles to help free their communities from the devastating effects of class and race exploitation. And significant historical events like the Great Depression and World War II were pivotal in motivating a new generation of activists ready to take on the barriers to equality. Cuarón and Cruz, then, represented the radical threads of advocacy who were determined—no matter how long it took—to achieve equality, first-class citizenship, and self-determination.

I chose to examine Mexican American participation in the Communist Party because not enough has been written about their contributions to the struggle for civil rights. Their presence in the literature and in the archives is ubiquitous, but not enough emerges on the details of their individual lives and on their choice to join this provocative organization. What the evidence does reveal is that these supposedly doctrinaire apparatchiks were more complex in their political and social views than the dogmatic anti-Communists have made them out to be. Despite the rigid—and often contradictory—nature of the party, many members remained free to approach local issues in more pragmatic ways. Mexican American Communists, like Cuarón, struggled to protect and enhance cultural, linguistic, and historic rights as they addressed community grievances and as they sought greater influence within the confines of the CP. They understood the central role of class struggle, but they were not willing to abandon their identity outright.

The overall image that arises from my examination of this radical activism is one of determined struggle to be counted in American society. And more than just the right to be seen. These radicals hoped that one day Mexican Americans would achieve equality among their citizen peers—that they, too, would have a place at the table. The acclaimed poet Langston Hughes expressed this sentiment eloquently in his poem "I, Too." In it, Hughes (whose work was frequently published in journals and press of the CP) recognized that he was an American, yet acknowledged that his country did not treat him as such. But he was also hopeful for a future in which he was present, as a whole and complete person, in a more inclusive America. Mexican Americans inside the party—and out—have struggled for this recognition, and the struggle has not ended.

Despite the overwhelming presence of Latinos in the United States today, this population is still largely ignored by mainstream America. When some media outlets (English language, specifically) do shift their gaze toward Latinos, and Mexican Americans in particular, the imagery and the discourse continue to represent this population as *outsiders*—foreigners in their own land. In effect, Latino Americans are often lumped together with immigrants—seamlessly bound and with little regard for their status and long history of contributions to American society. Discussions and debates generally revolve around issues of immigration, crime, gangs, educational deficiencies, language problems, poverty, and, more importantly, economic destabilization. Furthermore, this latter issue remains particularly contentious, especially during episodes of economic downturn. Rather than focus on the economic opportunities and cultural richness that Latinos contribute to the nation, discussions often devolve into harangues about job stealing—again, discussions generally devoid of meaningful and historic context. So, it should come as no surprise that when some Americans suddenly *discover* that Latinos now stand as the nation's largest ethnic or racial minority, they shriek in fear of *takeover* and loss of national, cultural integrity. And with the U.S. Census Bureau estimating that Latinos will represent almost a third of the national population by 2060, the reaction, in some circles, reaches levels of hysteria.[7]

The 2016 presidential campaign saw the rise of this hysteria yet again. Most alarming was the manner in which Mexican Americans, immigrants, and Muslims became political fodder, and how little recrimination befell its principal enthusiast—candidate at the time and now president—Donald Trump. Examples include his forceful removal of renowned reporter and writer Jorge Ramos at a press conference and his criticism of U.S. District Judge Gonzalo P. Curiel because of his Mexican heritage. According to Trump, the Indiana-born judge could not be trusted to be impartial in a lawsuit against Trump University because his ties to Mexico were too strong—and this conflicted with Trump's plans to build a border wall.[8] When Trump touted the success of President Dwight Eisenhower's deportation program of 1954, he did so not understanding that this episode stands as a shameful moment in American history.

At a major speech on immigration in Phoenix, Arizona, two months before the presidential election, Trump repeated his assertion that thirty million undocumented were living in our midst—a claim that was wildly inflated and uniformly discredited at the time. The speech was filled with vituperation as he conflated the undocumented with murderers, gang members, welfare abusers, and drug and gun smugglers. Indeed, from the standpoint of the speech, the undocumented had no redeeming value for American society whatsoever. As expected, Trump stayed the course and classified this population as a mammoth threat to our national security and economic stability. Without a doubt, Trump argued, undocumented immigration remains the "greatest challenge facing our country today." To confront this challenge, he proposed a deportation program that would remove these "criminal aliens" once and for all. Furthermore, Trump promised his enthusiastic supporters that on his first day in office he would commence construction of a border wall.[9] As my father, who is now eighty-five years old, watched the electoral pandemonium unfold, he could hardly believe what he was witnessing. He could never have imagined that he might live to see another nightmare that is mass deportation.

When my parents immigrated to the United States in the mid- to late 1950s, they did so in the wake of one of the largest efforts in U.S. immigration law enforcement since the Great Depression. Through aggressive measures that included expanded raids, roundups, roadblocks, indiscriminate interrogations, detentions as well as targeted campaigns such as Operation Wetback, the U.S. Border Patrol recorded over one million apprehensions of undocumented immigrants (largely Mexican citizens) between July 1953 and June 1954. The fear and uncertainty unleased by U.S. immigration law enforcement affected not only immigrant communities but also Mexican Americans with whom they remained closely tied. In 1954, my father, Enrique Buelna Echeverria, was an immigration officer for the Mexican government and was stationed in Nogales, Sonora, across from the Arizona border. He witnessed the deportation of thousands of hapless victims who understood little of the process that had ripped them away from their families, their homes, and their communities. My father eventually resigned his post out of profound disappointment over his government's failure to protect its citizens who had entered the United States without authorization as well as those working lawfully under the Bracero Program. My parents are now naturalized U.S. citizens, but they remain indelibly linked to the communities that Trump has vilified and has increasingly forced into the margins.

Beginning in early 2017, the administration stepped up its arrests of undocumented immigrants, including the removal of those who were brought to the United States as children. President Barack Obama had created the Deferred Action for Childhood Arrivals program (DACA) in 2012 to protect these young immigrants who came to this country through no choice of their own. Under DACA, these DREAMers, as they are called, were protected from deportation if they qualified for and fulfilled the necessary conditions under the policy. In addition, these young people were obligated to apply every two years with the federal government to be allowed to stay and receive work permits. But their status was never guaranteed.[10] Despite Trump's tepid public pronouncements that he would maintain DACA, he rescinded the program in September 2017. In a decision that defies logic, the lives of approximately eight hundred thousand young Americans were placed in jeopardy; their future uncertain, they were urged by their government to prepare for departure from the only country they had known.

The bluster emanating from the administration regarding stepped-up arrests, detentions, border walls, family separations, denaturalization as well as talk about ending family reunification (what detractors call "chain migration"), and indecision over DACA have caused profound anxiety for millions of families—citizens and noncitizens alike. Not surprisingly, many undocumented, mixed-status families, unaccompanied minors, and their extended support networks have been engrossed in a frenzied process of preparing for an uncertain future: maintaining low profiles and making plans in the event that family members are whisked away. There is little doubt that the principal victims will, again, be *American* children (born or raised in the United States)—a generation that will be stunted and lost because of the shortsighted whims of ignorance, prejudice, and fear. And yes, Mexican Americans, and Latinos in general, will be forced to revisit this cyclical history in which some cling to the view that this population—whether American-born or not—are outsiders and unfit to be Americans.

In spite of this portentous backdrop, I draw inspiration from the millions who have stood up time and again to defend our constitutionally protected rights as well as our democratic ideals. I look to the life of Ralph Cuarón, and those who embarked on similar paths, and take encouragement from a veteran activist who struggled against incredible odds, and who succeeded more times than not. At the height of McCarthyism, Cuarón refused to be intimidated and challenged power directly, regardless of the risks. And in the waning years of his career, he remained actively engaged in the struggle for equality, social justice, and self-determination, always driven to settle the indelible *Mexican question*: What role should Mexican Americans play in the larger scope of working-class struggle and revolution? Or, more simply, what place does this population have in American society? Though the answer to this set of queries would still lie ahead for Cuarón, the strategy to get there remained the same—*organize*. Only through persistent and sustained agitation in the home, in the streets, and in the halls of power, Cuarón would argue, can communities be restored and become forces for change. And as he would readily attest, nothing produces more change, moves more mountains, than the constant, irritating noise of a gadfly.

ACKNOWLEDGMENTS

FIRST AND FOREMOST, I want to acknowledge Ralph and Sylvia Cuarón for sharing their most precious memories with me and for allowing me to share them with the world. Ralph passed away in 2002 and was laid to rest at the Riverside National Cemetery in California. I have since remained close to Sylvia, who has been instrumental in clarifying the details of their lives. The stories that she shares are truly remarkable, but these are also emotional memories. It goes without saying that I owe my deepest appreciation to Sylvia and her children—Mita, Ralph Jr., Adel, and Fernando—who have been so patient in waiting for me to finally complete this story.

But there are many others who also need to be acknowledged for sharing their stories and memories with me: Steve Valencia, Albert Valencia, Sal Castro, Harry Gamboa, Celia Rodríguez, Julia Luna Mount and George Mount, Dorothy Healey, Carlos Montes, Edna Bonacich, Jim Smith, Enrique Buelna Echeverria, Gerome Salgado, Kevin Akin, Leland Lubinsky, and Frank Wilkinson. I am grateful to each one of these individuals for having taken the time to meet with me and share their memories; their participation was essential in bringing this story to life.

I wish to give special recognition to an old friend and mentor who passed away early in his life: Jeffrey M. Garcílazo. Jeff was instrumental in recruiting me to the graduate program at UC Irvine, guiding my studies, and introducing me to the Cuarón family.

This book would not have been possible without the support of the faculty at UC Irvine, who first reviewed this work many years ago and who provided me with exceptional mentorship, encouragement, and insightful criticism. Gilbert G. González was especially supportive during my early years in the graduate program and helped guide my studies and research. I appreciated those many talks in his office in which we discussed research, current events, and campus-wide politics. I want to thank Jonathan Wiener, who also helped inspire my intellectual pursuits. I enjoyed his classes very much, and his humor and wit were wonderful. And, finally, I want to thank Vicki L. Ruiz, who was the chair of my dissertation committee. With her guidance and first-rate editing, Vicki moved my work to a whole new level. She has not only been an inspiration to me, but was instrumental in opening publishing as well as career opportunities.

There are several institutions and archival collections that must be recognized for aiding my research for this project. I owe a great debt to the professional and volunteer staff of the Southern California Library for Social Studies and Research in Los Angeles—Sarah Cooper, Mary Tyler, Alexis Moreno, Chester Murray, Jenny Chynoweth, Teri Robertson, and Michele Welsing. It was in this library that I first discovered Ralph Cuarón's image dating back to 1948 and the campaign to elect Henry A. Wallace for president. The library remained a treasure trove of material that kept me working at this site for several years. Especially helpful were the CPUSA Collection, Civil Rights Congress Collection, Independent Progressive Party Archives, Edward Mosk Manuscript Collection, Robert W. Kenny Collection, Los Angeles Committee for Protection of Foreign Born (1950s–1960s) Collection, and the Pamphlet Files. Other important historical resources included the Carey McWilliams Archives, University of California, Los Angeles; the El Expectador Collection, the Josefina Fierro oral history interview by Albert Camarillo, 1995, and the Ernesto Galarza Papers, Stanford University; the Dorothy Healey Collection, California State University, Long Beach; the Clinton Jenks Papers, Arizona State University; and the CPUSA Collection, Library of Congress. Exceedingly helpful in my research were records of the reporting and surveillance conducted by the U.S. Department of Justice, Federal Bureau of Investigation. In 2005, through a Freedom of Information/Privacy Act request, I obtained the files for Ralph Cuarón and Sylvia Lucas Cuarón. The details were quite revealing, as they provided an impressive array of details about their activism and the degree of paranoia that so characterized anti-Communism in America.

I will always be grateful for the support given to me by the Chicana/o Studies Department at California State University, Northridge. I am especially indebted to Juana Mora, Mary Pardo, and Gerald Resendez. Through their support I was able to teach at CSU Northridge for several years. Juana Mora deserves special mention for helping me be selected for the California State University Chancellor's Doctoral Incentive Program.

This book took longer to complete partly because I began to teach full-time at Cabrillo College. In addition to our teaching, the faculty are also very involved in the day-to-day running of the institution—always innovating, always trying to make the educational experience that much better for the students that come to our campus. I am grateful for the support given me to continuously improve my teaching as well as the encouragement provided to all instructors to engage in academic enrichment. When I presented a paper in 2016 at the Third Bi-Annual Sal Castro Memorial Conference, hosted by UC Santa Barbara, the faculty in attendance was highly supportive of my work and encouraged me to get the manuscript published. That boost of confidence went a long way. Mario T. García was especially helpful by encouraging me to send the work out to publishers right away. I am immensely grateful for his support.

I cannot ignore other important individuals who have been sources of inspiration and important figures in my intellectual and professional pursuits: Alberto Garcia, Zaragosa Vargas, and Rodolfo F. Acuña. Alberto's many stories about his struggles to support democratic transition in Nicaragua impressed me immensely, and I am proud to have been one of his students. Zaragosa was a key mentor, who early on challenged me to be a better scholar, provided me with supportive feedback on my work, encouraged me to continue writing, and planted the seed for graduate study. Rudy's work, of course, was instrumental in developing my interest in history. His defiant stance against those who would neglect the contributions of Mexican Americans gave me the courage to question—and even to raise my fist in the air when the situation called for it. Later, he would provide guidance in my career path and academic pursuits.

And, finally, I am most indebted to my family. My wife, Elizabeth, has been especially supportive and patient during this long and arduous process. I do not know how I would have completed this work without her. To my daughter, Citlallin, and son, Teomah, who for many years have had to deal with me shut away in my office, reading and typing, and with the "Do Not Disturb" sign on the door—thank you for your patience. I would like to recognize my parents,

Enrique and Lilia Buelna, whose own immigrant experience from Mexico to the United States has been a great inspiration to me and to our entire family. My academic achievements and determination to succeed came directly from their sacrifices, their struggle to make it in a new country. I owe them a great debt. And finally, I feel fortunate for the support and love of my three brothers, Carlos, Rafael, and Gabriel, and their beautiful and still growing families. Gabriel deserves special mention, as he has been an important guide and confidant in our parallel journeys through the maze of academia and politics.

CHICANO COMMUNISTS AND THE STRUGGLE FOR SOCIAL JUSTICE

INTRODUCTION

Making Noise

But you are speaking to a man [Ralph Cuarón] who was instrumental in buck-ing a lot of the leadership of the [Communist] Party; not per se to knock it down but to educate the party itself on the need to organize Mexican American youth.
—Sylvia Cuarón, 1998

WHEN I FIRST MET Ralph Cuarón in 1998, he was seventy-five years old, staunchly defiant, and proud of his life's accomplishments. Despite having suffered a debilitating stroke that same year, Cuarón possessed a sharp wit and vivid memory. Sylvia, his wife and lifelong partner of almost fifty years, often felt frustrated that she could not accurately describe in words the person that Ralph had once been. But where details might fail her, she possessed a flair for the poetic and an urgency to get the story out. "The Ralph you see here today," she pressed, "is but a shell of the man he used to be." And in the course of our many interviews, there was one word she occasionally used to characterize her spouse, and which captured my attention—"gadfly." As the picture of Cuarón's life came into focus, I began to understand Sylvia's use of this intriguing word. Burned into her memory was the life of an individual habitually engaged in provocative criticism of social and economic inequality. Still, more than being a persistent and irritating critic as the word implies, Cuarón made it his lifelong mission to organize others to act on their own behalf. In different capacities, he engaged with young people to help them realize their true potential, always with the underlying goal of unleashing this energy on the world. He also hoped that this energy would be used in the pur-suit of building grassroots communities, with the ultimate goal of laying the foundations for a better world.

Ralph Cuarón was a product of the 1930s and the Left social movements that grew out of the Great Depression. For Cuarón, it was the Communist Party that ignited his passion to engage with social justice issues on behalf of the working class. Indeed, that passion led him toward a lifelong commitment to organizing. Filipino labor activist and writer Carlos Bulosan once wrote of his experience in a 1930 lettuce strike: "From this day onward my life became one long conspiracy. . . . I was so intensely fired by this dream of a better America that I had completely forgotten myself."[1] Cuarón came of age at a time of profound instability and uncertainty during the 1930s and early 1940s. He was swept up in a labor movement that he heartily embraced and made it his mission to spread. As Cuarón explained, "I had the advantage of having gained a greater worldview. . . . I understood why workers were in rebellion; in defense of their rights. . . . The Communist Party was supporting the movement, the worker. I understood, so I sympathized with them. . . . My history, my life, was a history of working-class support."[2] After returning home in 1946 from service in the U.S. Merchant Marine, Cuarón was ready to battle against structural inequality and discrimination. Like Carlos Bulosan, Cuarón's conspiracy was about to begin.

This study examines Mexican American labor activism between 1930 and 1970 in Southern California through the life of Ralph Cuarón, a member of the CP and an activist in the Congress of Industrial Organizations (CIO). Not unlike the life of labor and community activist Bert Corona, Cuarón exemplified what Mario T. García describes as "oppositional" struggle. That is, not only did Cuarón oppose social injustice, he also opposed "an American historical narrative that has excluded the roles, struggles, and even contradictions [contributions] of diverse racial and ethnic groups such as Mexican-Americans from the making of American history."[3] Cuarón represented a generation that took the mantle of leadership in this period as a personal challenge to better the economic and political conditions of this community. Yet, his project was not so narrowly defined that it excluded all but Mexican Americans. In fact, Cuarón's primary concern was the plight of the *working class*—regardless of race, ethnicity, and gender. He joined the CP because of its belief in the potential of the common laborer to transform society and make it more democratic and egalitarian.

Cuarón was not typical of the leadership in the Mexican American community in Los Angeles. By the mid-1930s, Mexican Americans were estimated at over two hundred thousand, or 16 percent of the city's total population.[4] Relatively few within this large community joined the CP. Indeed, according to one estimate, the total Mexican American membership may have hovered just over four hundred during this decade.[5] Regardless of the exact numbers, the lives of many Mexicans were influenced by the activities of the CP through organizations such as the International Labor Defense, Workers Alliance, and of course through their union activities, especially in the CIO.[6] This low rate of participation by Mexican Americans, however, may have had more to do with internal conflicts within the CP than with the desire of this group to join.

Despite the CP's claim that it welcomed all equally into its fold, it had problems. Prejudices based on race, ethnicity, and gender were not always cast aside. The fact that CP officials did not consistently regard Mexican Americans as on an equal plane with African Americans remained a sore point with Cuarón and other Mexican American activists. A theoretical rigidity led the party to identify African Americans as a key component in the ultimate demise of American imperialism, and this resulted in the belief that this population mattered above all others. The end result was that the party did not recognize Mexican Americans as central to its broader goals; they were simply viewed as a transient population, devoid of meaningful history and, for some, not worth the effort. As the record shows, however, time and again Mexican Americans refused to be marginalized within the party. In the streets and within the party's bureaucracy, Mexican Americans struggled to define a place for themselves.

Mexican Americans did manage to challenge the exclusivity of the "Negro question"—the party's doctrine outlining black liberation and self-determination—with its own countervailing position, appropriately titled the "Mexican question." The demand from this group was clear: Mexican American rights would not be subsumed beneath the rights of other groups. More importantly, Mexican Americans were also claiming that they had cultural and linguistic rights as well as a history every bit as legitimate as that of any other group. And by comparison, their history could be traced back to before the conquest of the Americas and, indeed, to a story of settlement before the founding of the United States itself. Nevertheless, the struggle by this population to achieve greater recognition and equal status with other cadres never fully succeeded. Despite the drawbacks, Mexican Americans did have influence within the CP and, more importantly, in their communities—where it mattered most.

The critique of the CP by Cuarón and fellow cadre members was at times jarring, as they did not shy away from questioning the obligations of top party brass. Still, some party leaders as well as rank-and-file members persistently failed to address the long-standing grievance that outreach and recruitment in poor and Mexican communities remained inconsistent and lacked commitment. In response, and at various times in his career as a CP member, Cuarón moved ahead of party directives, or he challenged them outright. He often asserted that party leaders were disconnected from the lives of average workers and regularly accused them of behaving in a manner that was distant, patronizing, and contemptuous—especially toward those not in the inner circles of organizational power. As this issue surfaced time and again, Cuarón brazenly denounced this cadre as *elitist*—a very serious charge, no doubt. With a dogged determination, and a flare for the dramatic, Cuarón chided any semblance of authoritarianism, even when it surfaced from the CP headquarters in New York. This picture of the CP as an organization characterized by complexity and contradictions has not been uniformly accepted within academia. Therefore, competing interpretations of American Communism persist.[7]

The historiography of Communism in the United States remains, as Maurice Isserman wrote over thirty years ago, "contested terrain."[8] The view of the CP as an appendage of the Soviet Union, as subservient and dogmatic, has long characterized anti-Communist scholarship. Theodore Draper set the tone in his 1957 work *Roots of American Communism*, in which he painted a picture of an organization hopelessly influenced by Soviet directives and unable to maintain an independent course. Half a century later, this rendering of the CP remains largely intact.[9] For example, John Earl Haynes and Harvey Klehr continue this traditional historical interpretation, and assail their revisionist colleagues for propagating a mythologized view of the CP.[10] In contrast, my study fits within a more multifaceted and nuanced historiography of U.S. social movements. The large body of literature produced by such scholars as Isserman, Bruce Nelson, Robin D. J. Kelley, Gerald Horne, Ellen Schrecker, Judith Stephan-Norris, Maurice Zeitlin, and numerous others provides a fascinating look at the contributions Communists have made to labor militancy, racial justice, and democracy. Nevertheless, this literature has not *denied* the real problems that plagued the CP. As Isserman explains, "the Communist party was, undeniably, an authoritarian organization that valued its members' discipline as the most potent weapon in its political arsenal."[11] And Cuarón certainly experienced this rigidity firsthand. Yet, despite its weaknesses and contradictions, the CP remained, for many of its members, a dynamic and evolving political organization. Therefore, we should also view the CP as an organization engaged "in the process of *becoming*."[12]

For some in the Mexican American and immigrant community, the CP was an important organization raising the political consciousness of workers. Douglas Monroy, for example, emphasizes the important contributions the CP made to early labor struggles among Mexicans in Los Angeles. Indeed, during the 1930s and 1940s, the CP took risks in helping to organize workers that few others dared. "For better or for worse," writes Monroy, "radicals in the United States, Mexican and Anglo, exposed them to working-class consciousness and organized them into working-class associations." The unions, and the radicals within them, therefore, provided Mexicans with "structural integration" into the United States.[13] And yet, as George Sánchez explains, the significance of the Communists to this community goes even further. The CP proved to be one of many Americanizing agents—a vehicle through which Mexican immigrants and their children were exposed to "American politics in the New Deal era."[14] This second generation, the children born in the United States of immigrant parents, were especially influenced by this exposure as they strove for changes in a country they identified as their own. Similarly, Ralph Cuarón's identity was forged by his experiences in the Depression, and by his interaction with the CP. When he became a member of the party during World War II, he joined because it promised racial equality and worker solidarity. But he would remain loyal to the organization even through its most difficult periods, because of its determined pursuit of these goals where it mattered most—in the streets of East Los Angeles.

This attraction to the Communist Party, and the impressive fealty of its members, remains intriguing. Why did some Mexican Americans join a marginalized political group that carried with it such inherent risks? Zaragosa Vargas sheds some light on this question in his examination of Tejana radical Emma Tenayuca. After several years of working to organize Mexican laborers in the 1930s, she came to believe that the "workplace required radical revision to achieve equity," and she joined the CP "because no one else but the communists expressed any interest in helping San Antonio's dispossessed Mexicans."[15] Labor organizer Luisa Moreno also joined the CP out of a profound commitment to change the conditions under which so many workers toiled. As Vicki L. Ruiz reminds us, "Moreno cultivated rank-and-file leadership as she fostered a sense of communal investment among workers as union members." She remained committed to Marxism despite leaving the party in 1935.[16] In his examination of the Asociación Nacional México-Americana (Mexican American National Association), for example, García describes the role of Mexican

American Communists as largely *reformist*, and certainly not subversive. These were activists "who had inherited an organic Mexican-American radical tradition and who, owing to their involvement in CIO organizing efforts, had found in the Communist Party a militant and supportive ally in the struggle to achieve democratic rights."[17]

When I asked Sylvia Cuarón if she felt any obligation to Moscow as a result of their involvement with the CP, she politely smiled and answered, "No." "This was East L.A.," she patiently reminded me. "This was our world." Their concerns, therefore, remained largely centered on local issues such as police brutality, labor rights, housing, and education.[18] Nevertheless, as important as local issues were to the Cuaróns, their desire to have an impact beyond the confines of Los Angeles was just as important.

Party members understood that they were part and parcel of an international movement, united under compelling slogans such as "Workers of the world, unite!" They readily accepted and took pride in an expansive brotherhood and sisterhood engaged in a struggle to end oppression everywhere. Indeed, the Cuaróns had become exposed to a set of values and ideals that helped situate their lives within this broader context. Therefore, they could see their community activism on the local level as seamlessly connected to an international movement for democracy and equality. This consciousness translated to a number of projects that included outreach across national boundaries. In 1948, for example, in the months leading up to the presidential election, Cuarón helped organize an event to celebrate labor solidarity between the United States and Mexico. The success of this event led to an invitation and subsequent three-day visit by members of the U.S. Progressive Party to a polytechnic institute in Tijuana, Mexico.

By the early 1950s, Cuarón and fellow activists were engaged in numerous activities to bring attention to the plight of immigrants unfairly targeted for deportation, including helping to organize the Los Angeles Committee for Protection of Foreign Born. In 1954, the FBI, having opened files on the Cuaróns, was investigating the couples' interest in Guatemala. The Cuaróns had made plans to visit the Central American country to assess, for themselves, the growing pressure by right-wing forces against the popular government of Jacobo Árbenz. But their plans were derailed when a military coup, engineered by the United States, toppled the government in Guatemala City. From their perspective, the Cold War was now intensifying and the forces of democracy were reeling from the pressure. Despite the ravages that the McCarthy era would impose on Left and progressive associations during this period, it did not dampen the Cuaróns' resolve to continue forward. By the start of the civil rights movement, they were prepared to entrust their knowledge to a new, and receptive, audience of young people ready to take on the world.

The social and political unrest that took place in the sixties did not come as a complete surprise to the Cuaróns. They had been heavily invested in the struggle for racial and class equality all their lives and therefore understood the yearning of this new generation for change. What was surprising, however, was the spirited energy and intensity that young people across the country demonstrated as they challenged the cultural standards of their parents, especially with respect to racial segregation, military intervention in Vietnam, materialism, women's rights, sexual mores, and the meaning of American democracy. Equally exciting for the Cuaróns was the added energy that young Chicanas and Chicanos gave to what historians call El Movimiento—The Movement. These young people, coming from the nation's barrios, not only demanded self-determination and a place at the table, they also challenged the very nature of their identity and place in history.

The Cuaróns, as did so many parents and community activists, welcomed this new spirit of rebellion and helped support and inspire these youths. Indeed, they reveled in the triumphs that resulted from the challenges against the schools, police, courts, political parties, and a host of other institutions that had for so long ignored and closed their doors to their communities. At the heart of these challenges, Marc Simon Rodriguez reminds us, was also a deep desire for "self-defense and self-protection." "Rather than anti-Americanism, this was a new, more militant form of Mexican Americanism."[19] And, as the War on Poverty programs invited ordinary people to engage in antipoverty activism, these communities responded by forging their own notions of economic, cultural, and political empowerment. In effect, this was *Americanism* in its purest form.[20] The challenge would now lie in sustaining these victories for the long haul. By the time I got to meet Ralph and Sylvia Cuarón, their activism had long passed. But as I sat at their kitchen table listening and recording their stories, those memories were as vivid and alive as if they had happened only yesterday.

Beginning in 1998, I made numerous trips out to Riverside, California. It seemed that in each visit something new was revealed about this remarkable couple. By this time, Sylvia was Ralph's primary caretaker, as he had already experienced a debilitating stroke and was diabetic. They lived in a modest apartment off Blaine Street, just minutes away from the University of California campus, where Ralph had last worked. It never mattered how pressed I was for time; Sylvia always had a way of drawing visitors in and making them feel like old friends. In fact, I came to understand why so many regarded the Cuarón home as a place of refuge, a family away from home. And I never left their apartment without something in hand: either food, a neatly folded article from a newspaper, or a book from their modest library. No matter how much I objected, they were adamant that giving things away, especially books, was important to them. By the time I met them, their library was largely gone.

In addition to their collection of books, I recall a handmade artifact hanging near the kitchen that always caught my attention. The art piece was the Star of David, completely covered in sequins, and in the colors of the Mexican flag—green, white, and red. Sylvia was proud of the art and always gazed at it lovingly. It seemed to signify the cultural harmony and complexity of this radical couple. Sylvia and Ralph were not religious, but the artifact appeared to represent a kind of juxtaposition or yearning for unity that bound their desire for cultural diversity and harmony—*humanistic relationships*, they would say. Sylvia's family is Jewish, but she could never fully accept the rigidity or absolutism she experienced in her religion growing up. And Ralph's experience with his Catholic faith was not that different. But that little art piece may have also expressed hopefulness: for unity and identity that helped give added meaning to their relationship as a couple, and to the lives of their children who were, clearly, a mix of both worlds.

This story of Chicano Communists is a quintessential American one and is absolutely relevant to our understanding of who we are as a nation. In their study of Southern California's largest metropolis, the authors of *The Next Los Angeles* remind us that in order to truly understand a place, we must expunge the vestiges of "historical amnesia." We cannot understand contemporary Los Angeles, for example, while neglecting "the intersection of race and community politics." Indeed, "by analyzing the political evolution of key individuals, we can understand how people shape movements as well as how movements shape the beliefs and values of their participants."[21] The Cuaróns and their radical compatriots are, without a doubt, part of a long tradition of Mexican American activism dating back over 160 years, since the end of the U.S.-Mexico War. Their lives exemplify the self-sacrifice of individuals ready to set aside personal ambitions for the greater good of society. They are examples of courageous individuals, of the sort that renderings of our nation's history have failed to identify among Mexican Americans, and Latinos in general. Their story helps fill an important gap in the historiography of radical activism, a story, largely, of the common folk who periodically rise up to demand their rightful place in American society. The Mexican American Left played a critical role, not only in organizing and providing a voice for this community, but by forcing the larger public to recognize Mexicans as *Americans*, as equal participants in the national polity. Ralph Cuarón's story sheds some light on the Communist Party, and also on the diverse approaches Mexican Americans took in their struggle to attain equality and first-class citizenship. For his part, Cuarón joined the CP not because of any romantic notions or wishful thinking about an egalitarian future. He cared profoundly about democracy and its promises of liberty, equality, and justice for all, and took part in radical activism out of a concern for the welfare of others. But in doing so, he did not leave behind his individual and ethnic identity. For Cuarón, then, the CP represented a vehicle—albeit an imperfect one—for achieving community-wide goals. While some party members experienced a loss of autonomy, organizational rigidity, and bureaucratic suffocation, Cuarón experienced *liberation*. Indeed, he acquired a new language with which to understand the depressed conditions of his community and how to challenge them. Henceforth, he made it his mission to make plain the contradictions of capitalism. But was Cuarón an unwitting dupe of the Soviet Union and, hence, a threat to national security? Hardly. Cuarón did not advocate the violent overthrow of the U.S. government, but he did work diligently to provoke activism among workers so that they might have a greater say over their lives. Ultimately, he believed in passionate persuasion in the hope of ushering in a shift toward revolutionary consciousness.

Historians and social scientists have only begun to scratch the surface of this rich history. The researchers who have studied this period of working-class activism have shed considerable light, yet much remains to be investigated. The intent of this book is to revise and add to this complex history of radical working-class activism by focusing on the life of Ralph Cuarón and those who worked alongside him as members of the Communist Party USA. Nevertheless, it is also crucial to situate this experience within the rich and complex history of activism that was already present—already fully conscious of its grander mission to bring about change and making certain that Mexican Americans were out front and helping to lead it.

Unlike some activists during this period, Ralph Cuarón was a lifelong member of the CP. This activism made him a very significant and visible Mexican

American CP leader in the twentieth century, but one whose legacy has been all but forgotten. Despite the repression unleashed by the Cold War, Cuarón remained actively engaged in developing leadership and political consciousness among Mexican Americans. The resurgent activism of the 1960s was, therefore, not cut off from its earlier roots. On the contrary, those roots, those strands of memory, were the fundamental building blocks that helped propel student activism and the Chicano Movement to new heights.

Since Ralph's death in 2002, Sylvia and I have continued to collaborate and to share our family's lives. Now in her nineties, Sylvia remains sharp, but time has taken its toll. There is no doubt that although the focus of this book is on Ralph, Sylvia played an important role. Throughout, I have made certain to include her, as she was present in every major decision in their family's journey. Even at this stage in her life, she continues to be rebellious in her own way. In 2011, I wrote down notes from a conversation I had with her. I have had countless conversations since then, but on this particular occasion, it exemplified her spirit, her zeal for life. On that day, she recounted a wonderful experience she had after reading a book by novelist and political activist Émile Zola. Her new mantra, she proudly proclaimed, was: "If you ask me what I came into this life to do, I will tell you: I came to live out loud." She didn't say as much that day, but I understood that she still wanted to live her life to the fullest, despite the obvious physical limitations. Sylvia wanted to let me know that if she had to depart this world, then she wanted to leave it with the full knowledge that she hadn't wasted a single moment. In her own way, she was telling the world that she refused to be silenced even now, and that she still wanted to make some noise.

1

FINDING THE MOVEMENT

It was easy for me to me to understand the persecution of the Mexican through an understanding of class struggle. It was very easy for me to understand my own suffering that I had endured as a child—the impoverishment and persecution as a young Mexican youth. So I gobbled it all up. My life was my education into Communism. And quickly I saw Communism as my way out of impoverishment and persecution. I believed it.
—Ralph Cuarón, 1998

ALPH CUARÓN CAME OF AGE at a time of profound instability and uncertainty during the 1930s and early 1940s. The Great Depression had turned the world upside down for millions of Americans—it was a period when traditions and old bonds were stretched to their limits. In her study of workers in Chicago, for example, Lizbeth Cohen writes that the loss of faith in "traditional organizations and authority figures—the ethnic leader, the priest, the boss, the father—created a crisis. Where should one turn now for protection and to ensure a future for one's family?"[1] For many Latinos, this question became increasingly urgent as the economic downturn further intensified their marginal status in American society.

Cuarón witnessed the selfless sacrifices made by his eldest sister and his mother as they struggled to sustain the family. That struggle became increasing difficult as his father's earning power deteriorated with every passing year. The mass deportations and repatriation drive that expelled tens of thousands in Los Angeles alone did not make life any easier for the Cuaróns, but they managed to survive the ordeal. By mid-decade, estimates show that the city lost up to one-third of its Mexican community.[2] Francisco Balderrama and Raymond Rodríguez argue that the exact numbers will never be known because census counts were inaccurate, as were the estimates of undocumented immigrants. Given the available data, the number of repatriated individuals nationwide probably reached as high as one million by the end of the 1930s. The devastating experience of persistent unemployment, harassment by public officials, and the antipathy of the general public forced many Mexicans to uproot families, abandon homes, and leave communities behind to take their chances in Mexico.[3] For those U.S. citizens among the uprooted (the majority of the repatriates), the experience was filled with that much more foreboding and angst as they moved to a country they hardly knew. These events remained seared in Cuarón's memory and shaped the contours of his political and social identity.

Throughout the country, responses to the economic crisis varied. Many, for instance, chose to retreat inside themselves, to take personal blame for their predicament. Others chose to perceive this crisis as proof of a failed system that could not be saved. Still others chose to organize, to take proactive measures to protect themselves from the ravages of an unstable economy and unscrupulous employers. Cuarón would come to embrace the latter choice.

Cuarón joined the Communist Party of the United States in 1942, at age nineteen, and never looked back. From our very first meeting in 1998, Cuarón expressed a firm and unequivocal belief in the correctness of his political choices. But why would a Mexican American, already facing discrimination, join an organization that itself was considered foreign, fringe, and worse yet, anti-American? As Benjamin Márquez explains, "what may seem to be a wrong-headed course of action to an outside observer could be a carefully considered long-term strategy guided by an informed analysis of U.S. race relations."[4] Cuarón became exposed to class struggle and to the politics of race from Communists and other leftists of varying ethnic backgrounds. He learned from them the advantages of multiethnic organizing.[5] Informed by a "revolutionary identity," Cuarón came to believe, as Márquez further explains, that Mexican Americans were "a working-class people whose interests lie in remaking the free-market system in order to achieve a more democratic and egalitarian society."[6] Hence, for Cuarón, joining the movement came to represent a journey of self-discovery and, above all, a moral imperative.

In 1888, Rafael and Geronima Ramos, and their two-year-old daughter, Micaela, immigrated to the United States from the state of Chihuahua, Mexico, eventually settling in the town of Morenci, Arizona. Their migratory route was not unique, writes Rodolfo Acuña, as thousands made a similar trek north in the wake of tremendous changes underway in Mexico. As the ruling oligarchy intensified their control over land, water, and politics (developments taking shape since midcentury), Mexican families had little choice but to move in search of better opportunities. Moreover, natural disasters such as droughts that affected the region periodically complicated the precarious existence of subsistence farmers and sharecroppers, who relied on rainfall. As the elite expanded the market economy and extended the reach of the railroads, the lives of average Mexicans became more insecure. When the Ramos family crossed the border, they were following a familiar path taken by their Chihuahua compatriots: a movement of people through the Camino Real and Mesilla corridors that led to extensive mining operations and expanding agricultural fields. Rafael Ramos was an experienced miner and, not long after arriving, gained employment with the Arizona Copper Company. But life in the Clifton-Morenci-Metcalf area was anything but ideal.[7]

Geronima Ramos maintained the home, which included managing the sparse household budget and caring for a total of nine children. She supplemented the family income by taking in boarders and selling homemade food items to local families. Additionally, Geronima produced her own "home brew," probably extracted from corn, from a still located beneath the house.[8] With opportunities for work limited to laboring as maids, cooks, or seamstresses, many women remained at home to help support their families. Restricted family incomes, strenuous mine and smelter schedules, poor housing, and neglect by civic authorities placed great burdens on these families. As Acuña notes, "the mines shaped women's work," which meant that most of their time was spent preparing food, fetching and heating water, cleaning clothes, caring for children, and growing whatever food they could to supplement their meager earnings.[9] These conditions were exacerbated by racist attitudes and beliefs held by Anglo Americans that relegated Mexican Americans to outsider status: a foreign race, regardless of citizenship. In addition, the idea that Mexicans possessed low morals, practiced poor hygiene, and spread diseases only worsened their degraded position, and further justified their neglect and abuse. In the mines, the exploitation of the Mexican workers often led to periodic revolts, which plunged entire families and communities into the struggle.[10] Yet, despite these obstructions, Mexican women carved out social spaces for their families and communities. These women, for example, planned, raised money, cooked, sewed, and decorated for baptisms, communions, weddings, and funerals. Through these activities, they helped build community bonds that all depended on.[11] A decade after the arrival of the Ramos family, and on the eve of the Mexican Revolution, Jesús Cuarón, another native of Chihuahua, left his parents' ranch in Ciudad Juárez (across from El Paso, Texas), entered the United States, and made his way to Morenci.

Jesús Cuarón left his home not as a direct result of the political turmoil engulfing his country of birth, but because of a disagreement with his parents over his future. After acquiring skills in carpentry, he hoped to apply his chosen craft outside the family ranch. But when his father refused, outright, to consider his son's plans, Jesús decided to leave. Not long after arriving in Morenci, he, too, found work in the mines, and in the employ of the Phelps Dodge Company. With Phelps Dodge being the most powerful company in town, in control of all copper mining and manufacturing, Jesús had few options. As Linda Gordon points out, by 1904 every resident served the copper industry directly or indirectly.[12] Sometime between 1905 and 1906, Geronima Ramos took Jesús Cuarón into her home as a lodger. Shortly thereafter, a relationship developed between Cuarón and Micaela, the eldest Ramos daughter. The couple eventually married, and in 1907 they had their first child, Margarita. After a few years of backbreaking work and with few opportunities for advancement, Jesús left the mines to venture out on his own.

Despite his skills, Jesús struggled to find work. Morenci and nearby Clifton were successful settlements, but largely the product of mining and related industries. Indeed, Morenci was, as Gordon describes, less of a town and "more a bunk for workers at the mines, mills, and smelter."[13] In addition to his carpentry skills, Jesús crafted string instruments such as violins and guitars. Jesús eventually found work in town as a piano player, of sorts, in the local "honky-tonk" bars. In addition, he also crafted and repaired musical instruments on a contract basis.[14] The change in employment not only opened the possibility of higher wages, but allowed for greater control over the pace and conditions of his work. It was also during this period, however, that Jesús began to drink heavily, a problem that would eat away at his health and affect his ability to work. By the early 1920s, Jesús resolved to leave Morenci altogether.[15]

Like many Mexicans in Arizona during this period, the Cuaróns decided that Los Angeles offered them the best opportunities for their economic future. "Los Angeles, for Mexicans as for others," explains Sánchez, "promised at least the possibility of a greater range of choice, possibly higher pay, and certainly a more exciting environment than many rural locals."[16] Ralph recalled that his father valued his independence as a skilled craftsman. "He never wanted to work out as a wage earner and work for somebody else."[17] In 1923, the Cuaróns— Geronima (the matriarch of the Ramos family) and her youngest children, Petra, Guadalupe, Rosa, and Carlos—moved to Los Angeles.

The move to the bustling metropolis could not have occurred at a more propitious time. The period 1910–30 saw great industrial and commercial expansion in Los Angeles, which directly affected the economic conditions of countless Mexican families.[18] As businesses moved beyond the central district, so too did Mexican Americans and new immigrants. By 1930, Mexicans accounted for 97,116 of the city's total population of 1,238,048. Soon, Mexican residents in Los Angeles outgrew those of San Antonio, Texas. And together with its county residents, the city would boast a Mexican population that rivaled "all but a few cities in Mexico."[19] Statewide, this population reached 368,013, with almost 200,000, or 52 percent, having been born outside the country. Significantly, almost two-thirds lived in urban communities.[20] However, this city of the future belonged, undeniably, in the hands of its Anglo-Saxon citizens. Therefore, Mexicans were tolerated largely as a workforce—expendable and inconsequential. The "racial logic" was clear for many of the region's prosperous businesses, such as the Simons Brick Company: "More Mexicans meant more workers. More workers meant more bricks. More bricks meant more money."[21]

As Mexican families increasingly took up residence in urban areas during the early 1920s, public health officials, writes Natalia Molina, felt challenged by the rapidly growing Mexican population. In fact, this community, including people of Japanese and Chinese ancestry, was identified as a significant threat to public health and civic well-being. White officials believed that this "foreign" population was the source of communicable diseases such as typhus and tuberculosis and, therefore, a danger to the health and welfare of the city's white residents. Rather than identifying structural factors such as access to clean water, sanitary waste disposal, medical care, malnutrition, poverty, low wages, segregation, and discrimination—they blamed the victims. Not surprisingly, Molina reminds us, linking Mexican communities to disease and "pathologizing Mexican culture" had a long history in the United States.[22] For the Cuarón family, however, the machinations of city health officials were secondary, if that, as they strove to survive and scratch out new lives for themselves in this modern metropolis.

The Cuaróns moved into a house located on North Gage Avenue in the hills south of City Terrace.[23] Since 1910, this community had become home to a large segment of the Orthodox Jewish population in the city.[24] And it was here that the family's third child, Rafael (Ralph), was born in October 1923. During this period, Jesús opened up a cabinet shop in the community of Boyle Heights, near the intersection of Boyle Avenue and Olympic Boulevard.[25] Despite Jesús's best efforts, the family business continually failed to generate sufficient income to support the household; he was struggling against economic forces beyond his control. Local as well as national furniture manufacturers had largely replaced the need for skilled craftsmen in the case of goods such as cabinets, chairs, and tables.[26] With Los Angeles a center for furniture manufacturing, it is not surprising that small, independent businesses could not compete. Still, in the early 1920s, the area around the shop remained a hub of expanding economic activity, and the Cuaróns hoped that business would eventually pick up.[27]

By mid-decade, the family's economic situation had improved, but probably not in a manner that Jesús would have imagined. Despite the family's economic situation, Jesús refused to allow Micaela to earn additional income through wage labor. Jesús appeared to be in step with his fellow countrymen in regard to traditional gender roles. The sexual division of labor was firmly engrained in the minds of many Mexican immigrant men: they expected women to remain at home and stay clear of work in the public sphere.[28] On the other hand, his influence over the lives of his children was more precarious. They, more than their first-generation parents, seemed adept at maneuvering the city's mainstream culture, language, and urban landscape. Certainly, their acculturation to American society allowed them some advantage in navigating across divergent cultural worlds.[29] In time, the older children secured employment, and their ability to generate income helped keep the family financially afloat. Economic necessity compelled Margarita, the eldest daughter, to seek employment outside the home, and very likely without the consent of her father. As Cuarón remembered, his father played a minimal role in his life and those of his siblings.[30] Soon, Margarita's salary would become more than supplementary income for the family; they would come to depend on it.[31]

When Margarita, now in her late teens, secured employment with the Diamond Walnut Company, she became, in effect, the family's primary income earner.[32] Margarita worked as a sheller at the factory, located downtown on Seventh Street near Alameda, earning approximately five to ten dollars a week. According to Cuarón, "that's what we survived on."[33] The conditions in these factories included long workdays, continuous repetitive motion, and demeaning employee-management relations. Reflecting on her experiences later in the decade, labor activist Julia Luna Mount described the corrupt and humiliating hiring practices by factory foremen. "Mostly, the men would come out and hire those ladies that they liked, the ladies that they could pinch in the butt" and "pat on the shoulder."[34] Indeed, a significant number of the industrial operatives in the city's expanding food processing plants were young, often single, Mexican immigrants and Mexican American women. Employers preferred to hire these women, hoping to capitalize on wage differentials based on race and gender (which placed Mexican women at or near the bottom of the pay scale) as well as on their inexperience and financial need. Though Ralph's recollection of Margarita's salary is not exact, it does conform to the $2.30 and $2.70 per day average wage paid to Mexican women employed in the canneries and packing houses at the time.[35] Margarita also sorted the walnuts and did so often without the use of gloves to protect her hands. As a result, her hands and fingers remained callused.[36] Despite her efforts to keep the family afloat, however, the family periodically failed to meet its financial obligations, such as paying the rent. The onslaught of the Great Depression in 1929 exacerbated matters further, as Mexican families, along with millions of other Americans, struggled with unemployment and hunger.

The Cuaróns moved periodically as they tried to situate themselves closer to the family business; but they also struggled to secure affordable housing. Cuarón recalled that the move away from their house in City Terrace, just prior to the outbreak of the Depression, was to an enclave popularly referred to as "El Hoyo" (the hole). This new home was located near Soto Street and Whittier Boulevard—a settlement he described as being little more than a "Mexican ghetto" nestled in a ravine.[37] As the economic conditions worsened, Cuarón remembered vividly that his family periodically had to scavenge for food and rely on the generosity of strangers to help fill their stomachs.

> I remember I had made a little wagon. My grandmother would then take me in the wagon and we would go to the central market by Alameda Street in downtown Los Angeles. We would pick up fruit and bits and pieces of vegetables in the garbage cans and bring them home. My grandmother would then buy a beef bone for a nickel and cook up a big bowl of soup.[38]

By 1930, and after several other changes of address, the Cuaróns moved in with Anita Ramos, one of Micaela's siblings. Two years later, the family finally moved to a house located in the Belvedere neighborhood of unincorporated East Los Angeles.

Once again, Margarita proved instrumental in supporting the family through its most challenging periods. Cuarón recalled that his father began to spend long stretches of time away from the family—often days on end. He worked at his rented garage on Seventh Street, near Euclid, where he stored his tools and "fabricated his little work as he earned his own living. He contributed nothing to us." It was through Margarita that Cuarón and his other siblings kept in contact with their father. "My sister, Margaret, would take us to his garage, once or twice a week to visit my father, to make sure he didn't forget us."[39] Through the assistance of Margarita's good friend Lupe Medina, the family moved to a home located at 3720 Princeton Street. Medina had purchased the house and allowed the Cuaróns to reside in the small, detached structure located in the back of the property. Micaela remained at this address, rent free, until her death in 1972.

Medina may have been a trailblazer, Cuarón recalled, as one of the first Mexican Americans to purchase a home on this block, in a neighborhood still considered exclusively white.[40] Despite her meager earnings from cleaning railroad cars for the Pullman Company, Medina had managed to save enough money to purchase the home on her own.[41] Even though some neighbors attempted to drive the family out, Medina and the Cuaróns refused to be intimidated; they held fast to their piece of the American dream.[42] The purchase of a home by Mexican Americans and Mexican immigrants symbolized more than a financial investment: it also represented an act of empowerment—taking control and claiming their rights while putting down roots and rearing their families.[43] Not only were the two families linked through friendship and living arrangements, they were also bound by a common desire to be respected members of the community.

In spite of the family's precarious finances, Cuarón's immediate world—as an adolescent—seemed filled with adventure and fascination. He had fond memories of growing up on Princeton Street, where he spent much of his time with schoolmates and neighborhood friends investigating local streets, adjacent neighborhoods, abandoned buildings, and empty railroad cars. He remembered selling newspapers on Alameda Street and Olympic Boulevard in the warehouse district below the towering Sears Roebuck store.[44] Eager to earn more money selling papers, Ralph expanded his area of operation by including more businesses in his daily route. And yet, in the midst of all the activity that filled the streets with people and the shops with eager customers, another reality loomed just beneath the surface—severe unemployment and poverty.

In Los Angeles, the unemployment rate soared. When the Mexican consular inspector, Enrique A. González, visited the area in 1931, the unemployment rate among Mexican families hovered between 20 and 50 percent.[45] Cuarón recalled the high concentration of unemployed men that congregated on street corners and in alleyways.

The men who hung around there, we called them "depression men," "idle men," men who worked a little in the day and some who didn't work at all. And they just hung around and threw pennies. They flipped pennies in a game whereby the one who got closest to a line would win everybody's pennies. And, so, every night there was some cause for interest on the corner. And, there was a lot of talk . . . a lot of talk about politics and other things. So, it was very, very interesting to me.[46]

As the nation sank deeper into economic depression, the nativism that characterized the 1920s became translated into public policy.[47] Mexican immigrants increasingly became the targets of scapegoating for the ills befalling the nation. In California, the "Mexican problem" was given particular attention by Governor C. C. Young in a special report titled "Mexicans in California," compiled by the Mexican Fact-Finding Committee in 1930. Despite an attempt at impartiality, the governor as well as the chair of the Fact-Finding Committee liberally sprinkled the preface and introduction with the phrases "Mexican problem" and "Mexican immigration problems."[48] As Carey McWilliams noted, references to Mexicans and Mexican immigration as dilemmas for American society were hardly new. The volumes of data collected on this population between 1920 and 1930 focused attention on the "social consequences of Mexican immigration," namely, delinquency, poor housing, low wages, illiteracy, and rates of disease. McWilliams noted the ramifications of such social science research:

> Mexicans lacked leadership, discipline, and organization; that they segregated themselves; that they were lacking in thrift and enterprise, and so forth. A mountainous collection of masters' theses "proved" conclusively that Spanish-speaking children were "retarded" because, on the basis of various so-called intellectual tests, they did not measure up to the intellectual caliber of Anglo-American students.[49]

Furthermore, Mexicans were not only a burden on the nation's overtaxed social and political institutions, they represented a potential danger to the genetic composition of the nation itself.

By the early twentieth century, the study of human races had developed into a serious academic discipline in several countries, including the United States, Canada, and many European countries. This new area of inquiry became known as *eugenics*. "Practically speaking," explains Nancy Leys Stepan, "eugenics encouraged the scientific and 'rational' management of the hereditary makeup of the human species." In fact, "it also introduced new social ideas and innovative policies of potentially explosive social force—such as the deliberate social selection against supposedly "unfit" individuals, including involuntary surgical sterilization."[50] In the United States, Mexicans as well as other groups became subjects of legitimate inquiry.

While eugenics theory in Mexico had, by the 1920s and early 1930s, largely elevated *indigenismo* (an appreciation of the contributions of Indian cultures) and *mestizaje* (racial amalgamation) as vital national elements in Mexican life, proponents of eugenics in the United States had come to view Mexicans— examples of "racial hybridization"—as anathema.[51] Racist commentaries, without the mask of scientific theory, were routinely treated as admissible evidence before governmental bodies. In 1930, for example, Dr. Roy L. Garis of Vanderbilt University—an authority on eugenics—included the following comments by "an American" living in the border region as evidence to illustrate the *real* concern over unrestricted immigration to this country.

> Their [the Mexicans'] minds run to nothing higher than animal functions—eat, sleep, and sexual debauchery. In every huddle of Mexican shacks, one meets the same idleness, hordes of hungry dogs, and filthy children with faces plastered with flies, disease, lice, human filth, stench, promiscuous fornication, bastardy, lounging, apathetic peons and lazy squaws, beans and dried chili, liquor, general squalor, and envy and hatred of the gringo. These people sleep by day and prowl by night like coyotes; stealing anything they can get their hands on, no matter how useless to them it may be. Nothing left outside is safe unless padlocked or chained down. Yet there are Americans clamoring for more of this human swine to be brought over from Mexico.[52]

In California, too, there was no shortage of vitriol, as numerous individuals, civic groups, public leaders, and government agencies lashed out against this population—regardless of citizenship status.[53] As the urgency to thwart race degeneracy increased, sterilization became an important tool in population control. Demonizing Mexicans as "oversexed, procreating families in excess of the 'normal' size of responsible citizens," writes Alexandra M. Stern, led this group to be disproportionately selected for sterilization. California eugenicists not only led the country in the number of all such operations, they were also at the forefront of the national movement to expel foreigners and undesirables.[54]

The clamor to expel "foreigners" from the country had become a famil-iar response in times of economic trouble. And the economic downturn that afflicted the nation after 1929 was markedly more severe than at any previous time. With American citizens put out of work in the millions, the focus on Mexican Americans and Mexican immigrants as undeserving outsiders became more acute.[55] This population had undergone significant demographic changes by the 1930s. According to the U.S. Census Bureau, Mexicans represented a total of 1,422,533 (619,998 foreign born and 805,535 native born).[56] In Los Angeles County alone, the Mexican population officially numbered 167,024 out of a total population of 2,190,738.[57] Gilbert G. González notes that the number may have been as high as 200,000.[58] Therefore, when the deportation and repatriation drives began in earnest in 1931, the results were, to say the least, devastating. Approximately five hundred thousand to one million Mexicans, nationwide, would be repatriated by the end of the decade.[59] The city of Los Angeles, with an official Mexican population count of 97,116, would lose some 35,000 individuals (a conservative estimate), or one-third of this community.[60]

Surprisingly, many of those directly affected by the Depression could not, or would not, respond critically to the economic system.[61] As some observers have noted, the thirties were not marked by any radical surge to the left by the general populous. On the contrary, most Americans viewed the crisis as a national disaster, with consequences outside of their control. As Studs Ter-kel explained, "Being unemployed seems to have been experienced more often as a humiliation than as evidence of class exploitation. A matter of personal fault."[62] Thus, the few voices that did speak out against these conditions were often perceived as misguided and irrational, voices pursuing *dreams* rather than *reality*. And, yet, these voices in the margins of American society began to have resonance for many who searched for answers. The Communist Party of the United States emerged as a visible contender for the hearts and minds of the American people.

In some respects, 1929 represented a rebirth, of sorts, for the CP. After a decade of internal strife, coupled with heightened repression from local, state, and federal authorities, the party came into its own, settling on a unified strat-egy as capitalism seemed on the brink of collapse.[63] The CP had moved away from its policy of *boring from within* established unions, such as the American Federation of Labor (AFL), to organizing revolutionary unions under the rubric of the Communist-led Trade Union Unity League (TUUL).[64] With slightly over ninety-six hundred members in 1929, the party launched a number of initiatives during the first half of the decade that generally helped broaden its appeal.[65] For example, it led mass demonstrations for unemployment relief and coordinated those efforts with the Young Communist League, TUUL, and the national Unemployed Councils. According to William Z. Foster, long-time union organizer and national party leader, "Among the mobilizing slogans were 'Work or Wages!' and 'Don't Starve—Fight!'"[66] The Unemployed Councils worked directly with communities, in neighborhoods, and in people's homes. As Foster explained,

> The councils fought for unemployment insurance, immediate cash and work relief, public work at union wages, food for school children, against eviction, against Negro discrimination, and so on. They used mass meetings, parades, petitions, picketing, hunger marches, and many other forms of agitation and struggle; they formed block committees to organize the workers in their homes.[67]

Despite the observations by some that a significant number of Americans were resigned to accept their fate during the Depression, many others were not. "The inadequacy of public relief," writes Fraser Ottanelli, "as well as the worsening of the depression generated a determination among many jobless not to suffer hardship passively, but to adopt radical, if not political, solutions to their problem."[68] Furthermore, the CP's unwavering commitment to defend and organize minority groups placed it in a unique position among radical mass organizations at the time.

Did the Communists pose a genuine threat to the nation by organizing communities of color? According to the director of the FBI, J. Edgar Hoover, the answer was yes. Hoover routinely railed against the CP for its involvement in civil rights work on behalf of African Americans and Mexicans, which he described simply as "alleged discrimination that is being perpetrated against them in national defense industries, the armed forces, etcetera."[69] He argued that the Communists were simply using these issues, especially the issue of racial integration, as a deception to sow division and dissension. "They [the Communists]," Hoover asserted, "serve to arouse people and to cause tension."[70]

The CP made great strides among African American communities, in particular, and made the concept of *self-determination* a centerpiece of their efforts. "One of the greatest achievements of the Communist Party during the big economic crisis," wrote Foster, "was its penetration of the South."[71] In an interview with Studs Terkel, William L. Patterson, a longtime African American civil rights activist, lawyer, and former member of the CP, explained that

> during the late Twenties, the concept of self-determination arose, as a means of sharpening the struggle. The rights of Negroes to have a part of the United States in which they constituted a majority. There were separatist movements at the time. They were sharply challenged by DuBois. Black Americans are not Africans. To consider themselves so would be to surrender their heritage to the very forces, which have been their greatest oppressors.[72]

He compared the concept of self-determination to the Black Power movement of the 1960s, describing it as a positive force far removed from any notion of separatism. By the late 1920s, the party had classified African Americans as a separate and unique *nation* within the United States. This designation meant, in practical terms, that the party would direct resources toward formulating and carrying out strategic policies to organize African American workers. The CP came to view the southern states as the natural boundaries of this nation.

This special attention was highly regarded by many African Americans who came to see Communists as the "defenders of the race."[73] But as Gerald Horne and Robin D. G. Kelley make clear, this relationship was complex. Jim Crow laws and the ravages inflicted by the Great Depression were not, in themselves, sufficient to move large numbers of African Americans to accept the precepts of the CP. More compelling were the day-to-day actions by the Communists in the streets—where it mattered. Indeed, many in the African American community would come to view this small group of dedicated radicals as courageous crusaders willing to engage the system that oppressed them at great personal risk.[74] The case of the Scottsboro boys in 1931 serves as a compelling example. Nine African American youths were indicted by a grand jury and convicted of raping two young white women. The International Labor Defense (ILD), the legal arm of the CP, took up the case, which lasted over a decade. The participation of the CP in defending countless African Americans convicted on fraudulent charges helped build the ranks of the organization and the CP-led ILD.[75] This kind of activism also endeared the party to many Mexican Americans throughout the country.

The Communist Party often tread, writes Douglas Monroy, where the "narrow, stodgy, and racist AFL feared" to go. CP members defended the rights of Mexican workers to organize and championed their integration into the CIO.[76]

And yet, the CP failed to recruit into its ranks significant numbers from this population because they often ignored the revolutionary and militant traditions that the Mexican working class already possessed. This failure to connect was due, in large part, to the party's reliance on Soviet policy and its lack of "theoretical creativity." In Los Angeles, where Mexican workers had been exposed to the traditions of the PLM and the IWW, the CP generally failed to bring these workers into their fold. "It could not do so," writes Monroy, "because of the Soviet influence which could not accept other revolutionary traditions."[77] Nevertheless, some within this community managed to overcome these shortcomings. In the city alone, for example, the party recruited over two hundred "Spanish and Mexican workers" in one period between 1936 and 1937.[78] Another estimate of the same shows the total membership may have been as high as 435.[79] Regardless of the exact numbers, the CP touched the lives of many Mexicans through its activities and organizations.

Celia Rodríguez, a longtime union organizer and civil rights activist, remembered how her uncle, Jesús Cruz ("Uncle Chuey"), helped organize the Workers Alliance of America in their neighborhood during the Depression.[80] Cruz had immigrated to the United States from Guanajuato, Mexico, and had worked on the railroads, eventually settling in Los Angeles. During the Depression, he looked for work in the orange groves, located east of the city, and it was there that he received, as Rodriguez recalled, a "rude awakening." When he joined the organizing efforts by the workers to form a union, he incurred the growers' wrath. The growers "came down hard on them," she remembered. "They hired the Red Squad from Los Angeles to quell that rebellion. They beat the hell out of him. They cracked his head open several times. . . . Boy, they treated him so bad [that] they made a Communist out of him."[81] Inspired by their uncle, Celia and her sister, Julia, participated in their first "sit-down strike" at a local welfare office, an experience they both found personally transforming.[82] "When they would turn off the gas, or turn off the lights," explained Julia, "we'd turn them back on. . . . When they were evicted . . . we would go and put all their belongings back into the homes."[83] The invitation by their radical uncle to "come and learn about what was happening" turned into a lifelong commitment of activism for both sisters.[84] The agricultural strikes from 1933 to 1934 in California proved challenging for the unflagging Communists, but their efforts gained them much credibility and admiration among Mexican workers.[85]

Agricultural workers soon embarked on a series of labor actions in the state. Thirty-seven major agricultural strikes occurred in 1933 alone, and the Cannery and Agricultural Workers Industrial Union (CAWIU) led twenty-four of these. Although the CAWIU had been a creation of TUUL, this did not mean automatic control by the CP. With reference to the San Joaquin Valley Cotton Strike, Vicki Ruiz writes: "While the union provided the umbrella leadership, Mexican families composed 95 percent of the rank and file. It was not as if the union were calling all the shots and the workers followed."[86] Regardless, as Gilbert González argues, the pressure to rid the CAWIU of Communist or leftist influence came largely from forces outside of the union, notably from the Mexican government. Thus, it seemed to matter little what the workers wanted.[87]

The Mexican government, through its consular offices in Los Angeles, acted to quell any independent voices among Mexican workers out of concern for its own political and economic fortunes. As González contends, Mexico, in its subordinate position vis-à-vis the United States, sought to placate the United States by cooperating with the State Department and growers. Priority was given to maintaining an economic status quo that situated the Mexican immigrant community as a major participant in the capitalist development of the southwestern region. Indeed, the wealth generated by *México de afuera* (Mexican immigrant communities in the United States) and remitted back to the home country had become a substantial source of income that the Mexican government felt compelled to protect. Despite this, Mexican agricultural workers organized on their own behalf to demand better wages and working conditions.

Dorothy Healey, labor organizer and leader of the Southern California District of the CP, recalled: "Despite charges by the growers that the Communists were conspiring to destroy California's agricultural economy, we were rarely the instigators of these strikes. They usually broke out spontaneously and then the workers would come and find us."[88] Healey (Dorothy Ray at the time) had been assigned to help organize workers in the Imperial Valley, and in the process, she gained tremendous respect for Mexican workers and their families. In return, the workers readily welcomed her into their ranks and into their homes. And yet, when she attempted to recruit them into the party, they often responded with measured pragmatism; they supported the revolution of the working class—they knew who the enemy was—but they drew the line at the party's more radical agenda and its bureaucratic formalities, preferring instead to focus on practical concerns. Indeed, they seemed to say, Healey wrote, "Just tell us when the revolution is ready. We'll be there."[89]

As workers struck throughout the country in 1934, over eighteen hundred strikes that year alone, the CP searched for ways to connect with the average worker.[90] They began to shift from their support of independent (dual) unions, represented by TUUL, to a policy of organizing within the AFL.[91] Despite President Roosevelt's efforts to allay workers' fears through a series of farm and union protections, the CP remained skeptical, if not critical, of attempts to reform and salvage what they believed to be a bankrupt economic system. The party came to interpret New Deal initiatives as incremental steps in the process of advancing corporate control over state power, which, if left unchallenged, threatened democracy and strengthened the forces of fascism.[92] By 1935, the CP had pressed forward with its plans to inaugurate a "Peoples' Front" strategy to confront fascism in the United States.[93]

Not all Communists accepted this party line, however. Communist union leaders often recognized and supported the upsurge in labor militancy within the AFL.[94] As David Brody argues, not only were workers, especially mass-production workers, reacting to labor-friendly legislation (e.g., the National Industrial Recovery Act, 1933; Wagner Act, 1935), they were "bursting with militancy" on their own.[95] When the rift occurred within the AFL, leading to the formation of the Congress of Industrial Organizations in 1938, the party's rank and file welcomed the new organization.

The CIO not only bucked labor's traditional position of organizing only skilled labor, it inaugurated a movement that lifted Mexican American workers to new heights within American labor.[96] With the support of the CP and progressives in the labor movement, Mexican Americans and Mexican immigrants became significant players in a number of CIO unions. These workers became key organizers and leaders in the International Ladies' Garment Workers' Union (ILGWU), the United Furniture Workers of America (UFWA), the International Longshoremen's and Warehousemen's Union (ILWU), the United Cannery, Agricultural, Packing, and Allied Workers of America (UCAPAWA), and the International Union of Mine, Mill and Smelter Workers (IUMMSW, commonly known as Mine-Mill), to name a few. Unions such as UCAPAWA became early models for democratic trade unionism. Union leaders, such as Luisa Moreno, Ruiz argues, led the way in organizing and nurturing a democratic work culture, "in which the workers controlled the affairs of their locals." In pursuit of these goals, Mexican women workers forged alliances with other ethnic workers, creating new "bonds of sisterhood" that helped mitigate the ethnic segregation that often prevailed in these workplaces.[97] Another pioneering union organizer was Rose Pesotta, a Russian Jew, who helped organize Mexican women in the dressmaking factories in Los Angeles during the early to mid-1930s. Pesotta recognized that the courage, militancy, and degree of organizational skills shown by these women came from a willingness to engage American culture and politics.[98] These unions not only became training grounds for Mexican American labor leadership, they helped to politicize their communities about issues affecting them every day, such as housing segregation, welfare rights, education, police abuse, and employment and gender discrimination. The Great Depression may have cast a long shadow over many lives, but the period also generated high-spirited optimism for a better future.

The Great Depression created a common experience among people of different ethnic origins. This shared experience often, though not always, created common cause among otherwise segregated and isolated workers to redress wrongs by employers. This movement did more than inaugurate a grassroots political front; it also produced a significant cultural and artistic renaissance. As Michael Denning has argued, the popular front culture was a movement that disseminated pro-worker, antifascist, and social democratic ideas that sprang forth from the combined influence of the emergence of labor, the New Deal, the growing class consciousness of second-generation immigrants, and the rise of mass communication. Denning also refers to this period as the "age of the CIO"—a time in which working-class men and women had tremendous influence on American culture and politics.[99] Workers in Chicago demonstrated this transformation as they negotiated new patterns of loyalty and allegiance with ethnic organizations, welfare agencies, employers, stores, banks, theaters, political parties, and unions. Armed with a new sense of political self-awareness, Lizbeth Cohen argues, workers strove for a new social vision for the nation, "a form of political economy that can best be characterized as 'moral capitalism.'"[100] This national union movement would also have a profound effect on Mexican workers. These workers began to see beyond their particular ethnic identity and experiences and to identify with a common, shared history with other workers. For Mexican immigrant labor as well as for Mexican Americans, this movement would help to redefine their national identity and the meaning of Americanism.[101]

The formation of El Congreso de Pueblos que Hablan Español (Congress of Spanish-Speaking People) in 1939 was a natural outgrowth of this growing political self-awareness. It represented the political manifestation of a population that increasingly perceived itself as a leading force for change and deserving of self-determination in its own right. El Congreso was, as one Communist party document observed, "the largest and most progressive organization ever to exist among the Mexican people."[102] Yet, from its inception, the organization was red-baited by the House Un-American Activities Committee (HUAC). According to activist and union organizer Bert Corona, El Congreso was identified as a source of "riots," of "revolutionary activity," and, most surprisingly, of plotting the creation of "a new republic or return [of] the South west [*sic*] to Mexico."[103] El Congreso's multiethnic network of liberal and radical activists managed to ignite a greater awareness of Latinos as a significant force throughout the nation and not just an isolated, regional population. Hence, the unity of all Latinos became a central theme in its political work and outreach activities.[104] In the organization's historic gathering in April 1939, its participants proudly declared: "For the first time we were united."[105]

El Congreso was different from other organizations in the Mexican community. Corona, for example, observed that the new organization, from its inception, made every effort to make no distinctions between immigrants and those born in the United States. Unlike LULAC, which stressed, above all, integration, assimilation, and middle-class conservative values, El Congreso "stressed the unity of all the Spanish-speaking, U.S. citizens or not."[106] The need for such an organization was so evident that within two years its membership climbed to over six thousand.[107] El Congreso was an outgrowth of grassroots activism in the Southwest and was launched in Los Angeles largely through the auspices of UCAPAWA and under the vision and leadership of veteran labor organizer Luisa Moreno.

Moreno understood the need to develop a "true national conference" and, therefore, worked diligently to steer this civil rights assembly in that direction.[108] The other key leader of the organization was the executive secretary, Josefina Fierro. Through her tireless dedication and organizational abilities, and that of other activists, El Congreso moved forward on several fronts to bring attention to problems in housing, education, immigration, civil rights, racial and gender discrimination, citizenship, political representation, and police brutality, to name a few.[109] El Congreso, for example, would help establish the Sleepy Lagoon Defense Committee, a multiethnic coalition that in 1942 defended a group of Mexican American youth accused of murder. As Healey recalled, El Congreso epitomized the meaning of the "people's front" that developed in Los Angeles during this period.[110]

The ideological line in the sand, however, had been drawn well before El Congreso had an opportunity to fully develop. The participation of such prominent CIO unions as UCAPAWA, IUMMSW, ILWU, Steel Workers,

Electrical Workers, Furniture Workers, and local chapters of the Workers Alliance certainly signaled their leftist politics. The pronouncements by El Congreso's California affiliate, in December 1939, that it opposed the entry of the United States into any war, opposed intervention in Latin America, opposed limitations on civil liberties, and condemned the "practice of discrimination, intimidation, and deportation as a means of solving the economic, social, and cultural problems of the Spanish Speaking and other minority groups" may have been too radical.[111] This shift in position from an all-out offensive against the growing tide of fascism (before the August 1939 signing of the German-Soviet Nonaggression Pact) to an urgent call for neutrality certainly illustrated its close affinity with the CP. And with prominent radical labor activists in Los Angeles such as Armando Dávila, Frank López, and Ramón Welch helping to maintain this oppositional viewpoint, El Congreso became a target for conservative politicians.[112]

Although the CP claimed to have played an important role in founding the organization, it was, as George Sánchez explains, far from having been "captured."[113] The CP not only supported El Congreso's goals but also hoped that it could become more than a bread-and-butter organization. Leading CP activists and labor organizers such as Emma Tenayuca and Homer Brooks, Mario García notes, called on the new organization to broaden its appeal across class and ethnicity. "In all, the Communist Party saw El Congreso and the struggle by Mexican Americans for basic civil rights as part of the CP's strategy for a Popular Front of democratic forces."[114] As one CP document concluded, El Congreso's "work in raising the political level of the people in obtaining concessions from the government, and in bringing about a closer understanding between Anglo-American progressives and the Hispanic Americans was incalculable."[115] Nonetheless, the political stance adopted by the CIO and CP as a result of the nation's entry into the global conflict, which called for wartime unity and the playing down of civil rights cases, significantly affected the militant activism of El Congreso.[116] Although El Congreso was short-lived, both Healey and Corona concurred that it helped embolden "a generation" of Mexican American community leaders into the next decade.[117]

Not surprisingly, many Mexican American families remained on the margins of the tremendous changes taking place within the labor movement. The Cuaróns, for example, had managed to survive the worst of the deportations and repatriation drives that occurred early in the decade, but despite all their sacrifices and hard work, they failed to raise their economic status. In 1938, Jesús

Cuarón finally gave up his dream of independent entrepreneurship. Margarita continued to meet the family's needs, even as she delayed her own plans for financial independence, marriage, and a family of her own.[118] At age fifteen, Ralph Cuarón recalled meeting Armando Dávila for the first time. Dávila had set up an upholstery shop on Indiana and Sixth Street and hired Ralph's father. He had a contractual arrangement with Fishman Upholstery, a larger shop. Ralph recalled that Fishman was a former Socialist from Europe and was very supportive of unions and issues affecting the working class in general.[119] Interestingly, Dávila had opened his shop at a time when the furniture industry in the region began to recover and in the same year that the United Furniture Workers union had gained local strength.[120] Ralph was impressed by Dávila's knowledge of unions and learned a great deal about labor history and local struggles in the community. Dávila would later be instrumental in recruiting Ralph into the CIO in Los Angeles after the war and would himself become a leader in the newly formed UFWA Local 576.[121] But for the moment, Ralph had more pressing concerns—the need to contribute financially to the family.

In 1940, at age seventeen, Cuarón dropped out of school. As he recalled, "My school life and my school learning, somehow were something else. I did not feel that my school learning was relevant to my real life, my street life, my home life."[122] He acquired a job during this period at a local "mom and pop store," where he learned to drive a truck. His job routine began at five o'clock each morning with a trip to the central market on Seventh Street, in downtown Los Angeles, where he purchased fresh produce and general supplies for the store.[123] His school attendance at Garfield High School now seemed more sporadic as he spent increasing time at work earning a meager income. School officials regularly granted requests by Mexican American students for work permits regardless of how this might affect school performance. In fact, this disregard for their education was part and parcel of a general attitude that identified Mexican children as possessing limited learning abilities and, by extension, limited employment opportunities.[124]

The result of this alienation from school as well as from society as a whole led many young Mexican Americans to join street gangs.[125] Bert Corona recalled that membership in these gangs began as early as thirteen. "Gangs represented," Corona explained, "a way of dealing with their alienation and providing a support system outside of the family among their peers."[126] Cuarón remembered that many of his friends joined local street gangs but that he carefully managed to keep a distance from the "gang warfare and gang fights" that erupted with great frequency on and off school property. The danger and violence associated with some of the pachucos, notwithstanding, Cuarón was impressed by their bravado and their defiance of authority. In their struggle for identity—for a place in American society—many young Mexican Americans chose to stand apart from the culture of their first-generation parents.[127] Cuarón would later focus his energies on organizing these youth into the labor movement in Los Angeles. With few options available to increase or supplement his own income, Cuarón joined the Civilian Conservation Corps (CCC) and headed out for the mountains of San Bernardino.

Cuarón recalled the day he departed from East Los Angeles on the back of a pickup truck along with other young Mexican American recruits. He relished his new independence and the opportunities that lay ahead. As F. Arturo Rosales argues, New Deal agencies such as the CCC and the National Youth Administration became important avenues by which Mexican American youth were exposed to mainstream American society, the positive as well as negative aspects.[128] For Cuarón, as for so many young men, the CCC also represented an opportunity to leave a depressed community, earn needed income, and gain work experience. Almost fifty years later, he remembered with great detail the path that truck took as it left Los Angeles and wound its way into the San Bernardino National Forest. The experience away from home would be a significant turning point in his life.

For the young and impressionable Cuarón, the camps seemed like worlds unto themselves. The CCC had been formed in 1933 during the first few months of President Roosevelt's administration called the "Hundred Days." As Mariá E. Montoya notes, the administration believed that through the CCC "it had found a partial solution for the two overwhelming problems of youth unemployment and environmental deterioration. The CCC enlisted the young men of the nation to fight a war against poverty, ecological waste, and idleness."[129] After completing two weeks of a scaled-down version of basic training, the new recruits were shipped out to their assigned work camps run by the army. As Cuarón recalled, the young recruits were assigned to specific sleeping quarters and provided with "rations"—a pair of pants, a shirt, and boots.[130] Most important, however, was the thirty dollars a month allotment that each received. Despite the fact that twenty-five of those thirty dollars went directly home, the five dollars each corps member retained represented a substantial amount. The daily routine began at five o'clock each morning, Cuarón recalled, with breakfast served in a large mess hall. He and his companions worked for the U.S. Forest

Service—repairing and servicing picnic areas and campgrounds, building new campsites, clearing and constructing new roads, and of course fighting forest fires. The rigor and the close quarters in the work camps promoted a degree of camaraderie among many of the enrollees. However, some differences remained difficult to overcome.[131]

Although the camps were far removed from cities and towns, the new environment was not always successful in mitigating neighborhood and regional differences among the youth. On numerous occasions, Cuarón had to diffuse physical confrontations between competing groups, often between young men from agricultural areas (Redlands) and those from more urban areas (Los Angeles). One of the more difficult challenges, as he recalled, was persuading many of the young street toughs to cut off their distinctive "pachuco style hair" in accordance with dress code regulations. They "did not feel good about having to separate themselves from their hair," Cuarón recalled, "so they put up a struggle. . . . Then they would threaten me. They'd say, 'If you cut my hair, I'm gonna get you back in Los Angeles.'"[132]

Cuarón also remembered that among his cohort were a significant number of immigrants. Sometimes conflicts flared between members of this group, who maintained a strong identification with their Mexican heritage, and the more acculturated second (or more) generation of Mexican American youth. Cuarón strove to bridge what he considered an artificial divide between the groups. Part of his motivation was to reconnect with, if not relearn, the cultural roots of his parents. He recalled one young recruit that stood out above all the others. He had been schooled in Mexico City, and his education and level of maturity surpassed that of most in the camp. This, of course, brought him into direct conflict with the "pachucos who didn't like him," Cuarón recalled. Despite the pressures to not associate with such *outsiders*, Cuarón mentored the young man and in time helped him acquire a job as an "infirmary attendant" inside the camp. In exchange for his intervention, the young man tutored Cuarón in Mexican history and Spanish.[133] Cuarón's display of fellowship among camp enrollees and his leadership skills soon gained him the respect and admiration of camp supervisors. And though the work was dangerous, physically demanding, and required long hours, Cuarón felt exhilarated by the whole experience. He came to be proud of the work they did to preserve the nation's natural resources.[134]

A short time after arriving in the camp, Cuarón was assigned to oversee the orientation of new recruits. Because the camps practiced de facto segregation, however, he worked exclusively with Mexican American enrollees. In her study of the CCC in northern New Mexico, Montoya describes the overt and the hidden racism that Latinos faced. Despite the CCC's rhetoric that promised America's young men, irrespective of race, better lives as a result of their new skills and abilities, old prejudices proved difficult to overcome. Indeed, CCC officials in New Mexico, for example, readily dismissed the educational and leadership abilities of Latino enrollees, believing instead that they were "mentally and physically inferior." As a result, Latino enrollees were marginalized within the camps and passed over for higher-paying skilled jobs and leadership positions. Furthermore, as Montoya explains, "the CCC may have been uneasy about giving these higher-paying jobs to Hispanos when there were 'more-deserving' Anglos who 'needed' the extra money to maintain their standard of living." In the CCC camp located at the Bandelier National Monument, for example, only one Latino ever held a position higher than basic enrollee in its ten-year existence.[135] Cuarón recognized the segregation that existed in the camps, but he placed high hopes that through hard work and dedication he could impress his supervisors. He had his mind firmly set on becoming a tractor/bulldozer operator—a skill he could use to gain employment once outside the camps.

The work camps had a number of training facilities that provided skills instruction for more specialized work, such as operating heavy equipment. The schools, as Cuarón recalled, admitted students on a six-month rotating schedule and only two trainees per camp could attend. He had acquired some experience in the forestry truck garage, had performed some blacksmith work, and had regularly operated the tractors on light duty assignments. Thus, Cuarón felt confident that his request for admission to the school would receive priority consideration. The response he received from his superior, however, caught him by surprise. As Cuarón remembered, the captain responded by saying, "Well, I'll tell you what Ralph . . . I like you a lot. But I'll tell you, I'm gonna try my damnedest to send you there. But I'm gonna tell you right now that we don't send Mexicans to that school." The response shocked Cuarón; he was humiliated and profoundly angered by the experience. "The floor fell out from under me. This was the last of my days in these camps."[136]

A dramatic change occurred within the work camp after the Japanese attack on Pearl Harbor in December 1941. Cuarón recalled that Latino enrollees soon became targets of military recruiters, actions that he perceived as hypocritical and insulting. Cuarón was appalled at how readily Mexican Americans were being drafted to defend a country that treated them with such disdain.

FIGURE 1 Ralph Cuarón joins the Merchant Marine, 1941. Cuarón Family Collection.

Nevertheless, many Mexican Americans enthusiastically joined the armed services: as an opportunity to defend their country and to prove their loyalty and commitment to broader democratic ideals. But Cuarón had experienced injustice directly, blatantly, and it burned inside him. Despite the treatment that he and other Mexican Americans experienced, he also felt torn by the feelings of loyalty to his country of birth. The war against fascism touched a sensitive cord with Cuarón. "Although I felt that I had had nothing to do with what had happened in the world, I was beginning to feel a sense of responsibility that I had to participate in this war whether I wanted to or not." Rather than entering the armed forces, however, Cuarón chose to join the Merchant Marine.[137]

Since 1940, the nation's shipyards had been humming with activity as factories filled orders to produce hundreds of Liberty ships, including various levels of C-class vessels, T2 tankers, ore carriers, seagoing barges, and tugs.[138] The production capacity of the United States was so impressive that, by 1942, it equaled that of Germany, Italy, and Japan combined.[139] Merchant seamen played a critical role in transporting and delivering vital materials (including munitions for the beleaguered Allies) to destinations overseas. These maritime workers learned firsthand—in fact several years before the country officially entered the conflict abroad—that the sea-lanes were the "front lines." In fact, these seamen, many of whom were members of the National Maritime Union (NMU), became the nation's earliest casualties as the war spread beyond the European theater.[140] In a publication produced by the NMU titled *On a True Course*, the union proudly described the courage and sacrifice of its members during this period.

> As factories and training camps increased their output and our military commitments became larger, the loss of ships rose. Men and material could not be moved fast enough. In the month of April 1942, allied sinkings totaled 800,000 tons, the equivalent of 80 Liberty ships.
>
> Seamen were dying with scorched lungs in seas of blazing oil barely a mile off the U.S. coast. Others were going down in the icy waters of the Arctic, in the Pacific, off the coast of Africa. The Seven Seas were a combat zone and they ran red with the blood of American seamen.[141]

Although the work aboard ships presented numerous hazards to life and limb, even in good times, the significant pay (approximately $180 a month) attracted many sailors, and would-be sailors.[142]

Cuarón trained for two weeks at a seamen's camp located in Avalon, on Santa Catalina Island, prior to being assigned to a Liberty ship. Aboard the SS *Yancy*, a 10,000-ton displacement cargo vessel, "fresh off the wharf," his principal work assignment was as an "oiler" in the engine rooms, a member of what were termed the *engine gangs* or *black gangs*.[143] In the hierarchy of seafaring men, this was a position just above the bottom rung. As Bruce Nelson describes, on top were situated the masters and mates, then came "deck sailors a considerable notch below, followed by the engine room men, or black gang, and then the stewards' department." The work was dirty and the hours long. Cuarón's hearing would be permanently impaired as a result of prolonged exposure to the intense noise emanating from the engines and boilers.[144] Each new assignment to ship out represented another adventure—working on different ships, visiting new ports of call, and joining new crews.

The excitement of these trips, however, may have been tempered by the realization that these work assignments came with great risks. Later in life, Cuarón, for example, captured this undercurrent of foreboding as his ship left the San Francisco harbor:

> Finally, we were out on the high seas and some of us began to feel a little nauseous, a little wheezy [*sic*] in the stomach, a little afraid of what we were heading into. And slowly we watched . . . we watched the skyline of San Francisco disappear into the sky. . . . And, finally, all of a sudden, there were no lights. There was nothing. There was only water; water below us, water on all four sides of us. We had been consumed by the high seas.[145]

Sailors realized that their universe had now been drastically reduced and that survival depended on the contributions and support of every shipmate. "The crewmembers," Cuarón recalled, "were a conglomeration of American society crossing all genders [men and women], nationalities, religious beliefs, cultures, etc." Cuarón also remembered the loneliness and depression that many crewmembers experienced as a result of being away from their families for months at a time. The fear and anxiety associated with the ever-present danger of perishing at sea—of being bombed or torpedoed—kept the crews on edge. These stressful conditions often exacerbated social and racial tensions rather than diminished them. Solidarity on the high seas seemed to rest squarely, though not always, on racial exclusiveness. Despite his disappointment with the racism aboard ships, he soon discovered that the CIO's National Maritime Union could be an important ally in the struggle for equality among all seamen.

Cuarón was soon thrust into the rancorous and political world of the NMU. Formed in 1937 and led by the stodgy veteran sailor Joseph Curran, the NMU had become a formidable union competitor to the AFL's Sailors' Union of the Pacific. Described as "strong-willed and self-righteous," Curran became popular with fellow seamen because of his long history of struggle, independence (though he was routinely accused of being a Communist and toeing the party line), and commitment to workers and their issues.[146] Six months prior to the attack on Pearl Harbor, Curran provided the following statement at the union's Third National Convention in 1941: "We love our country far more than those who wave the flag and make patriotic speeches. We work at defending our country . . . at defending our union . . . at defending the democratic institutions of this country and we are attempting to expand those things, for we believe this is real national defense."[147] Moreover, for members of the NMU, especially its radical and progressive leadership, democratic ideals did not hinge on race.

From its inception, the NMU worked aggressively to end discrimination and build a racially integrated union. The most committed to ending Jim Crow on the high seas were the Communist members of the union.[148] William Standard, lawyer and general counsel for the NMU from 1937 to 1948, wrote proudly of the NMU's commitment to fighting discrimination. "The NMU fought for racial equality," Standard asserted, "by practicing it and proving that it was not only possible but a positive good."[149] The same can be said of the leadership of the International Longshoremen's and Warehousemen's Union (ILWU), where Harry Bridges, its president, championed the rights of African Americans. But as Nelson correctly argues, that vision of racial harmony hinged on local conditions, the degree to which European American seamen and longshoremen would engage their darker-skinned union brothers on an equal basis.[150]

Notwithstanding Nelson's observations that Mexicans benefited from having better ethnic relations with European Americans than did African Americans, that *acceptance* remained fickle.[151] Indeed, the U.S. Census Bureau in 1940 may have classified Mexicans as "White," but on board ships and on the docks, as Cuarón experienced, they also remained "spics"—out to get the jobs of deserving white men.[152] Some 10 percent of the NMU membership in 1947 was African American, or over seven thousand, and its "Spanish-speaking" members represented 25 percent, or approximately twenty thousand.[153] Though Latinos were one-quarter of the union, they were not uniformly accepted.

Cuarón could recall numerous incidents in which he was forced to defend himself against racist diatribe and physical intimidation. During one occasion, for example, a crew member standing nearby turned his invective toward Cuarón, yelling, "You're not equal! What makes you think you're equal? You're just like the rest of them blacks. You're not equal, you're brown." Almost immediately, Cuarón recalled, another crew member entered the fray by adding, "That son-of-a-bitch, spic, thinks he's equal. He thinks he's too good for his own skin. We'll take care of that." Cuarón recalled vividly how he and his companion left the scene immediately. In fact, the racial tensions on that particular trip reached such a fevered pitch that a "committee" was formed to mete out discipline against Cuarón, as he explained, to "teach me who I was and where my place was."[154] In another incident, Cuarón jumped ship during a scheduled stop to escape from two crew members who had threatened his life.[155] Responding to conditions of discrimination affecting workers of color throughout the country, President Roosevelt issued Executive Order 8802 (banning discrimination in the employment of workers in defense industries or government) in 1941. But the measure proved difficult to enforce.

Time and again, the numerous public hearings conducted by the Fair Employment Practices Committee (FEPC), charged with carrying out Executive Order 8802, revealed the endemic discrimination against Mexican workers. The reality, however, was that Executive Order 8802 and the FEPC were, as Clete Daniel argues, feeble at best and "little more than a gesture" toward correcting any wrongs perpetrated against Mexican American and Mexican immigrant workers. The federal government understood the economic segmentation of Mexicans through its own studies conducted in the spring of 1942 but chose to set them aside. As Daniel illustrates, those studies clearly identified Mexicans as victims of a historic pattern of discrimination and disenfranchisement that, as one study concluded, followed "much the same pattern as Jim Crowism." With the war effort being paramount, the administration appeared eager to appease minority concerns only in so far as to silence their public protests and retain their full support and loyalty during the war. In response to a request by the FEPC for greater support from the administration, presidential aide Marvin McIntyre said to Roosevelt himself: "Personally, I am a little leery for fear of stirring up the animals at this time."[156]

In spite of the administration's weak support, there were some positive outcomes. Indeed, most committee members, field investigators, and, above all, CIO unions (most notably Mine, Mill and Smelter Workers) made great strides in documenting and publicizing discrimination and racism experienced by Mexicans throughout the country. And as Elizabeth Escobedo reminds us, Mexican women in particular gained significant opportunities through the FEPC. As aircraft plants in Los Angeles experienced labor shortages during the war, for example, they turned to women of color to fill vital production needs. Though they still experienced discrimination at the work site, it was significantly abated by hiring practices and job assignments that allowed for "intermixing between groups." This intermingling of groups, Escobedo argues, helped lead to "cross-cultural understanding and a breakdown of traditional racial boundaries."[157] And despite the fact that both the Communist Party and CIO chose to play down "civil rights activity in order to promote wartime unity," radical leaders such as Luisa Moreno and Frank López eagerly served on the FEPC in California. No doubt both leaders must have participated as members of the regional office (Region XII) located in Los Angeles. While Mexican American leaders struggled to gain the attention and respect of federal officials, Cuarón carried on his own struggle to survive as a maritime worker.[158]

Despite Cuarón's experiences, he did not immediately join the NMU or the Communist Party. His initial reluctance to join the seaman's union, for instance, was based on the recurring violent conflict between navy sailors and private merchant seamen. As Cuarón recalled, navy sailors regarded merchant seamen as nothing more than "draft dodgers." Even more significant, Cuarón emphasized, was the charge that the union activities of the merchant seamen were "anti-American."[159] Against this backdrop of history and conflict, Cuarón began to ask questions.

Cuarón's political education in the NMU opened his eyes to other, larger issues of class, race, and power. He remembered, for example, how a good friend explained to him "why things were the way they were in the world." "He explained to me that there were two social systems existing [that] were colliding with each other. He explained to me the nature of the class struggle—the workers and the capitalists." Rather than spend his time aboard ships playing cards or engaged in other such leisure activities, Cuarón began to read books. It was at this time that he acquired a book titled *The Nature of Dialectical Materialism*, which he enthusiastically consumed "word for word, over and over again."[160]

This emphasis on education and mentorship practiced by CP unionists at sea and on the docks reveals far more than simple membership recruitment activities by disciplined party cadres.[161] As Michael Torigian argues in his examination of the ILWU during the war, these activities go to the core of "Communist unionism": a vision guided by an understanding in which labor and the working class would transform American society in order to bring about a just world. Thus, Communist unionism went far beyond "'business unionism' (which responds mainly to labor-market needs) or social-democratic unionism (which creates an institutional extension of itself in the political system)."[162] The focus on this grand vision for a new world meant having to reach out to all workers; it meant organizing people of color, women, poorly paid workers, and other laborers neglected by the union movement. For the forces of anti-Communism, however, any interest shown by the Communists in ending discrimination was wholly insincere; they were simply putting on a front to obscure their true intentions. According to this argument, the most important goal of the Communist Party was building the "Communist machine," a machine whose goal it was to sow chaos.[163] As Cuarón delved deeper into the politics of class struggle, events at home would soon prove decisive in his joining the CP.

While waiting to load a shipment of nitrate off the coastal town of Iquique, Chile, Cuarón became aware of the rioting in Los Angeles between navy sailors and Mexican American youth. The "Zoot-Suit Riots," as the frenzied media labeled the weeklong disturbances, occurred between June 3 and 13, 1943, in the areas of downtown and East Los Angeles. The event made headlines across the nation and, apparently, reports had reached as far as South America.[164] Indeed, wartime patriotism and unity had done little to ameliorate race relations. Celia Rodríguez, who by this stage was engaged in union organizing, believed that the political, economic, and social marginalization of Latinos on the Eastside, accentuated by the wartime patriotism, allowed the servicemen to generate great havoc in the community. "It felt very hopeless, helpless . . . but [we were also] very angry."[165] Another eyewitness to the rioting, Chester Himes (writer for the African American magazine *The Crisis*), echoed Rodríguez's memories of the roaming "gangs" of white servicemen and was very critical of "nazi-minded citizenry" that appeared eager to condone those attacks.

> The papers of Los Angeles crowed. "It was a good job," they said. They rooted and cheered. What could make the white people more happy than to see their uniformed sons sapping up some dark-skinned people? It proved beyond all doubt the bravery of white servicemen, their gallantry. Los Angeles was at last being made safe for white people—to do as they damned well pleased.[166]

For some observers of these events, like Celia Rodríguez, the riots had the effect of waking many Mexican Americans out of their patriotic complacency. Bert Corona recalled that various community leaders, including members of El Congreso, "sprang into action" to defend the countless Mexican American youth arrested and detained by authorities.[167] The attacks may have emerged out of some psychological need by European Americans to emasculate young Mexican Americans, but these rituals were nothing short of terror for those who lived through them.[168] More significant, however, was the fact that Mexican American youth were targeted because of their perceived inherent criminality. As wartime anxieties fed irrational beliefs of internal enemies, and as law enforcement officials increasingly linked crime to race, anti-Mexican hysteria took hold of the imagination and spread like wildfire.[169] For Cuarón, the news further convinced him that Mexican Americans had to organize themselves with greater urgency and that their fight for civil rights could lead to allegiances with people around the world. He soon discarded any notions that Mexican Americans could achieve full integration in American society without concrete action to achieve that goal.[170] The events in Los Angeles confirmed Cuarón's decision to join the Communist Party.

Sometime after the events in Los Angeles, Cuarón wrote a letter to his eldest sister, Margarita. The letter reflects newfound confidence and a sense of mission:

> Dearest sister Margaret,
>
> I am very worried that you had a cold and that I have left you. I am concerned that everyone is so preoccupied with my absence. Please don't mourn for me, organize, talk to the people, tell them that a great change is coming, and that their lives shall be emancipated from the cruel and inhumane conditions they now live in.
>
> Margie, . . . We truly are a different kind of people in that neighborhood. Our name is strength of love, determination and willpower to stick together. We shall demonstrate that faith conquers all, heals all wounds, and opens all hearts. And so always remember that my [participation in the war effort] is necessary for my health, my faith and my love. Let me do my honors well, let me be faithful to God. Please pray for us all and give lots of love to my little babies.
>
> Your loving brother.[171]

Indeed, his letter appears infused with what Nelson describes as "Pentecostal" unionism. The term, according to the author, has no religious connotation, but captures how the union leadership of the seamen attempted to "sanctify and revitalize conventional institutions and commitments" during the labor upheavals of the 1930s. This period was "accompanied by a zealous commitment to new leaders and new, or transformed, institutions and by an apocalyptic sense of urgency."[172] This pentecostal spirit appears to have remained a powerful influence as the nation entered the war.[173] For Communists and liberal progressives, the spreading threat of Nazism meant a redoubling of their efforts to defeat the ominous enemy. When the call went out to Cuarón and his comrades to help rescue partisans from the defeated Republican forces in Spain, he enthusiastically joined the international crusade.[174]

At the end of the civil war in Spain (1936–39), many of the former Republican guerrillas, including former members of the International Brigades, were systematically persecuted and hunted down by the newly triumphant, and fascist, government of Francisco Franco. Communist parties around the world heeded the call to assist these partisans by extricating and resettling them in friendly nations. Cuarón worked closely with the CP-organized Anti-Fascist Refugee Committee, based in New York, that transported partisans to the United States. He remembered one such operation in which he helped to rescue a Portuguese Communist from the port of Le Havre, France. As a union steward, Cuarón not only became an important conduit of information between the union leadership and rank-and-file workers, but he managed to gain some freedom and control over his daily activities. In this capacity, he played a key role in getting the stowaway boarded under cover of darkness, dressing him in a sailor's uniform, and providing him with false documentations to complete his trip. When they arrived in New York, they handed over their comrade-in-exile to the Anti-Fascist Refugee Committee, which then helped to resettle and integrate him into society. Cuarón's participation in these clandestine activities helped to redefine his identity, as he increasingly saw himself as a member of a world community—a brotherhood of activists.[175]

The fellowship and education Cuarón gained from his shipmates overwhelmed and inspired him. Sailors had a penchant for telling stories with creative embellishments and passing on the lessons of their struggles to new, impressionable seamen—and to those who would listen. Dorothy Healey recalled, for example, how captivated she was by the sailors she met in San Pedro. "They were already veterans of great labor struggles, very courageous, militant, and politically sophisticated. I can remember sitting in the headquarters listening spellbound to the yarns they would spin of life aboard ship in the ports they visited."[176] In a short period, Cuarón had traveled around the world, participated in labor organizing, and engaged in CP militant action. He recalled, with great relish, the day he walked straight to the local bookstore of the Communist Party in San Pedro and joined the organization. He was now, officially, a "soldier of the working class."[177]

By war's end, however, the labor movement that had transformed the structure of American society came under heavy assault. Leading the charge were corporate leaders who, emboldened by a strong sense of entitlement and self-confidence, strove to regain what power they had lost to labor over product pricing, market allocation, and the shop-floor work environment.[178] The emergence

of an intransigent anti-unionism, chronicles Nelson Lichtenstein, had been evident as early as 1944. Indeed, labor's successes in organizing workers in sectors
of the economy that had not known union activity "awakened and politicized
elements of the business community that had not been active on the national
scene before the war."[179]

Though polls indicated significant public support for labor, persistent unemployment, a high inflation rate, and rising tension between the United States
and the Soviet Union began to shift the national mood in the other direction.
The 1946 Republican Party victory in the Congress accelerated the attacks on
New Deal programs, and anti-Communism became a revitalized tool in this
assault.[180] Indeed, when the House Un-American Activities Committee was
made a standing (permanent) committee in that same year, the hunt for subversives and spies gained further legitimacy.

The NMU became an early target of the anti-Communist campaign. Indeed,
not only had the union been identified as a hotbed of radicalism going back to
the late 1930s, maritime workers were increasingly perceived as key elements in
Moscow's plans to take control of the marine industry.[181] The anti-Communist
barrage, however, often originated from conservative union leaders themselves,
who utilized this tactic as a key component in their strategy to control independent unions and rival leadership. For example, Joseph Ryan, president of the
International Longshoremen's Association, frequently accused the NMU and
the ILWU of Communist intrigue as a result of their support for striking workers within his own union.[182] In California, the legislature's Joint Fact-Finding
Committee on Un-American Activities played host to witnesses (former Communists and union members) eager to expose the "Stalinists on the waterfront."
During committee hearings held in 1946, in the city of Oakland, state senator
Jack B. Tenney learned from these witnesses that Communists resembled fan-
tastic, lurid creatures with incredible regenerative powers.

> You can defeat them today; they'll come back tomorrow, or they will come back
> tonight. If they can't come in through that door, they'll come in through the
> window. If they can't get in through the window, they'll come in through the
> roof. They get in.[183]

Thus, if the CP "hacks" ("disciplined Communists") did not *capture* a union
through intimidation and brute force, then it was accomplished through cun-
ning and deceit, as innocent seamen fell victims to the intoxicating rhetoric

of the "Communist-fronters."[184] But this portrayal of Communists was, and remains, as Howard Kimeldorf explains, little more than a "caricature," a weak argument by anti-Communists against the fact that their prime nemeses "were usually more effective organizers" and more popular leaders among the rank and file than they cared to admit.[185]

Cuarón was soon spending more time on the docks in the company of hundreds of other idle workers waiting to join crews and to ship out. The passage of the Taft-Hartley Act in 1947 would have tremendous consequences. Indeed, as George Lipsitz argues, Taft-Hartley became the first major volley by political conservatives and corporate leaders to beat back labor. Thus, the mass picketing, sympathy strikes, and secondary boycotts that erupted nationwide in 1946 were seen as great abuses by unions that needed to be "corrected." The act also placed restrictions on closed shops, allowed states to pass legislation that outlawed union shops, and provided the federal government with the power to obtain strikebreaking injunctions. Although the legislation would not answer the concerns of most small businesses (in a national economy increasingly moving in favor of monopoly capital), section 9(h)—the anti-Communist affidavit—did prove surprisingly effective.[186] As Ellen Schrecker explains, these affidavits became "too tempting a weapon for the foes of the left-led unions to ignore." Despite the courageous stance by these unions to rebuff this assault on the constitutional rights of members, "their failure to submit the non-Communist affidavits barred them from participating in NLRB representation elections." Without this support, the Left-led unions were less and less able "to protect their members' economic interests."[187] In that year, the anti-Communists prevailed at the NMU convention. The union's president, Joe Curran, made an about-face and moved against his Communist allies, apparently in an attempt to save the union from expulsion from the CIO.[188] As Cuarón recalled, the government "clamped down. They took our shipping papers, our seamen's papers. They took them away from us, which made it impossible for us to ship out anymore. We became automatically blacklisted."[189] For over a year Cuarón struggled, with little success, to find employment. In San Pedro, the environment became increasingly inhospitable.

In late 1947, Mexican American Communist Party activists held a picnic gathering at Lake Elsinore, in Riverside County, to introduce new members and for old members to become reacquainted. Frank López, longtime Communist Party activist and UFWA leader, invited Cuarón. At the event, Cuarón met a core of the activists on the Eastside, including Frances Lym, Ben Cruz,

Leroy Parra, Delfino Varela, Francisco and Lydia Moisa, Ramón Welch, and Gilbert Orosco.[190] Through their mentorship, he became integrated into the local political milieu. Fifty-two years later, Cuarón still fondly remembered this early encounter: "I just thought they were great. I [had] finally found the Movement."[191] Soon after the event, Cuarón was offered employment at the Crest Pacific Furniture Company located on North Broadway near Chinatown. Almost immediately he became immersed in the politics of the UFWA Local 576.

2

INSURGENT COMMUNITY

Justice for Salcido

*When things would happen in the community, we didn't go to the [Communist]
Party and say, "Do you think we should do such and such?" We did [it on our
own]. The Party was not the myth that it has come down to [be].*
—Sylvia Cuarón, 1998

T
HE KILLING OF SEVENTEEN-YEAR-OLD Augustino Salcido in 1948 by
two Los Angeles police officers generated a flurry of activism on the
Eastside that demanded an end to police brutality.[1] The degree of
organization and coordinated response by the supporters of the Salcido family
illustrated that the relationship between the community and the police had
changed significantly. The Sleepy Lagoon case (1942), the Zoot Suit riots
(1943), and World War II helped transform Mexican American communities in Los Angeles so that their responses to police misconduct increasingly
involved widespread and collective mobilization. These events would inspire
not only ethnic solidarity but also a "sense of political identity," which Mexican
Americans would employ to advance their civil rights.[2] In the period following
the end of the war, however, anti-Communism increasingly negatively affected
these struggles.

The defense attorney for one of the officers implicated in Salcido's death,
Joseph Scott, would situate the ensuing trial squarely within this ominous political environment. "The America we all love, the citadel of freedom," he declared,
"is at the crossroads of destiny today. . . . We find men and women [Salcido
supporters] raised here by the accident of birth joining with Godless Communism to destroy our nation. . . . We must never forget that where Moscow
rules, there is no God."[3] To some, the plaintiffs in the case clearly had crossed
the Rubicon in daring to question authority and its right to act with impunity.

Drawing an ideological line in the sand, Scott attempted to portray the trial as a struggle between good and evil, patriots and traitors.

In contrast, the Civil Rights Congress (CRC) of Los Angeles and its Eastside branch sought to situate the Salcido case within the context of racism, discrimination, and police abuse. In the introduction to the CRC pamphlet *Justice for Salcido*, Carey McWilliams—journalist, lawyer, and one-time director of the state's Immigration and Housing Commission—provided an important counternarrative to Joseph Scott. "Always unwilling to acknowledge this ugly, underlying motivation," McWilliams reminded his readers, "the dominant group invariably develops a set of rationalizations, or social myths, by which it justifies to itself and to the world the suppression which it practices."[4] In spite of all the efforts by the CRC and other supporters of the Salcido family to shift the debate, the struggle for civil rights in Los Angeles would be subsumed within the politics of the Cold War and McCarthyism. Ironically, as Mexican Americans and liberal activists increased their demands for equality, they also became suspects in the eyes of the anti-Communist crusaders.

This chapter examines the surge of activism that arose from the Mexican American community in Los Angeles following the end of World War II. A new generation of Mexican Americans would come of age determined to make America's promise of democracy and equality a reality for all.[5] I argue that the Mexican American Left represented an important element in this activist upsurge. Indeed, they would mount courageous public campaigns against injustice and help influence the course of politics in the city and region. For Mexican Americans like Ralph Cuarón, the 1930s and 1940s were a time of personal discovery filled with optimism, euphoria, and, most importantly, a desire to change the world.[6]

For many young men of color who went off to fight in the "people's war" against fascism, the struggle for freedom and democracy abroad would correspond with a struggle for civil rights at home.[7] The contradiction between America's professed principles and its practiced prejudices, writes Ronald Takaki, marked the United States during this world conflict.[8] In *Double Victory: A Multicultural History of America in World War II*, Takaki eloquently weaves together numerous stories of those who hoped that by making the ultimate sacrifice for their country, their families could be accepted as equals and, thus, accorded the same rights and privileges as all Americans. By war's end, over one million men of color had served in the armed forces, and of these, over five hundred thousand were Mexican Americans.[9] But what awaited them back home was not what these veterans, or their families, had expected. In one community after another, the message remained clear: Mexican Americans were to maintain their pariah status. Even Congressional Medal of Honor recipients were not spared the humiliation. The case of Silvestre Herrera is poignant. When Governor Sidney Preston Osborn of Arizona proudly declared a day of honor for Herrera, Lorena Oropeza explains, he had to "order Phoenix businesses to take down signs that read "No Mexican Trade Wanted" in advance of that day."[10] In addition to "racial threats and slurs, public signs, and social restrictions," Henry A. J. Ramos reminds us, Mexican Americans would additionally suffer from the "neglect of American institutions."[11] But while conditions at home remained stubbornly resistant to change during and after the war, returning veterans were no longer the same.

Mexican American war veterans were increasingly unwilling to accept their traditional status in American society as outsiders. Changed by their experiences overseas, these veterans were determined to open up the necessary space to advance American democratic and egalitarian principles.[12] "World War II, then," explains Maggie Rivas-Rodríguez, "imbued the ongoing Mexican American civil rights movement with new leadership and a new attitude of entitlement—Mexican American men had, in large numbers, served their country as Americans; now it was time to reap the benefits of full citizenship rights."[13] When Ralph Cuarón entered his service in the U.S. Merchant Marine, he had serious doubts about ever gaining equality. By the time he returned home in 1946, however, he was determined to assert his rights. As he recalled, "I had faith in the system. I had faith in the American democratic system. And I felt that Mexicans could learn to live and to build organizations—democratic organizations. I felt that we could be good Americans."[14]

And yet, this broader struggle for democracy did not preclude discord within the Communist Party. As Cuarón immersed himself in the daily struggles confronting Mexican Americans in Los Angeles, he often felt exasperated by what he regarded as endless party meetings, rigid organizational procedures, and unnecessary formalities. Indeed, his irreverence toward party bureaucracy was indicative of the famous irreverence practiced by the CP waterfront section.[15] As Howard Kimeldorf explains, the "radical propensities of seamen and loggers were partly an outgrowth of their extraordinary geographical mobility."[16] Arguably, these workers were exceedingly cosmopolitan, as they had witnessed poverty on a worldwide scale. Thus, Cuarón had come to embrace a very "itinerant lifestyle" as a member of the CP's Harbor Club.[17] The Mexican American community, Cuarón believed, required urgent organization and defense; therefore, he was often impatient with party pronouncements of Mexican American self-determination *at a future date*. In other words, Cuarón cringed at the notion that Mexican American liberation would have to wait behind that of African Americans, whom many within the party believed took priority over all other minority groups. As Cuarón recalled, "I came into the Communist Party [in Los Angeles] from the outside; I was recruited by the sailors in San Pedro. I was a seaman. So, I brought with me a very militant [orientation]. I came into East Los Angeles and I quickly got involved with a small group of Mexicans from the CP."[18]

Within a short period, Cuarón recalled, he had been elevated into the party's local leadership ranks, "where I began to raise many questions about the CP and why they weren't able to organize the Mexicans."[19] As a member of the Mexican Commission of the Communist Party, which he maintained dealt largely with theoretical problems, Cuarón remembered that

we began to talk about Mexicans in the U.S. and the national question. It aroused the curiosity of the Los Angeles County Commission of the CP. They were furious about this young Mexican seaman who was raising questions about the national question. . . . Dorothy Healey quickly became acquainted with us . . . and joined us in our discussions.[20]

In fact, FBI documents confirm that as early as 1948, Ralph had set his sights beyond Los Angeles. Accordingly, Cuarón had become "active as a section organizer in the CP in Denver, Colorado," in addition to being "very active in the CP in the Los Angeles area."[21] Outside the CP orbit, Cuarón also directed his criticism toward Mexican American organizations that he perceived were counterproductive.

Cuarón was particularly distrustful of middle-class groups, especially of leaders in organizations such as the League of United Latin American Citizens (LULAC), the American GI Forum, as well as the Community Service Organization (CSO). He believed that such groups privileged assimilation and reform as the end-all product of American citizenship—a tendency he regarded as "dead-end." "Their ideas," Cuarón explained, "had no [class] struggle. . . . The idea was that if you went to school and you got educated, you could help yourself—you could be successful. You could end your despair merely by getting a high school diploma."[22]

This stinging rebuke reflected what Cuarón believed was a "chasm" that affected organizing efforts in ethnic communities and among working-class families during this period.[23] Indeed, the Cold War and McCarthyism helped sharpen that ideological divide as different advocacy groups vied for the attention and loyalty of their respective constituencies. Irrespective of political and ideological positions, however, organizing efforts—on a number of fronts— flourished within Mexican American communities after the war.

As noted earlier, the end of the war had not dramatically changed the social, political, and economic dynamics for many communities of color back home; their second-class status remained entrenched. "The de facto exclusion of Mexicans from public facilities, schools, trade unions, juries, and voting," writes Rodolfo Acuña, "was common in many sections of the country."[24] Resistance to this exclusion, however, emerged in both small and large communities. In her study of Santa Paula, California, Martha Menchaca provides a compelling example of how returning veterans and an expanding middle class helped alter race relations in a town dominated by citrus interests—a battle not easily won. "For Mexicans to run for political office and to purchase property in Anglo American neighborhoods was in essence to break social taboos, to violate the political and social boundaries imposed by members of the Anglo-American community."[25] Organizations such as LULAC, El Congreso, the American GI Forum, and CSO led the way in challenging the segregation of Mexican Americans.

Established first in Corpus Christi, Texas, in 1929, LULAC remains "one of the most important of all Mexican American civil rights organizations."[26] And despite the organization's middle-class origins, LULAC was keenly committed to combating racism by demanding their rights as *Americans*. "Their members were among the first to assert a Mexican American identity," Cynthia Orozco writes, "and claim their U.S. citizenship by arguing that they possessed the rights accorded them by the U.S. Constitution."[27] In its first two decades, LULAC's active membership base was engaged in a wide range of activities including "protest, petition drives, community education campaigns, and litigation."[28] Specifically, the group organized voter registration and poll tax campaigns, legal battles against segregation in public facilities, and public campaigns to demand greater political representation of Mexican Americans on juries.[29] LULAC was highly committed to individual achievement and to full integration into the American mainstream. Indeed, their goal was to "develop within the members of our race the best, purest, and most perfect type of a true and loyal citizen of the United States."[30] Although the organization sought first-class citizenship through acculturation and ethnic uplift, LULAC avoided being identified, as one official noted, as a "minority organization."[31] LULAC founders were very conscious of their status as American citizens and therefore felt compelled to exclude non-U.S. citizens from membership. Although LULAC members, and those of like-minded civic organizations, continued to "profess respect for Mexico and for their Mexican heritage," writes David G. Gutiérrez, "they insisted that the best way to advance in American society was to convince other Americans that they too were loyal, upstanding American citizens."[32] Still, their insistence, for example, on English-only during regular organization meetings and their support of restrictive immigration legislation led to strained community relations and some divisions among their own members.

LULAC's faith in education as a vehicle to create change and to transform the individual, writes Benjamin Márquez, "was reflected in the energy it invested in education reform."[33] In 1946, for example, LULAC provided assistance during the landmark lawsuit *Mendez v. Westminster School District*, which successfully argued that racial segregation in schools violated the equal protection clause of the Fourteenth Amendment. The case was pivotal in that it successfully utilized social science and education research to make the argument that segregation had a negative psychological impact on Mexican American children. Thurgood Marshall and the NAACP in *Brown v. Board of Education* would use this strategy with great success. The *Mendez* case was so impactful that it led to the passage of the Anderson bill the following year, repealing all California school codes requiring segregation. And finally, the effect of *Mendez* reverberated as far away as Texas and Arizona, where communities challenged their own segregated schools.[34] In these efforts to advance civil rights, LULAC collaborated with like-minded groups such as the American GI Forum to bolster legal challenges and to broaden the struggle for first-class citizenship.

In 1948, Mexican American veterans organized the American GI Forum to address the intolerable conditions facing returning veterans, their families, and communities at home. The newly formed organization was thrust into national prominence with the case of Private Félix Longoria. Longoria had been killed in the Philippines in the line of duty but was denied funeral services in his hometown because of his Mexican heritage. The GI Forum, led by founding member Dr. Hector P. García, directed a campaign that gained the support of then-senator Lyndon B. Johnson, who arranged for Longoria to be buried in Arlington National Cemetery. Despite its veteran base, writes Ramos, the GI

Forum made concerted efforts to incorporate all its membership, including women, youth, and entire family networks, into its organizational framework. Notably, women in the organization not only organized fundraising events around *tamaladas* (tamale sales), barbecues, dances, and beauty contests, they were also an integral part of the leadership: developing new GI Forum chapters, pursuing initiatives, organizing voter registration drives and community service programs, and lobbying for equal opportunity legislation.[35] Activists involved with the newly formed CSO in Los Angeles also helped galvanize Mexican Americans in confronting long-established barriers to equality.[36]

In postwar Los Angeles, Mexican Americans remained marginalized from meaningful participation on a number of vital community issues ranging from zoning and land use to public health and politics. As the Mexican American population in California increased dramatically between the 1930s and the 1950s (368,013 in 1930; 416,140 in 1940; and 758,400 in 1950), concerns rose over the changing color of the city's inhabitants.[37] "In a city built upon a regional myth of whiteness," writes Eric Avila, "the racial transformation of postwar Los Angeles incited profound anxieties among white working class and middle class residents, who drew nostalgically upon a contrived memory of a city that never was—a white city."[38] By 1950, for example, Los Angeles County alone was home to some 287,614 "white persons of Spanish surname." Furthermore, in a sign of the deep-seated racial anxieties, "the 'darkening' of the urban population overshadowed other coexisting concerns" such as urban sprawl, pollution, Communists, and even the Soviet Union.[39] These concerns went far beyond Los Angeles, however. For most European Americans, writes Thomas Borstelmann, returning to a peacetime life "meant a life grounded in segregation and white domination of people of color." Moreover, "for most white Southerners, the reestablishment of Jim Crow far surpassed other Cold War priorities like promoting democracy."[40] From East Los Angeles, however, Mexican Americans challenged that citadel of white domination—the Los Angeles municipal government—by supporting one of their own in a race for city council.

With the support of family, friends, veterans, and labor activists, Edward R. Roybal challenged the political establishment in 1947 by announcing his bid to run for the city council's Ninth District seat, which represented parts of downtown and the Eastside. Many Mexican Americans gave Roybal their enthusiastic support because of his years of service, outreach, and familiarity with issues that affected their community. The author Beatrice Griffith wrote in 1949: "As educational director for the Los Angeles Tuberculosis Association, he [Roybal] knew their health problems. He knew the ugly face of discrimination in employment, for doors had been slammed in his face, too. He knew the value of a democracy; he fought and his brother died to preserve it while fighting overseas."[41] But Roybal's campaign was also buttressed by a coalition of Jewish American, African American, Japanese American, and Euro-American supporters. In her study of interracial cooperation, Shana Bernstein writes that moderate civil rights activists concerned about the repressive nature of anti-Communism worked diligently on the Eastside to support someone who would advocate for their needs. Fearing that their activism on behalf of civil rights would be tainted as un-American and subversive, some in the Jewish community and other groups (mostly liberals) worked to dissociate themselves from radicals—specifically Communists. Significantly, this interracial community of activists would play a key role in providing moral, financial, legal, and political support in the development and success of the CSO.[42] Although Roybal did not prevail in the election, he gained tremendous respect and admiration for the effort.

With Roybal losing by only three hundred votes, the campaign learned that success in a future attempt would require an extensive voter education and organization campaign.[43] Indeed, by 1948, voter registration mobilizations on the Eastside paralleled similar efforts elsewhere across the nation. In El Paso, Texas, for example, "30,000 Mexican-Americans paid their poll taxes to vote in the primaries—the largest number recorded in history."[44] The CSO in Los Angeles grew out of the excitement and optimism generated by the campaign. The organization worked diligently, through countless open forums, to inform and consider vital community issues such as housing, health, education, citizenship, and political representation. The participation of women in the CSO moved them to new heights of political and civic engagement. As full-fledged members with voting rights, they helped build and expand the CIO.[45] With the leadership of Fred Ross—undergirded by Saul Alinsky's concepts of mass organization for power—the CSO helped launch a major campaign to get new voters registered.[46] The success of this campaign led to Roybal's triumph over the incumbent, Parley Christianson, in 1949, with a comfortable margin of over eighty-five hundred votes.[47] Without a doubt, the CSO played a major role in the election, and its impact would continue to be felt for generations. However, despite the increased sense of citizenship and belonging gained through these activities, many others shied away from this kind of public display.

The memories of xenophobia and ostracism experienced by immigrant and nonimmigrant Mexican families during and after the Great Depression certainly shaped their view of American society. "Although thousands of Mexican Americans did begin to think of themselves more as Americans than as Mexicans during the 1940s," writes Gutiérrez, "thousands more remained deeply ambivalent about their cultural and national identities."[48] Mexicans had reason to distrust the value of citizenship. Indeed, for many, citizenship proved to be no protection against deportation, discrimination, and police brutality. By the mid to late 1950s, Gutiérrez notes, some Mexican American leaders and organizations would begin to reassess traditional positions that blamed the presence of Mexican aliens for the misfortunes plaguing Mexican American communities.[49]

Not only did Cuarón steer away from placing blame on immigrants for economic woes affecting Mexican Americans, he remained a vocal critic of ideological positions that advocated conformity, patriotism, and free market capitalism. For example, whereas LULAC believed that racism represented "a blemish on the American record of fairness and justice," Cuarón viewed racism as an essential component of American capitalism and its imperialist policies.[50] LULAC's call for limited social change "in the hope that it would prevent social cleavages from exploding into class and racial warfare" was precisely what Cuarón found counterproductive.[51] Contrary to LULAC's emphasis on the middle class, Cuarón believed that leadership had to be nurtured and developed from within the ranks of the working class, and rejected any notion of an educated elite lifting up the masses.

Despite his sharp criticism, Cuarón as well as other Communists did not dismiss altogether the contributions of reformist Mexican American civil rights organizations. In fact, Cuarón spent a great deal of his activist career working and collaborating with such organizations. During Edward R. Roybal's second attempt at public office, for example, Cuarón supported him and the fledgling CSO. "I raised some funds for him once," he recalled, "and he accepted it. I was his great supporter in the [Furniture Workers] union."[52] Cuarón also acknowledged participating in CSO forums and meetings but did not hold official leadership positions within the organization. In another example, Henry Steinberg, "known in his neighborhood as a fighter for the rights of the Jewish people and Mexican Americans," was a well-known CP activist on the Eastside who helped organize the CSO.[53] Irrespective of political ideology, activists on the Eastside were engaged in a historic period, "which highlighted a special sense of urgency, not only to improve educational conditions, but also to advance justice and equal opportunity."[54]

Notwithstanding his propensity to move ahead on his own, Cuarón surrounded himself with a number of mentors who would help guide and instruct his activism in Los Angeles. Among these early mentors were Frank López and Armando Dávila. Cuarón recalled that López, in particular, played an important role in his life. Indeed, by the time their paths crossed, López had had a long career as a labor organizer and community activist in Los Angeles. Beginning in 1933, López became a key leader and organizer in the fledgling militant labor movement taking shape across the country during this decade. His election in 1935 as vice president of Furniture Workers Local 1561, a CIO union, was a significant victory. As Luis Arroyo explains,

> López had developed the quickest. An articulate, dynamic, inquisitive person, he soon became a confirmed believer in industrial unionism and in the need for unions to protect the rights of the workingman. Initially elected to the vice-presidency, a "token" position, López learned quickly and was next elected recording secretary—a true decision-making office. . . . His victory . . . marked a radical change in the union's politics.[55]

López would go on to help organize and direct the upstart UFWA Local 576 in a long and bitter struggle against the American Federation of Labor. The stature of Mexican workers in Local 576 would also be raised by the work of other radical leaders, including Ben Cruz, Armando Dávila, Manuel García Jiménez, and Eddie Valles, to name a few.[56] When López helped Cuarón secure employment at Crest Pacific Furniture in 1947, Cuarón quickly moved up the ranks of Local 576.

Within a year, Gus Brown, a prominent labor organizer in the CIO and business agent for Local 576, appointed Cuarón as an organizer. As an officer in charge of the stewards' council, Cuarón found the avenue by which to implement his own efforts to develop and nurture Mexican American leadership. Cuarón did not take his union position lightly. He initiated an educational program to bring young workers into the union, intending, as a part of that project, to instill class consciousness. In other words, he sought to engender among the workers an understanding that they were more than merely *wage earners*: they were the vanguard of a democratic workers' movement. Moreover, Cuarón believed, as Maurice Isserman argues, that Communist leadership was essential in elevating the "elemental confrontation at the point of production . . . to a higher political level."[57] Cuarón strove to dispel what he described as the highly seductive, yet illusive promise of personal fulfillment and economic security that materialism offered. Indeed, American society in the postwar period was increasingly infused with ideologies of the home and new technologies that promised to restore the American family and make it a bulwark against an uncertain world.[58] But for Cuarón, security could only be attained by organizing the masses—nothing else sufficed. He was in his midtwenties—ambitious, brash, and impatient. However, the tendency to move and act on his own volition, as conditions and events demanded, would lead to friction with some in the CP leadership. The first confrontation would come when Cuarón answered a call for assistance by the newly organized Civil Rights Congress (CRC).

The CRC developed out of the need to counter the growing attacks on civil liberties across the country. In addition to its focus on racial equality and labor rights, what set the CRC apart from other organizations was its aggressive use of the courts in conjunction with mass action.[59] In fact, the activists behind the CRC understood that the most effective way of challenging the assault on civil rights was to confront it head-on, by using direct action—"the mass pressure of the people."[60] The CRC, Gerald Horne explains, did not view the judiciary system as a neutral dispenser of the law, but as a "tool of reaction" that could be influenced to produce positive outcomes.[61] The people who made up the core of the CRC—attorneys, labor leaders, community activists—were very passionate about civil liberties. So, too, was the organization's support network, which one newspaper angrily complained included "Protestant bishops, judges, university professors, movie stars, lawyers, and Henry A. Wallace."[62] The CRC was an interracial organization dedicated to promoting racial equality, educating the general public about their rights, and, more importantly, encouraging them to act.[63]

The CRC in Southern California proved to be particularly effective. In addition to having an active working-class constituency, the organization could also count on the support of prominent Hollywood personalities. "Their sponsors in 1946," notes Horne, "included Artie Shaw, Lena Horne, Dalton Trumbo, John Garfield, Gregory Peck, Frank Sinatra, and others."[64] According to a CRC pamphlet, "The program of the CRC is threefold; the defense of the rights of labor, of Negro, Mexican, and other national groups, and the rights of political minorities." In addition,

CRC participates in campaigns for the repeal of the Taft-Hartley Law and other labor-repressive measures. CRC fights for the rights of the Mexican and Negro workers to jobs and against discrimination on the job. It conducts educational campaigns in the trade unions on the meaning of Jimcrow [*sic*] and anti-Semitism and their causes. It supports every action leading toward unity of Negro and white, Jew and non-Jew, native and foreign-born in the struggle against fascism and for economic security and peace.[65]

The CRC's courageous stance against police brutality, segregation, and human-rights abuses helped assure the organization of important public support at a time when confronting the status quo was viewed with suspicion. And indeed, for cold warriors the CRC's program reeked of "communism"—pure and simple.

Leading the charge against Communists, alleged Communists, and progressives in the state was Senator Jack B. Tenney, a Democrat from Los Angeles. "Tenney, a former piano player and song writer," wrote David P. Gardner, "entered public life in 1936 when he was elected to the California State Assembly on the Democratic ticket." Indeed, for the next three years, he was associated with "liberal and 'left-wing' causes." But then something changed. "Following defeat in his bid for reelection as president of Local 47 in December of 1939," writes Gardner, "Tenney turned against several of the same liberal causes he had supported only shortly before. In the next session of the California Legislature, he emerged as a leading proponent of a bill designed to deny the Communist [P]arty the right to a place on the ballot." In the following year, he was appointed as chairman of the Fact-Finding Committee on Un-American Activities.[66]

Senator Tenney wrote that one of the most important weapons in the Communist Party arsenal was "the 'front' or 'transmission-belt' organization."[67] In fact, he reduced these organizations to being simple "Stalinist satellites" of the Soviet Union.

The general purpose of a Communist 'front' organization is to secure the services of distinguished persons, whose very names aid in concealing the real character of the organization, thus extending Communist agitation and propaganda to non-Communist masses.[68]

And, yet, the rabble-rousing that seemed to irk Tenney the most was that which targeted or emanated from communities of color.

Tenney was vehemently opposed to any legislation that attempted to outlaw discrimination, attacking these as deliberate interferences with employer rights and the free flow of trade. "Every American should denounce," Tenney declared, "the crime of raising the flames of hope in the hearts of innocent

and uninformed people for a Utopia of brotherly love."[69] Attempts to outlaw
discrimination were promptly situated within this cold war prism that reflected
Communistic plotting and intrigue.[70] Thus, the Sleepy Lagoon case and the
Zoot Suit riots were prime examples of how Tenney believed the Communists
stirred up "racial agitation." This strategy was not peculiar to California, however. Conflating anti-Communism and racial discrimination appears to have
dovetailed neatly with Dixiecrat efforts to maintain Jim Crow policies. As the
national Democratic Party increased its support for racial equality after 1948,
explains Borstelmann, Dixiecrats, by comparison, raised the "rhetoric of anti-
communism" as a cover for segregation. "If Communists and other radicals
supported racial equality, they asked, what clearer evidence could there be of its
subversiveness? They played on rising fears of domestic subversion in an effort
to fend off Truman's liberal racial legislative goals."[71] In all of the analysis and
evidence presented by Tenney, Mexican Americans appeared as hapless pawns,
bending and shifting with the political winds. The reality, of course, was altogether different.

In Los Angeles, as elsewhere across the nation, Mexican communities had
long struggled against pervasive police brutality. In his study of the relationship between Mexican Americans and the Los Angeles Police Department
(LAPD), Edward Escobar explores how race has been a defining factor. From
their inception, police departments have functioned, writes Escobar, as "agents
of social control," working to uphold and defend the rights and privileges of
the elite class.[72] And central to this coercive mandate has been law enforcement's role—at the behest of the state—in "maintaining racial inequality."[73]
Despite the police reform movement launched in the 1930s to "professionalize"
law enforcement, the antagonism toward Mexican American communities in
the Southwest remained largely intact.[74] Minority communities were increasingly identified by the LAPD as cesspools of criminality. During the first three
decades of the twentieth century, Mexican Americans became not only the targets of yellow journalism, but also the recipients of increased police surveillance,
harassment, and arrest. For their part, Mexican Americans would increasingly
organize to challenge this "policing" of their communities and in the process
form, as Escobar contends, a new "Mexican American political identity."[75]
Needless to say, McCarthyism and the Cold War made it increasingly difficult
for activists to bring these issues to the attention of the general public.

From its inception, some CRC activists understood that their charge had
to be broader than a focus on African Americans.[76] Under the leadership of

attorney William L. Paterson in 1948, the national organization was initially oriented toward the civil liberties of the African American community. In a letter to Marjorie Robinson, CRC organizational secretary of the Los Angeles chapter, Patterson wrote, "He who has the leadership of the Negro people for equal rights, has the leadership of the whole American movement for constitutional liberties, civil and human rights. . . . There is no problem, no issue, no project . . . that takes priority over the Negro question."[77] In contrast, Aubrey Grossman, West Coast director of the CRC based in the Bay Area, reminded Patterson that the success of the CRC and, indeed, of the progressive movement in general, had to be built by making serious inroads "in the Mexican community."[78]

The CRC in Los Angeles proved ill equipped to meet the tremendous need for its services on the Eastside. The sheer volumes of cases, wrote Horne, meant that the local chapter "faced the problem of growth" and not demise, as was the case with so many affiliates throughout the Southwest.[79] By June 1947, William R. Bidner became the organization's executive director, and Anne Shore would serve as the organizational secretary.[80] Marguerite Robinson joined the CRC in 1948 and two years later would become its executive director. Other important leaders included: Emil Freed;[81] Rose Chernin, active for many years in the CP's International Labor Defense (ILD);[82] and La Rue McCormick, longtime head of the ILD and co-founder of the Sleepy Lagoon Defense Committee.[83] Celia Rodríguez, the only Mexican American on staff, was the financial secretary.

Rodríguez joined the CRC from the onset and immediately became its principal liaison with the Mexican community on the Eastside.[84] She was a valuable asset to the CRC because of her activism on behalf of cannery workers and dedication to civil rights. As one CRC booklet boasted, "Her leadership has been a major factor in making CRC known to the Mexican people and the problems of the Mexican people known to the community at large."[85] Despite her efforts, however, the workload proved overwhelming. Ralph Cuarón heeded the CRC's call for help and opened up a storefront office. His success was due, in part, to the ease with which he was able to collect funds and other resources from the residents of Boyle Heights and surrounding neighborhoods, including assistance from UFWA members sympathetic with this cause. He soon referred cases to the CRC main office located on South Spring Street in downtown. The operation did not last very long, however. Within approximately two or three months, Cuarón was forced to close his doors; the order didn't come from local authorities but from the CP.

FIGURE 2 Celia Rodríguez, Civil Rights Congress, 1951. Courtesy of Celia Rodríguez.

The local CP leadership seemed distrustful of Cuarón's activities. Indeed, his apparent ad hoc approach is what unnerved some. As Cuarón recalled, he had already made his priorities known to many in the party, and it appeared that some felt he might use this opportunity to create a personal power base from which to launch a separate organization—outside the CP's orbit.[86] This seemingly irrational response by party leaders, however, appears to have precedents dating back to the early 1930s. As Robin D. G. Kelley reveals in the case of African Americans in the South, the Communist Party's central leadership had long committed itself to retaining control—or, "its leading role"—in the struggle for equality and self-determination.[87] For his part, Cuarón made no secret of the fact that he would use this opportunity to educate Mexican Americans about their rights as well as recruit them into the party. Party leaders, however, were not prepared to let loose this young, energetic comrade onto the Mexican American community.

For the Cuaróns, the decision to shut them down sent a clear message: the party was principally concerned with "toeing the line, following policy . . . their policy."[88] Thus, as Sylvia Cuarón pointed out, Ralph "was a *travieso* [naughty] child, almost a bastard child."[89] The closure of this CRC satellite office forced Cuarón to rethink his strategies, as he aimed to focus his energies on the Mexican American community. Far from being discouraged as a result of the party's rebuke, Cuarón felt compelled to organize beyond East Los Angeles. "Well, I became more active, more active nationally. I ended up in a national convention in Salt Lake City [Utah] to discuss these questions. And I met vocal friends in the Midwest."[90] Try as it might to control and monitor the activities of its members, the party simply could not compel complete obedience; nor could it be everywhere at once.

In 1947, the party selected Cuarón to attend a conference in New York organized to oppose military conscription. As the crisis between the United States and the Soviet Union heated up in Germany, so too did calls for a peacetime draft. After completing his work in New York, Cuarón did not return immediately to Los Angeles as scheduled. Instead, he attended a Communist Party meeting in Denver, Colorado. There he met with Arthur Bary, "the head of the western region of the CP," representing Colorado and the Midwest, and with Patricia Blau, the secretary of the CP's local office in Denver.[91] Bary had become familiar with Cuarón's outspoken position on national minority rights and convinced him to make a presentation at a party convention of the Rocky

Mountain region. Cuarón recalled that the majority of the delegates at the Salt Lake City convention agreed with his assessment that a new position on the Mexican American national question was necessary and that it ought to be a national priority for the Communist Party. Cuarón firmly believed that Mexican Americans were not a foreign element in the United States, but instead were an oppressed national minority that should be incorporated fully into the struggle to destroy imperialism at home and abroad. The delegates agreed that this issue should be presented at the national convention of the Communist Party scheduled for 1948.[92]

On his return from the conference in Utah, Ben Dobbs, Los Angeles County labor secretary of the CP, castigated Cuarón for his impromptu presentation. As Cuarón explains:

> Then I came back to Los Angeles and Ben Dobbs got a hold of me and started chewing me out. He wanted to know where the hell I was and why I had not come back right away. I told him who I had met with and what we had done. He was pissed off. I had stepped on his toes. I had got him in trouble with the national office.[93]

Even Dorothy Healy, his strongest advocate within the top leadership, was not amused with Cuarón's unscheduled trip. "Dorothy Healey was furious," Cuarón recalled, "because we were interfering with national politics in the CP. This was their territory."[94] Nevertheless, there were no serious repercussions. Instead, his popularity appears to have risen within the rank and file, especially among Mexican Americans.[95] Despite the CP's efforts to curtail Cuarón's activities, his actions had the effect of getting the wheels turning toward the formation of a separate CRC, one specifically charged with addressing issues in the Mexican American community.

In March 1947, the Mexican Civil Rights Committee, a new affiliate of the Los Angeles chapter of the CRC, had formed.[96] In June, Leroy Parra, the organization's first chair, co-authored a letter with CRC executive director William R. Bidner, requesting the support of the membership and the public in yet another case of police abuse. Two months earlier, William J. Keyes and another LAPD officer from the Hollenbeck Station shot and wounded two young Mexican American veterans, Albert Rodríguez and Joseph González, "in the back without reason."[97] The officers had accused the young men of attacking them with "knives" and charged them with assault with a deadly weapon. The criminal charges moved both organizations to hire longtime activist and CRC lawyer Leo Gallagher to defend the young men.[98] This new case of police abuse also served as a rallying cry for the fledgling organization that by August had been formally renamed the Mexican-American Civil Rights Congress (MA-CRC). To inaugurate the new organization, a "Fiesta and Celebration" was held at the end of August at the Sons of Hermann Hall, located on East 25th Street. Margo Albert, a Mexican American film actress and dancer, and the wife of actor Eddie Albert, was the chair of the program and helped facilitate the event.[99]

The Mexican-American CRC received support from several progressive sectors in this historically diverse section of the city (Boyle Heights, Hollenbeck, Maravilla, Belvedere, and City Terrace).[100] A partial list of the key individuals and organizations that formed the support network around the MA-CRC included Ralph Cuarón, Frank González, and Alexander Martínez of the American Veterans Committee (AVC); Frank López, United Electrical Workers Local 1421; Bruno Cano, Nicolas Ramírez, and Oscar Castro, UFWA; and Juanita Madrigal, YWCA.[101] Other organizations present at the fiesta included the American Jewish Committee; News Vendors Local 75; International Ladies' Garment Workers' Union; Progressive Citizens of America; and the Aliso Village Residents Council.[102] In the days leading to the grand fiesta, the *Eastside Sun*, a local weekly newspaper, carried a short announcement from the executive board of the Progressive Citizens of America "strongly" urging its members, and the community at large, to support the MA-CRC.[103] For fiesta participants and observers, the Saturday event was a resounding success.

In less than a month, the MA-CRC was embroiled in another case involving the local police. In September 1947, two plainclothes LAPD officers attempted to disrupt a meeting of the MA-CRC and the Belvedere chapter of the AVC. The meeting had been called to discuss the recent brutal beating, by Officer William Keyes, of Bruno Cano, a UFWA Local 576 member. In a public letter co-authored by Cuarón, Oscar Castro, and the CRC's William Bidner, they noted that the officers (Keyes and Ernest R. Sánchez) had publicly admitted that they were acting "under orders of Police Chief C. B. Horrall to break up any meetings which they considered subversive." The letter continued by stating:

> This is the third incident of this nature, which occurred recently. Obviously, this
> is the beginning of a reign of terror in the Boyle Heights-Belvedere community
> to break up and intimidate meetings of trade unions, progressives and minority
> organizations.[104]

In October, a committee of thirty organizational representatives, headed by Assemblyman William H. Rosenthal, met with assistant chief of police Joseph Reed to demand that police officers "respect the civil liberties of the citizens and organizations and that Chief Reed guarantee that such provocative police activities stop."[105] Yet, by December it was clear to community activists that no disciplinary action would be taken. The consequences of that decision became glaringly clear to many when on March 10, 1948, officers Keyes and Sánchez were implicated in the brutal shooting of Augustino Salcido.

The death of Salcido shocked and angered Eastside residents. The news that patrolmen Keyes and Sánchez were directly involved, and then exonerated of any wrongdoing by the county coroner's office, ignited further indignation in the community. The facts in the case were murky, at best, and the coroner's inquest did little to clarify what had happened in the predawn hours. Keyes testified that he and Sánchez had "received information that stolen jewelry was being peddled" in the Bunker Hill section of the city.[106] Novelist and screenwriter Guy Endore had noted that the inquest did not attempt to investigate why these two officers, assigned to the Hollenbeck Division, located "across the bridge on the other side of the city," had responded to the call.[107] At the El Conocito cafe on Temple and Grand Street, the officers concluded that Salcido had been connected to a robbery that had netted fifty watches, and escorted him outside for further questioning and possible arrest. Instead of taking Salcido to their patrol vehicle, the officers walked the youth some seventy feet from the cafe to the entryway of a locked and dimly lit building. While escorting Salcido up the stairwell leading to the main door entrance, a scuffle took place in which Salcido, while trying to "escape," received four fatal gunshots to the upper body.[108] Endore described the bullet wounds:

> One bullet crashed through the head approximately from ear to ear. Two drilled almost parallel holes through the back of the boy's head, starting at the base of the brain and coming out of [the] forehead and temple. . . . A fourth shattered one of the bones of the forearm.[109]

One of the shots had been fired at such close range that it left "powder burns" on the victim's face. The degree of the violence perpetrated against the teenage victim as well as the coroner's jury verdict of "justifiable homicide" caused outrage.[110] Endore recounted the ensuing reaction.

AUGUSTINE SALCIDO

FIGURE 3 Augustino Salcido, 1948. Courtesy of the CRC Collection, Southern California Library.

But this decision did not sit easily with the residents of Bunker Hill. It did not sit easily with the *People's Daily World*, the only paper to give the case full coverage from the beginning. It did not sit easily with such people as Ralph Cuaron of the Belvedere chapter of the American Veterans' Committee, with Frank Pestana of the Community Services Organization, with Reverent Hugh Weston, with Oscar Castro of the CIO, with Jack Berman of PCA, and others, all of whom kept calling upon William Bidner and Anne Shore of the Local Civil Rights Congress to push for a re-opening of the case in the interest of justice.[111]

The day after the inquest, the MA-CRC and the Los Angeles CRC arranged a meeting with District Attorney William Simpson. The large delegation scheduled to meet with Simpson included a host of progressive organizations active on the Eastside and throughout the city.[112] The most prominent figures included Ralph Cuarón; José R. Chávez, assembly candidate in the Fifty-First District; Ann Shore, CRC; Jesse Parra, MA-CRC; Rudy Salcido, brother of the victim; Leticia Innes, Soto-Michigan Jewish Community Center; H. Nava, Community Service Organization; and William Belton, Los Angeles CIO Council.

The delegation, however, never met with the district attorney. Simpson refused to meet with the group, and letters to various officials, including Chief Reed, went unanswered.[113]

The intensity of the police harassment and brutality was such that the pro-Salcido activists found it increasingly difficult to inform the public about the case and their organizing activities. Nine days after the killing, the Los Angeles CIO Council passed a resolution reiterating its "support to the Mexican-American and other minorities in their fight against the intimidations, brutalities, and terror tactics of the police department." They also condemned District Attorney Simpson and LAPD chief Reed for their refusal to hear the petitions of community leaders and citizens.[114] The resolution demanded that Simpson open a public meeting to "hear testimony and protests against Patrolman Keyes and the policies of the Police Department." The resolution also emphasized that the three main witnesses in the case, Guillermo Gallegos, Ella Moody, and Oscar del Campo, had been victims of ongoing harassment by LAPD. Indeed, they had been "arrested, beaten, and intimidated" on numerous occasions. Because Gallegos was the only eyewitness to the shooting, the reprisals against him were particularly intense.[115]

Cuarón stepped up his public presence in the community with a series of appearances before local organizations on the subject of police abuse. In fact, the FBI would note that Ralph Cuarón had become "very active" and "had developed favorable CP relationships with the Mexican-American community in Los Angeles and was active in propagandizing alleged police brutality towards Mexican Americans."[116] Cuarón remembered: "I was making speeches all over the city . . . I was getting people aroused." These activities did not go unnoticed by local authorities. The police heightened their surveillance of Cuarón wherever he and his cohorts traveled by making their presence known at meetings—usually by brandishing their side arms to amplify their intimidation. It was also common practice for the police to follow—and on occasion detain—the intrepid activists with their "prowl" (patrol) cars.[117] In one incident, Cuarón recalled, he was pulled over by police, near Hollenbeck Park, and his car was searched. The questioning that night intensified when one of the officers discovered a large quantity of "books about Marxism" and other political literature in the trunk of the car. When Cuarón responded to one of the interrogating officers with, "It's not against the law to read, is it?" the retort from the officer was, "For this kind of stuff it is."[118]

It was at one of these numerous community meetings that Cuarón would meet his future lifelong partner, Sylvia Lucas. Sylvia's parents, Samuel and Adel, emigrated from Ukraine, Russia, between 1917 and 1918 at the start of the Revolution and spent several years in eastern Europe. In the early 1920s, the family finally immigrated to the United States. On entering Ellis Island, immigration officials shortened Samuel's family name from Lukachevski to Lucas.[119] The family opened up their first grocery store near Prospect Place and Harvard Avenue in the largely Jewish community of Crown Heights, New York. Of the four siblings (Ruth, Alex, Rose, and Sylvia), Sylvia was the youngest and the only one to be born in the United States—"the Americanski in the family," Sylvia recalled with humor and some nostalgia. And, as such, she was afforded some degree of leisure to experiment, and even traverse beyond the seemingly sheltered and limited world that her parents inhabited.[120]

After graduating from Thomas Jefferson High School in 1941, Sylvia decided to pursue her interest in the arts. She joined a local art school owned and directed by Moi Solotaroff, an émigré who had trained in the Moscow Theatre School. From her home, several times a week, Sylvia made the trek to Manhattan on the subway where Solotaroff's studio, The Group Collective, was located. Here, Sylvia was exposed to a unique social environment, "a cross-culture of people," as she recalled warmly, that exuded community and comradeship. In one of her fondest memories of living in New York, Sylvia recalled the time when she played the lead role in a theatrical production at the Barbizon-Plaza Hotel.[121] The proceeds generated from this one and only performance in 1943 were donated to Secretary of the Treasury Henry Morgenthau as a contribution to the war effort.[122] But her time in New York did not last long; in that same year, her parents decided to move to California.

Sylvia remembered that her parents yearned to escape the extreme weather of the East Coast. Manya, Adel's sister, had recently moved to Sierra Madre, California, and sent "glowing pictures" of the warm climate in Southern California, convincing the Lucases to move west. Samuel Lucas traveled ahead to Los Angeles to open up a new business and to make preparations for Adel and Sylvia, who followed the next year. In a short time, he succeeded in establishing a small store called the Chicago Creamery on Brooklyn Avenue and Saint Louis Street in Boyle Heights.[123] Their first home was an apartment on Folsom Street, just a few blocks away.[124] As Sylvia recalled, "There was one Mexican family across the street from us on Folsom Street . . . the rest were Jewish residents."[125]

Sylvia proudly noted that her father churned and sold his own butter and, as a result, gained a steady clientele coming from as far away as Tujunga, some twenty miles away.

Sylvia's introduction to progressive politics did not happen by choice. Her political "awakening," she remembered, happened while working for the Los Angeles City Housing Authority (CHA).

> I had arrived in California from New York in February of '44. So I was quite new, not only geographically for that area, but not at all attuned to anything radical, until I met the people working for the Housing Authority. They were the beginning of my awakening of radicalism. And that's where I met a group of people where Frank Wilkinson was a supervisor of some kind. . . . I would meet him and a group of other like [minded] people. When I say "like," I mean politically active people.[126]

During a weekend excursion to the San Bernardino Mountains, organized by and for CHA employees, she first became aware of the intense political world that permeated her work environment and the surrounding community.[127] The young people she met at the CHA also impressed on her the need for education. With their encouragement, as well as her father's, Sylvia enrolled at Los Angeles City College in 1945. When her father became ill, however, she withdrew. Tragically, within a few months, Samuel passed away. Devastated by the loss, Sylvia immersed herself in the family business where she worked for the next two years. Nevertheless, she yearned for the stimulating environment of the Housing Authority. Despite the heavy work schedule at the family store, she found the time to volunteer at the Soto-Michigan Jewish Community Center.[128] It was here, in 1948, that Sylvia met Ralph Cuarón.

The occasion was a community meeting at which Edward R. Roybal, candidate for the city's Ninth District seat, was invited to speak. After his presentation, Sylvia remembered, Roybal "called a young Mexican American to speak about issues at hand of police brutality and discrimination against Mexican American youth. And on the stage walks this handsome, beautiful, self-effacing, but so articulate, young man that he took my breath away."[129] The passion Sylvia saw in Cuarón that night impressed her; one year later, they married.

On that night, Cuarón stood on stage hoping to convince the largely Jewish audience that the civil rights of all Angelenos were imperiled. The persistent refusal by the district attorney's office, the city council, and the police department to investigate the death of Augustino Salcido prompted the pro-Salcido supporters to take the case directly to the public. On March 29 and 31, 1948, the *Daily People's World* ran articles detailing the plans for a combination memorial meeting for Salcido and "public trial" against Officer William Keyes. Margo Albert, again, played a key role in organizing the mock trial.[130] News of the impending trial in absentia for Keyes apparently created enough of a stir within the LAPD to compel the agency to act. Within hours of the start of the event at the Moose Lodge, the venue suddenly—and without explanation—became "unavailable." Philip M. Connelly, secretary-treasurer of the Los Angeles CIO Council, expressed little patience with Frank Grillo's decision to renege on the Lodge's contractual obligation.

> I am . . . amazed that you, a former trade union official, took the position you are reported by the press as having taken in regard to the wanton killing of a Mexican boy by a trigger-happy cop. Apparently, you have quickly forgotten your own experiences as a fighter for people's right [*sic*] in the United Rubber Workers. I would have assumed that the Moose Lodge, with its tradition and background would be on the side of oppressed minority people, not identified with the current drive to Nazify America by persecuting minorities, denying free assemble of the people and encouraging police brutality and murder.[131]

The mock trial took place instead at the Embassy Auditorium, located in the Ambassador Hotel in downtown Los Angeles. The event was well attended, with a "standing-room-only audience" of over six hundred people. The Embassy had served as a haven for minorities and progressive organizations (between the 1930s and the 1950s), chronicles Dolores Hayden, "when severe racial discrimination, increasingly strong antiunion sentiment, and McCarthyism limited the availability of meeting places."[132] The presiding "judge" was attorney and activist Richard Ibañez and the "prosecutor" was CRC attorney Leo Gallagher in the case of "the Mexican-American Community vs. the Los Angeles Police Department."[133] The citizens' jury included a number of community activists, such as Charlotta A. Bass, publisher of the *California Eagle*, and Edward R. Roybal. The jury was unanimous in its verdict against Keyes: "guilty of murder in the first degree."[134]

When, on April 3, Guillermo Gallegos signed a manslaughter complaint against Officer Keyes before Justice of the Peace Stanley W. Moffatt, in Huntington Park, the case took a new turn. Judge Moffatt's decision to issue a warrant for the arrest of Officer Keyes drew a sharp reaction from the LAPD, the city council, and the district attorney's office: the red-baiting was unleashed with all earnestness. Cognizant that the political heat had now reached a new level, Cuarón, Sambrano, Frances Lym, Celia Rodríguez, and Julia Luna Mount acted with greater determination to keep Gallegos from appearing in public and risk confrontation with the police. Celia Rodríguez remembered the exhausting work involved trying to keep Gallegos out of sight of the LAPD. This work included having to move him from one house to another, while minimizing his contacts so that only a select few knew his whereabouts at any one time.[135] Cuarón, too, recalled all the work involved to keep "Willie" from falling into the wrong hands: "We could never show him out in public or the cops would pick him up. . . . Then, one day, he got out. The next day, the cops picked him up and arrested him for possession [of marijuana]."[136]

On April 6, the *Herald-Express* reported that officers D. J. Medina and D. Molino had taken the "26-year-old transient" into custody for possession of "marijuana cigarettes." According to the arresting officers, Gallegos voluntarily provided them with the following incriminating *confession*: "I found the marijuana cigarettes. I like the stuff. I smoke it all the time."[137] Coincidentally, Gallegos was "booked on suspicion of violating the narcotics act" only hours after Officer Keyes had surrendered to Judge Moffatt's San Antonio Township Court.[138] Gallegos's *confession* lacked credibility, but the police obtained what they wanted all along—the opportunity to discredit or remove Gallegos as a key witness in the preliminary hearing of Officer Keyes, scheduled for April 12.

Meanwhile, eyewitnesses Oscar del Campo and Ella Moody had also been arrested, and they too faced court appearances. Del Campo was arrested on a vagrancy charge, and he faced trial on April 15. Officers Molina and Medina arrested Moody on a charge of public drunkenness, and she faced trial on April 23. With the principal witnesses entangled in the court system and on the defensive, the supporters of Keyes, which included the Los Angeles Fire and Police Protective League (responsible for providing Keyes's legal defense and $2,000 bail), moved to discredit Judge Stanley Moffatt himself.

As the *Daily News* reported on the day of the preliminary hearing, Gallegos now became "a forgotten man" as anti-Communism took center stage.[139] The opening volley was a seven-page affidavit introduced by defense attorney Joseph Scott, asking Judge Moffatt to disqualify himself from presiding at the preliminary hearing on "the grounds of his own affiliations and principles."[140] According to a *Herald-Express* report, the document accused the judge of "having been associated with known Communists and Communist sympathizers and having been an active member of Communist Front organizations in Southern California for 12 years."[141] Scott denounced what he called the "masquerade trial" and berated Judge Moffatt for his apparent weakness of character for allowing himself, and the court, to be duped by the "Communist program."[142] The *Daily News* accurately assessed the unruly atmosphere when it captioned its photo of Scott pointing at Judge Moffatt: "Ideological Warfare in the Courtroom."[143]

SCOTT: Why was it [the preliminary hearing for Officer Keyes] brought down here? Why was it brought down here? To make you a sucker and fall guy for those people.

JUDGE: They are not making me a sucker. I am trying to bring about justice in this county. This court is open to all who want to file a complaint.

SCOTT: In that affidavit it states that back of this whole movement is a Communist program that is behind this thing.

JUDGE: You don't have to do any red baiting out here.

SCOTT: It is not red baiting. I don't like that kind of language used, even if you are the chief justice, I would resent it. I am no red-baiter, don't tell me that.

JUDGE: There is no law in California against a man being a Communist, so don't try to make out . . .

SCOTT: You don't tell me you are a Communist, do you?

JUDGE: I will put you in jail for contempt if you call me a Communist.[144]

The thrust and counterthrust went on throughout the hearing despite the judge's admonitions. However, Scott gained the upper hand when he succeeded in publicly labeling attorney Leo Gallagher—who appeared as a friend of the court—as a "known Communist." Judge Moffatt accurately observed that Scott had wasted the court's time by singularly managing to place "everybody on trial except the defendant."[145] Undeterred, Judge Moffatt informed the courtroom that he would ask for a grand jury investigation for the failure in Los Angeles to issue a complaint against Keyes and held him over for trial to be arraigned for April 27.[146]

City elites were quick to respond. In an editorial that appeared two days after the preliminary hearing, the *Los Angeles Times* stated that Judge Moffatt had "plainly stepped outside normal procedures and his customary jurisdiction."[147] The editorial questioned the legality and efficacy in a law that would allow an "alien" district to arrest an officer simply for attempting to "enforce the law."

More important, it seemed, were the two other "elements" that weighed heavily on this case. According to the editorial,

> one of them, that Leo Gallagher, who has been a Communist candidate for office more than once, was allowed to take a prominent part in the prosecution after the District Attorney's representative closed his case, and that organizations declared by the Tenney Committee to be part of the "Communist front" urged that the charges be brought. Justice Moffatt appears as one of the sponsors for these organizations, the so-called Civil Rights Congress and the so-called American Youth for Democracy.[148]

The editorial closed by stating that "some forceful method should be found to remind Justice Moffatt that his bailiwick is Huntington Park and that the rest of the county should not be annoyed by him." Ironically, the editorial attempted to place distance between the *Times* and the case itself, claiming that "this paper takes no stand on the question of Officer Keyes' guilt or innocence."[149]

The CRC's main chapter in Los Angeles regarded the *Times* editorial as an outrageous interference in the case.[150] On the same day that the editorial appeared, the *Daily People's World* reported that the city council suspended its rules and unanimously adopted a motion "asking the city attorney to suggest ways of amending a California law that permits any county judge to issue warrants for arrest of persons within that county."[151] In a sharply worded letter to the city council, the CRC's William Bidner and Anne Shore charged that council members Lloyd Davies and Ed Davenport were helping to promote the bigotry and hysteria "whipped" up by Keyes's defense counsel.[152] "They do this," wrote Bidner and Shore, "in order to completely obscure the real content of this whole matter—that is, that citizens of minority groups have the full right to equal protection by law and that police malpractices against members of minority groups must be stopped by every proper and lawful means at our disposal."[153]

From April through June, pro-Salcido activists continued their efforts to publicize the case. The CRC led the charge with letter-writing campaigns, press releases, mass rallies, and delegations to individual council members' offices. Bringing new organizations into the struggle remained an important and ongoing strategy. By mid-April, the Los Angeles Bar Association and the National Lawyers Guild agreed to investigate charges that the district attorney had been negligent in prosecuting Keyes.[154] During this time, the Mexican-American CRC initiated new plans to rally the support of Mexican Americans on the

KEYES ON TRIAL!

WHAT IS YOUR VERDICT?

Policeman William Keyes

He pulled the trigger five times on March 10, 1948. And Augustin Salcido was dead.

Salcido's crime? Trying to evade two burly policemen who had him cornered in a dark stairway, held by one and covered by the pistol of Keyes.

This is the same Keyes who has three shootings to his record of the past eighteen months and who boasts of many more.

This is the police officer about which District Attorney William Simpson, Ass't Chief of Police Joseph Reed, and the City Council have done nothing. . . .

It was only an aroused people who have brought Keyes to trial.

Augustin Salcido was his victim.

17-year-old Mexican-American, Augustin Salcido was born to poverty and reared in an America which denied to him and millions of others the right to decent jobs, decent homes, and freedom from fear.

One of many thousands, Augustin was used to the bullying and brutality of police who enjoyed pushing him and his friends around.

Is it any wonder that cornered—he was afraid and tried to get away?

The Victim, Augustin Salcido

WILLIAM KEYES GOES ON TRIAL ON CHARGES OF MANSLAUGHTER, THURSDAY, JULY 8th, 1948, DIVISION 41—HALL OF JUSTICE, 9 A.M. LET THE DISTRICT ATTORNEY'S OFFICE KNOW THAT THE PEOPLE DEMAND A FULL PROSECUTION OF KEYES AND A COMPLETE INVESTIGATION OF THE CITY'S POLICE PRACTICES.

A complete review of the case will be given at a PUBLIC MEETING to be held on FRIDAY, JULY 9, 1948—the day after the beginning of the Keyes trial.

MASS MEETING

- ● **FRIDAY, JULY 9th, 1946**
- ● **CONVENTION HALL - EMBASSY**
  9th and Grand—8 P.M.
- ● **ADMISSION FREE**
- ● **HEAR:** Leo Gallagher, Attorney
  Guy Endore, Author of
  "Justice for Salcido"
  and others.

YOUR BALLOT . . . COME TO THE MEETING, HEAR THE FACTS AND CAST YOUR BALLOT

I believe that Police Officer William Keyes is   GUILTY ☐   INNOCENT ☐

OF THE MURDER OF AUGUSTIN SALCIDO

Issued by the Civil Rights Congress of Los Angeles, 307 South Hill — MA. 6-5121 - 5122

FIGURE 4 Flyer for public show trial against Officer William Keyes on charges of manslaughter, 1948. Courtesy of the CRC Collection, Southern California Library.

Eastside.[155] Three months later, however, Keyes's trial ended in disappointment for pro-Salcido activists. According to the *Labor Herald*, on July 13, Judge C. C. MacDonald "was imported from Yolo County to try the case." A conservative Northern California judge, MacDonald acquitted Keyes of manslaughter.[156] Undeterred, the Justice for Salcido campaign rallied its forces. Soon, the Independent Progressive Party (IPP) weighed in to support the pro-Salcido activists.

The IPP reached out to the Mexican American community and sought to incorporate them into the new party's organizational structure. The IPP had been formed with the goal of electing former vice president Henry A. Wallace of Iowa as president in 1948.[157] Under the leadership of Hugh Bryson, president of the National Union of Marine Cooks and Stewards, the IPP in Southern California made strong inroads into East Los Angeles. Cuarón divided his time between civil rights work on the Salcido case and campaign activities for the IPP. In fact, he and Frank López were actively campaigning for the election of José Chávez, candidate for the Fifty-First Assembly District, on the IPP ticket. This trio proved instrumental in forming Amigos de Wallace, a new political group on the Eastside charged with promoting Wallace. On the day of Officer Keyes's acquittal, Cuarón spoke before the IPP's Los Angeles County central committee informing them that "no young Mexican American is safe from brutal treatment and gunfire of the police if this verdict is allowed to stand unprotected by the people of Los Angeles."[158]

From its central office located on Whittier Boulevard in Pico Rivera, Amigos de Wallace issued a strongly worded press release condemning the Keyes verdict and demanding a grand jury investigation into the practices of the Los Angeles Police Department.[159] The CRC, too, responded by issuing and distributing the pamphlet *Justice for Salcido*. In a forceful postscript, the author of the pamphlet, Guy Endore, wrote that "Keyes walked out, free, and more than ever entitled to believe that the season on Mexicans is never closed." By mid-July, the Hollywood Arts, Sciences and Professions Council also added its support to the pro-Salcido cause.[160] Writer Howard Koch, president of the council, condemned the acquittal of Keyes and demanded the "immediate dismissal" of the officer. Such notable Americans as Lena Horne and Dr. Linus Pauling[161] voiced their support for justice in the case.[162]

On July 19, the pro-Salcido activists held their largest event to garner support for their cause.[163] That evening, more than one thousand people gathered at the Embassy Auditorium to hear new voices in the struggle to bring justice in the Salcido case.[164] While twelve uniformed policemen watched the gathering, Philip Connelly, secretary-general of the Los Angeles CIO Council, warned the audience that they might also become victims of the "sickening thud of the [policeman's] night stick . . . if Keyes and others like him and their political bosses in high places get away with the murder."[165] Alvah Bessie, a veteran of the Abraham Lincoln Brigade and a member of the Hollywood Ten, connected the Salcido case to a broader and more ominous movement afoot in the country: "There is an immediate and obvious link between what has been happening to us (the Hollywood 10) and what happened to Augustine E. Salcido."[166]

Gallegos's first trial ended in a deadlock. During the second trial, the same judge who acquitted Keyes, Judge C. C. McDonald, would also preside. But despite the judge's attempts to discredit Gallegos by constantly referring to him as the "marijuana witness," the jury found him innocent of the charges.[167] In early August, Gallegos married Ethel Luna, the younger sister of Celia Luna Rodríguez and Julia Luna Mount. Although he now held a steady job, trouble was never too far behind. On October 11, Gallegos was taken into custody once again, this time on "suspicion of robbery." During the arrest, Raymond E. Varela, a homicide officer assigned to the Salcido case, warned Gallegos "to get out of town" or die.[168] Gallegos's run-ins with the police created great instability and personal stress that would mar his life for some time.

Despite the Communist Party's propensity to aim at ideological purity and organizational discipline, some voices demanded greater pragmatism. In fact, some called for working collaboratively with a greater variety of groups in the hope of broadening a progressive movement for democracy.[169] In a 1948 report delivered to the Los Angeles County convention of the Communist Party, Pettis Perry, an African American and chair of the county Nationalities Commission, exhorted fellow party cadre to work harder to form coalitions around vital community issues. The undertone of Perry's remarks was clear: the CP should step back from rushing to take *the* leading role in every grassroots mobilization. In other words, the party should function as a catalyst—contributing its knowledge and experience where necessary. He gave the example of how the party's Carver Club in Midtown successfully joined forces with social clubs, the Urban League, the NAACP, and even the Inter-Denominational Ministries in a local struggle to demand jobs at Ralph's supermarkets. Perry castigated party activists for spending more time "discussing" the need for coalitions than acting on their own advice.[170]

Perry also spoke passionately for the need to work more closely with the Mexican American community, especially on the issue of police brutality. In the case of fifteen-year-old shooting victim Eugene Montenegro, he credited the work of Communists and liberal progressives in having broadened the contacts and relationships between the progressive movement and the Mexican American people. "The movement around the shooting of this youth," Perry remarked, "immediately brought reactions from the Mexican-American Legion posts; the LULACS . . . and many other broad forces which joined hands with the Civil Rights Congress in protest again[st] this outrage."[171] Although he expressed a strong need to be pragmatic, Perry also believed that the party should make every effort to be open about its activities. "We must understand how to develop coalition work," he carefully explained, "and increasingly bring forth the face of the Party."[172]

Through creative means, the CRC and the Mexican-American Civil Rights Congress succeeded in bringing together a multiracial and cross-class coalition of organizations and individuals in a struggle to defend basic civil and human rights in the city. Los Angeles progressives identified the Salcido killing protests as connected to a broader struggle for civil rights. Nevertheless, a persistent problem for the CRC remained its struggle to convince the broader public of the danger inherent in the relentless attacks on civil liberties. Its liberal allies, too, often ignored the warnings.[173] For many Americans, the postwar period represented a new beginning—an opportunity to relax and enjoy the period of prosperity.

Progressives and radicals alike plunged into the political maelstrom in 1948 intent on electing as president one of their own—Henry A. Wallace. The campaign to elect Wallace, however, would become a lightning rod attracting both admirers and detractors. Under the banner of the Independent Progressive Party, this third-party movement represented an opportunity to change the course of national and international politics. But as the nation descended deeper into a cold war with the Soviet Union, some Americans perceived the IPP as divisive and naïve. Others saw in this fledgling movement the signs of foreign intrigue and treachery. As one author wrote in the literary magazine the *American Mercury*, the IPP was far from being "indigenous" to American politics. Instead, "it [the IPP] is the first party in all American history that is foreign in its conception, in its basic ideology," and with a direct connection to the Communist Party USA.[174] As Cuarón recalled, the charge of foreign conspiracy by the right wing against the Left was altogether unfounded:

I don't remember ever thinking of accepting some doctrine or some order [from abroad]. Of course, I was a very ardent reader. I read the science of Marxism. I didn't consider that as an order from Moscow. . . . I considered it a science of the working-class. I adhered to that. I believed it.[175]

Mexican Americans in Southern California would play an important role in this progressive movement. Indeed, the campaign in support of former vice president Wallace would result in the formation of the Mexican American National Association in 1949. These activists would also place sincere hope in the world that Wallace promised: peaceful coexistence with the Soviet Union and the continuation of Roosevelt's New Deal policies. In the words of Albert Einstein: "Only men who are above the petty bickering of the day and without any selfish interest can save us from the threatening domestic and international situation. Such men were [Franklin Delano] Roosevelt and [Wendell] Willkie, and such a man is Henry Wallace."[176]

3

MARCHING TOWARD A
PEOPLE'S WORLD

*In order to bring an end to the long series of abuses and discrimination which
we, the Mexican people, have suffered down through the years, and for the purpose of defending our economic, political and social rights as well as developing
our culture and democratic traditions, we are holding the founding convention
of the local section of the Mexican-American National Association.*
—Ralph Cuarón, national executive secretary, ANMA, 1949

HE BRUTAL SLAYING OF Augustino Salcido in 1948 raised the level of
political activism on the Eastside to new heights. The campaign to
bring justice for the Salcido family assumed new meaning as progressive activists pursued broader social and political goals that reached beyond the
confines of East Los Angeles. As a natural extension of their activism, Frank
López, Josefina Fierro, Armando Dávila, Ben Cruz, Celia Rodríguez, Julia
Luna Mount, Francisca Flores, Ramón Morán Welch, Ralph Cuarón, and others joined the third-party movement, led by the Independent Progressive Party.
Contrary to the public pronouncements by political conservatives that these
organizing efforts represented nothing more than a smokescreen—orchestrated
by "Godless" Communists and under the direction of Moscow—this grassroots
activism was homegrown. For some members of the CP, toeing the party line
and maintaining organizational discipline remained high priorities, especially
as the Cold War climate intensified. But for others, successful navigation of the
political waters meant adopting more pragmatic approaches.

World War II had unmasked the fallacy of racist ideologies and inspired
movements worldwide for democracy, liberation, and self-determination. This
rising chorus of voices at home and abroad increasingly viewed civil and human
rights as essential elements in a new postwar world. Yet, some Americans were
not ready to accede to these growing demands. Many in positions of power

remained content with the world as it was—"a world marked by European power, Third World weakness, and nearly ubiquitous racial segregation," writes Thomas Borstelmann.[1] And little in their experience informed them that these conditions needed to change. As colonial rule began to tear at the seams, American leaders, especially those representing southern states, looked wholly askance at these movements. To his credit, however, President Harry S. Truman responded positively to domestic demands by moving ahead on a number of fronts, such as desegregating the armed forces and the federal civil service. Nonetheless, Truman was also motivated to respond to perceived pressures emanating from the Soviet Union and politics at home. By 1948, he had to contend with the Republican Party and the rising popularity of Henry A. Wallace and his Independent Progressive Party.[2] In fact, even Communists got swept up in the grassroots fervor behind the IPP candidate.

Many party members in Los Angeles did not wait for leadership approval to join the Progressive Party bandwagon. As Dorothy Healey explains, "There were all too many occasions on which we shaped our approach to domestic politics in response to some Soviet diplomatic declaration or policy, but this [the third-party movement] was not one of them."[3] This third-party movement represented a challenge and break with the growing postwar consensus that equated freedom and democracy with containment of Communism at home and abroad. By contrast, many progressives had hoped that a new world order would prevail after the war, one in which international cooperation and peace would replace the need for expanding armies, atomic weapons, and military aggression. This election also represented for many activists an important, if not crucial, opportunity to disarm, what one CRC pamphlet delineated as the ever expanding "political persecution and developing Fascism in the United States."[4] This growing optimism, however, did not dissuade criticism of the nation's position vis-à-vis the Communist world. The CP had come to the conclusion, writes Robbie Lieberman, that the United States, with its monopoly on the atomic bomb, "posed the greatest threat to world peace."[5] By early 1946, CP leaders identified the growing anti-Communist policies as evidence that the United States was moving toward war and fascism. And yet, Healey, too, remembers that Communists viewed the postwar period as a time for genuine political change:

> With the exception of a few years during the war, Communists had believed that the breakup of the existing two-party system and the emergence of a new

independent party representing the labor movement, Blacks, and other groups was a necessary and long overdue step. Just as "organize the unorganized" had been the central slogan of the 1930's and had largely been accomplished in the course of the decade, we now felt that it was possible that the historical moment had arrived for the emergence of the new third party.[6]

This grassroots movement, however, was paralleled by an equally determined movement gaining ground within the CIO's national leadership to rein in the power and influence of its Communist organizers.

The CIO leadership believed that to survive in the climate of rampant red-baiting, the organization had to distance itself from any semblance of CP influence. The need to remain unified on the "crucial Cold War issues" compelled the CIO to move against union Communists.[7] Before 1947, this move to enforce rank-and-file discipline did not necessarily mean expelling Communist members. Indeed, some CIO leaders felt confident they could weather the rising ideological storm by enforcing, as Nelson Lichtenstein explains, "at least a paper CIO unity." Even the highly controversial Taft-Hartley Act of 1947, which sought to isolate and expel Communists, did not threaten the federation.[8] The candidacy of Henry A. Wallace and the third-party movement, however, changed this precarious accommodation with the CIO's left wing.

The Wallace campaign represented a break with the Democratic Party—a position hard-won by progressives and radical activists. CIO president Philip Murray, on the other hand, dared not risk losing his organization's growing power within the party. "A powerful Wallace movement," explains Lichtenstein, "threatened to taint the CIO with the badge of disloyalty in much the same way that opposition to the no-strike pledge represented an intolerable deviation during the war."[9] For some Mexican Americans, the Democratic Party had already abandoned its New Deal roots, thus placing them at greater risk within the rising tide of conservative unionism. Consequently, they plunged into this maelstrom enthusiastic over the prospect for change, despite the inherent conflicts involved.

In September 1948, the *Daily People's World* emphasized the upbeat mood in the Mexican American community around the candidacy of the former vice president. Staff writer Helen Taylor used cultural nationalist tropes in gauging Progressive Party support. "Just as the Mexican people rallied swiftly and joyously to the banners of the priest [Miguel] Hidalgo," went the analysis, "so today Spanish-speaking people in all parts of the new world are marching with the new third party, the people's party led by Henry Wallace."[10] In noting important gains in the previous year such as increased voter registration and the creation of Amigos de Wallace, Taylor gave much credit, naturally, to the Communist Party in Los Angeles as having played a "leading role." She clearly situated the third-party movement as viable and wholly compatible with the CP and its longer vision for Mexican American and working-class liberation. Reaching for cultural relevance, Taylor concluded: "Much more remains to be done. . . . But the Mexican people will continue to go forward under the impetus of the new people's party. In the tradition of Hidalgo, Jose Maria Morelos, [Benito] Juarez, [Lazaro] Cardenas and other Mexican heroes, they are marching toward a people's world with Wallace."[11]

By 1944, Vice President Henry Wallace had amassed enough enemies within the Democratic Party apparatus to find him effectively sidelined and eventually booted off the presidential ticket. Some political insiders increasingly perceived the vice president as a social engineer, at best, and a "candidate of the radicals of the country," at worse.[12] Still others began to associate Wallace with Communism—including President Franklin D. Roosevelt. The impressive gains by the Republicans two years earlier had raised concerns within the Democratic Party and prioritized stopping the impending conservative tide. In response, Roosevelt's inner circle succeeded (with his blessing) in removing Wallace from the presidential ticket in 1944 and replacing him with Harry S. Truman. Underestimating his popular appeal with the Democratic rank and file, and perhaps feeling guilty, Roosevelt promised Wallace a job in his administration.[13]

As secretary of commerce in 1945, in the Truman administration, Wallace worked tirelessly to influence the course of reconversion of the nation's economy, remaining staunchly committed to the New Deal.[14] He viewed peace in the postwar period as closely tied to jobs, civil rights, and increased cooperation around the world. Wallace envisioned taking social and economic programs, crafted and tried during the Roosevelt years, and expanding them further to create a "People's Peace" that would make the "American standard of living a reality for all of our people."[15] This vision of progress, however, had its detractors. As Charles Kramer, a former research director for the Independent Progressive Party, explained, a "new power orientation" within the Truman cabinet had gained ascendancy and was determined to take the nation down a dangerous path. According to Kramer, "Wallace saw the two alternatives emerging from the Second World War. Either we made peace with socialism, recognized that it was here to stay—or we carried out Churchill's 1919 dream of 'drowning

Bolshevism in blood.'" In effect, one way meant partnership with the world to free people from the yoke of colonial rule, while the other meant "an unending commitment to police the world against socialism in the guise of 'containing Russian expansion.'"[16]

The conservative Right, and detractors within the Democratic Party, increasingly perceived Wallace's views as the rantings of an impractical visionary. His brand of ambitious liberalism was described by one high-ranking administration official as the work of "socialist-minded uplifters."[17] More importantly, Wallace's ideas for a postwar order were now on a collision course with those of the military, the State Department, Republicans, and a growing number of Democrats. Despite the concerted efforts of Democratic Party leaders to dissuade the former vice president from challenging Truman for the White House in 1948, Wallace embarked on a campaign "with an untried third party."[18]

For many progressives and radicals alike, the news of Wallace's decision to run for the presidency was nothing short of electrifying. The concern over the conservative shift on the national scene, and the increasing resort to an aggressive and unilateral foreign policy, pulled many away from the Democratic Party. In fact, this growing disenchantment led directly to the formation of the Progressive Citizens of America (PCA) in 1946, an amalgamation of several liberal organizations and various constituent groups, including labor, small farmers, urban middle class, veterans, and blacks.[19] Many within the Democratic Party feared that any weakening of the Democratic base might allow the Republican Party to gain the White House after sixteen long years of Democratic ascendancy. Equally concerned, Wallace made every effort to work with the Democratic Party apparatus and, thus, did not make his official break until very late in 1947. That delay may have hindered the IPP's ability to mount a more effective campaign.[20]

For some progressives, labor activists, and Communists, the opportunity could not have been more auspicious to set a new course. Indeed, CP members welcomed the IPP. The endorsement by William Z. Foster, head of the Communist Party USA, in fall 1947, gave rank-and-file members the green light to participate in the building of a third party.[21] And according to William Schneiderman, chair of the Communist Party of California during this period, "The progressive upsurge in the ranks of the Democratic party, particularly in Southern California, is one of the many signs of political realignments beginning to take place as a result of the reactionary course of the Truman Administration, and its betrayal of the Roosevelt policies." Still, Schneiderman was adamant that attempts by progressives to "capture" the Democratic Party from within would be doomed to failure. He also warned party activists and progressives to be leery of "straddling double-talk" by liberal advocates of a "middle policy."[22]

Schneiderman criticized the motives of the state leadership of the Democratic Party headed by James Roosevelt, the son of the late president. According to Schneiderman, James Roosevelt's apparent heroic stand against the conservative impulses within the Democratic Party amounted to little more than "appeasing and apologizing for reaction."[23] Unfortunately, Schneiderman may have misread Roosevelt's genuine disagreements with the Truman administration as well as the actual power struggle among those holding opposing views within the Democratic Party organization.[24]

But how was the CP going to justify to its membership the building of a political movement around a liberal party and candidate committed to making the capitalist system work? The party leadership seemed not to see a conflict of interest. In an educational pamphlet distributed to its membership in 1947, the leadership clarified its position on this issue:

> While Communists do not agree that this is possible, and while Communists may differ with Wallace on one or another specific position he takes, we recognize the important political role he plays as a leader in the developing coalition. Taken generally, the domestic and foreign policy for which he fights represents a programmatic basis for this broad coalition.[25]

The party called on all Communists "to cooperate wholeheartedly with all elements who will fight to defend the interests of the people."[26] By December 1947, the CP had endorsed Wallace and "urged like-minded trade unionists to do likewise."[27]

Though the CP had identified a number of key constituents—workers, urban middle class, veterans, pensioners, and blacks—it failed to address the role of Mexican Americans. In general, the consensus and attitude within the party seemed to be that this latter group had been firmly ensconced within the category of "other minority groups," which therefore meant that no further consideration was necessary. African Americans, on the other hand, merited special attention:

> The Negro people represent one of the most militant and advanced sectors of the developing people's coalition. They are already developing various forms of

independent political action in alliance with labor—as in the Oakland and Los Angeles elections—and will undoubtedly be one of the most important forces in the building of a third party.[28]

But the CP had underestimated Mexican Americans as a political force; this was surprising considering the activism of this community among trade unionists and civil rights activists.

Labor would take the early lead in setting the stage for a third party in California. In July 1947, the Joint Labor Committee for a Third Party was formed in San Francisco by an amalgam of seventeen labor organizations, including the AFL, CIO, and railroad unions.[29] Local 576, of the Furniture Workers union, sent three delegates—Ralph Cuarón, Frank López, and Ben Cruz—to this historic meeting. Cuarón recalled, with great nostalgia, how the three were very cognizant of the significance of this gathering. As the junior partner in this small contingent of Mexican American radicals, Cuarón was thoroughly impressed by his comrades—especially with López. Indeed, he took every moment to absorb as much as he could on this first trip to San Francisco. "And at this trip, I learned a lot from Frank. He spoke about the founding of [Local] 576 and the [Communist] Party." The formation of this Joint Labor Committee generated much excitement as delegates returned home to spread the word and prepare for a meeting scheduled for the following month in Los Angeles. According to Cuarón, "When we came back, I became very active in the founding of the Independent Progressive Party."[30]

"There's a fresh, clean breeze sweeping through California politics today!"[31] This was the opening statement of a pamphlet produced by the IPP. In late August, some fourteen hundred delegates gathered in Los Angeles "to set up an organizing committee for a new political party in the state." At this meeting, Hugh Bryson, president of the National Union of Marine Cooks and Stewards, became chair of the newly formed Organizing Committee of the IPP.[32] Among the union endorsers were the United Electrical, Radio and Machine Workers; the International Fisherman and Allied Workers of America; the United Packinghouse Workers of America; and the National Union of Marine Cooks and Stewards. Bryson believed that the mere existence of their party would "frighten those in command of the Democratic Party" and force them to shift their positions.[33]

Sensitive to the issue of racial discrimination, Bryson was critical of both Democrats and Republicans for their lack of leadership and courage on civil rights. He, like Henry Wallace, understood that employers used racism to divide the power of labor. "Race hatred means cheap labor and cheap labor means increased profits," Bryson told the gathered delegates.[34] And race hatred also meant race exclusivity. At the end of the war, explains Eric Avila, the "racialized fantasies that depicted the region as a southwestern outpost of white supremacy" began to take shape as ethnic minorities were excluded (and expelled) from choice employment and housing opportunities.[35] Employers in critical industries such as aircraft, for example, remained committed to Jim Crow and actively pursued policies that gave preference to returning white veterans. This system hinged not only on the support of the culture at large, but also on the support of white employees—many of them members of unions.[36] And yet, despite the seeming intractability of this system, some people of color, and women in particular, successfully negotiated opportunities for both work and social interaction across diverse racial and ethnic lines.[37] Regardless, the push for a return to traditional gender roles remained a powerful impulse in postwar America. The fact that Republican *and* Democratic congressional representatives had voted to end the Fair Employment Practices Committee and the Race Relations Service in federal housing provided further evidence that significant numbers in both parties were unwilling to deal concretely with discrimination and segregation.[38]

By late September 1947, the organizing committee of the IPP of California included one prominent Mexican American, Ben Cruz. Cruz was a former president of the United Furniture Workers of America Local 576. He had a long record of political action that included "naturalization and fundraising drives, civilian defense, trade union and community politics, labor unity and racial equality."[39] Cruz had also served as a key mentor to a number of young Mexican American workers, including Ralph Cuarón. On October 17, the *Eastside Sun* reported that activities were underway in the Nineteenth Congressional District to qualify the IPP for a place on the ballot in the next elections. Volunteers circulated more than two hundred petitions. Their activities were bolstered by the news that two area trade unions, the AFL's Painters Union Local 1348 and the CIO's UFWA Local 576, had officially endorsed and pledged their support for the IPP.

In November, the IPP staged a major weekend effort to gather signatures for the new party. With headquarters on South Spring Street in downtown Los Angeles, IPP volunteers marched across the city and county with the goal of reaching one hundred thousand signers by mid-November. A provisional committee that included Leroy Parra, a founding member and chair of the

Mexican-American Civil Rights Congress, headed the "full-scale campaign" on the Eastside.[40] As reported in the *Eastside Sun* newspaper, "Community leaders and representatives of labor, fraternal and civic groups" had elected Parra among a group of thirty activists. The campaign had gathered so much momentum that Local 576 approved, without hesitation, Ralph Cuarón's request for a temporary leave from his union duties to work full-time on the IPP campaign.

Cuarón's organizing work included both direct outreach for the IPP as well as civil rights work on behalf of the Mexican American community. Discrimination against Mexican Americans, especially youth, at public facilities was common practice—though sometimes it could be selective. Certainly, not all Mexican Americans experienced the same discrimination—the lighter one's skin hue, the easier it was to navigate the maze of racial exclusivity. But the facts remained glaringly clear: many white Americans continued to see Mexican Americans as *foreigners*. In his 1954 study, sociologist John H. Burma wrote:

> For one thing, Mexicans are often dark, and darkness of skin was already a badge of alleged inferiority before most Mexicans came upon the scene. Second, they are predominantly poor, and so suffer from class discrimination. Third, their culture is different, and hence is looked upon as inferior. Fourth, they are Catholic in a predominantly Protestant country. Fifth, theirs is a different language, and when used in public it accentuates differences and may make Anglos feel excluded, fear insult, and so forth.[41]

Although there were few legal barriers in place by the late 1940s, *extralegal* barriers (de facto segregation and exclusion), Burma contended, remained a significant impediment to equality.[42] As demographic shifts accelerated on the Eastside after the war, increasingly tipping in favor of a larger Mexican American presence, so too did racial tensions.[43] Demographic shifts have often meant significant changes (particularly for the incoming group) with respect to public institutions. "Sometimes local officials chose to move major public programs out and away from the barrio," explain Antonio Ríos-Bustamante and Pedro Castillo; "more often, however, libraries, schools, and parks were simply allowed to deteriorate." Creative administrative practices (diverting and reducing funds) often meant that Anglo communities received superior facilities and services, while "Mexicans were left with neighborhood eyesores and architectural dead weight."[44]

On behalf of the Mexican American CRC and the American Veterans Committee, Cuarón began a series of presentations to urge local religious and civic leaders to open public facilities to Mexican American youth and to address the growing problem of police brutality. As Cuarón recalled:

> We were trying to open up the Jewish centers [to Mexican American youth]. There were two of them in East L.A.: the Menorah Center . . . and the Soto/ Michigan [Jewish Community] Center. They were very active and very prominent youth centers. But the centers were not available for Mexican youth. And, of course, we were shooting to get the Jewish community to allow Mexicans to go to these centers.[45]

Edward R. Roybal (who would soon announce his candidacy for a second bid to capture the city's Ninth District council seat) supported Ralph's efforts despite the inherent political pitfall involved. Many moderate civil rights activists on the Eastside, such as the Community Service Organization, shunned any cooperation with organizations labeled as Left extremism, specifically the Communists. They rightly feared that their activities would be labeled subversive. But extremism from the Right also posed a serious threat for these activists, especially on the issues of racial justice and equality. Roybal remained particularly concerned about the chilling effect anti-Communist legislation would have on the Latino community as well as on the nation's democratic institutions. As evidenced by his actions and public statements, Roybal feared red-baiting and anti-Communist hysteria more than the local Communists.[46] Cuarón soon gained the support of another important community member, Leticia Innes, of the Soto-Michigan Jewish Community Center.

Innes was a prominent member of the Eastside community, working primarily with Mexican American youth. As Sylvia Cuarón recalled, Innes was "a cultural dancer," who had been to Mexico on several occasions to learn the country's national dances.[47] But Innes's interest in working with youth took her beyond dancing. A year earlier, in 1947, she was selected as the delegate by the Los Angeles Youth Council to attend the World Festival of Youth and Students in Prague, Czechoslovakia, held July through August. In the context of rising anti-Communism and the Cold War, participation in this cultural festival (seventy-two nations were represented) was certainly perceived as being radical. So radical indeed, that it did not escape the attention of the House Un-American Activities Committee.[48] By September, she had also attended the World Federation of Democratic Youth "as an official delegate."[49] When Cuarón and some of his cohorts wanted to send Gilbert Orosco, a local youth, to Budapest for the second World Festival of Youth and Youth Congress, they went to Innes for help.[50]

Sylvia became aware of the problems of her Mexican American neighbors while performing volunteer work at the Soto-Michigan Jewish Community Center. Encouraged by Innes's liberal ideas about race relations, Sylvia began to venture beyond her more familiar Jewish surroundings to work with young Mexican Americans in the barrio. The death of seventeen-year-old Augustino Salcido in March not only heightened the deteriorating relationship in the community with local police, but it also galvanized the community into action like no other event. Seeking to capitalize on this increased political consciousness among Mexican Americans, the IPP announced in mid-March its support for Roybal in the race for the Ninth District council seat.

The decision by IPP leaders to support Roybal was politically astute and illustrated their commitment to support minority candidates. Jack Berman, Eastside chair of the IPP, recognized the problems plaguing the area and believed that the district needed "a courageous and fighting young progressive" at the helm.[51] The IPP's endorsement of José Ramón Chávez (candidate for the Fifty-First State Assembly District) two weeks later demonstrated their keen interest in gaining favor and support among the Mexican American community.

A group of largely Mexican American activists, including Cuarón and Frank López, supported the idea of promoting Chávez for public office under the IPP banner. Chávez had been a member of Shipyard Workers Local 9 (CIO), and, according to the *Eastside Sun*, was "widely known to local residents because of his activities in various community organizations."[52] Chávez had already gained some notoriety when he ran as a Democratic Party candidate for the State Assembly in 1946. Although he lost against the Democratic Party stalwart Elwyn S. Bennett, the election generated great enthusiasm among Mexican Americans in the Belvedere community. Actively campaigning for Chávez, Cuarón also increased his visibility through making public presentations on the issue of police brutality.

Labor organizer and civil rights activist Bert Corona recalled in later life the aura that surrounded the IPP and Wallace.

Mexican-Americans could identify with Wallace, and he had the charisma, as Kennedy would have, to attract them. I was surprised at how many Mexican-Americans sympathized with the IPP. It was, however, the only party speaking out against racism, for integrated housing, for better education, and for many other issues vital to minority communities. The Democrats were being very cautious in opposing the growing right-wing reaction. But not the IPP. It faced the right wing head on.[53]

Ignacio López, editor and publisher of the Spanish-language weekly *El Expectador*, echoed Corona's sentiment: "The enthusiasm today among the county's Spanish-speaking people is very large, because Henry Wallace has always championed the rights of our countrymen."[54] As some historians have already noted, López was a true muckraking journalist and one of a very few newspaper editors willing to expose and challenge the inequalities and injustices perpetrated against Mexican communities in Southern California.[55] López considered Wallace "one of the most courageous and progressive statesmen in the modern era." Wallace's firm stance on the defense of human rights, at home and abroad, struck a chord with López and some within the Mexican American and immigrant community.[56] Julia Luna Mount and her husband, George, also remembered how the entire Luna family became enthusiastic and supportive of the Progressive Party ticket. "We knew Truman stunk," recalled George. "We'd heard the radio reports of Henry Wallace . . . during the political campaign. Man, if he didn't sound like John L. Lewis. He was great."[57] This enthusiasm for Wallace moved one step further when Mexican American progressives, radicals, and trade unionists from several organizations (Mine-Mill; United Furniture Workers of America; Food, Tobacco, Agricultural, and Allied Workers of America; and United Packinghouse Workers of America) formed their own political group to support this progressive upswell.[58]

Cuarón recalled with much nostalgia how he participated in the founding of this new organization: "First it was 'Mexicans for Wallace' and then it was 'Amigos de Wallace.'"[59] Ignacio López's support for the new group was evident by his participation as master of ceremonies for their first major rally held at Lincoln Park Stadium on May 16, 1948. This was the first West Coast stop by Wallace on a speaking tour across the nation, and it proved highly successful. "History was made," wrote Helen Taylor in the *Daily People's World*, as ten thousand Mexican Americans participated in this, "the largest political meeting of Mexican Americans on record."[60]

Wallace appears to have made every effort to connect with his audience at Lincoln Park. The *Los Angeles Times* reported the following remarks, which Wallace made in Spanish:

'He spoke our language . . . ,' say 'Amigos de Wallace'

FIGURE 5 Amigos de Wallace rally in East Los Angeles, 1948. Courtesy of the CRC Collection, Southern California Library.

My attitude is one of strongest friendship for the fine Mexican-American people whose work and sacrifices have done so much for California and for North America as a whole. . . . I wish I could say that you Mexican-Americans have been rewarded, decently and fairly, for everything you have contributed to California. But you have not been rewarded. And it is a shame upon our country that you have not. This disgrace of injustice and ingratitude is one of the many disgraces, which has made necessary a new political party in the United States of America. And it is the kind of disgrace that I, as the leader of this new party, am determined to atone for—so help me God.[61]

Wallace acknowledged the presence of large numbers of farmworkers who had traveled to the rally by reminding the assemblage that it was they "who create the real prosperity of California." He recognized the heavy burdens and insecurities under which these workers lived every day and denounced this as a national disgrace. "It is the intention of our new party," Wallace told the crowd, "to guarantee equal justice and dignified treatment for all people—citizens and non-citizens alike. . . . In a genuine democracy there are no second-class citizens—there are no aliens—there are only people."[62]

On that evening, Frank López was officially designated as coordinator of Amigos de Wallace. Cuarón remembered the entire event at Lincoln Park, and especially the speech given by López. "And Frank López made a beautiful speech there which just astounded me. I just became exalted at the whole thing. I felt all my progressive activities were coming together. This spurred me to organize my young people and teaching them [*sic*]."[63]

Amigos de Wallace managed to bring on board community notables such as Camilo Camacho, president of the Mexican Chamber of Commerce as well as the Latin-American Protective League and the Federation of Spanish-American Voters. Also present were Latino elected officials from the communities of Chino, Colton, Azusa, and Oxnard. Abigail Alvarez provided the musical entertainment along with orchestra bandleader Bobby Ramos, cousin to labor activist and former executive director of El Congreso Josefina Fierro.[64] Indeed, Fierro was not only prominently featured on the panel of speakers, but played a key role in the IPP by running in the congressional race for California's Ninth District seat.

Living in the city of Madera, located in California's Central Valley near Fresno, Josefina Fierro (then married to Pete Daniels, a local farmer) placed her name on the IPP ticket. This decision was a direct challenge to the Democratic Party candidate, Cecil F. White. Fierro recalled that she undertook a spirited campaign that included registering citizens to vote, distributing campaign literature (produced from her home), and appearing at a local radio station in Fresno. Although she would withdraw before the November vote, Fierro recalled that her efforts helped generate enthusiasm among the Mexican American community for the election.[65] Indeed, IPP leaders came to believe that challenging Democratic Party candidates helped pry them away from strict party control, thus allowing them to move toward what Curtis D. MacDougall maintains was a "more constructive liberal path."[66] As the June 1 Democratic primary neared, there was excitement among IPP supporters that change was in the offing. Others, however, were clearly perturbed by the enthusiasm that Wallace generated among audiences in Los Angeles and across the country. In California, the *Los Angeles Times* appeared determined to derail this progressive train.

Staunchly conservative, fiercely anti-Communist, and particularly insensitive to Mexican Americans, the *Times* began its dogged assault against Wallace and the IPP following his weekend visit to the city.[67] After correcting the *Times*'s apparent slip that Wallace had delivered his speech in "Mexican," staff reporter Chester Hanson went on to report at length the method by which the campaign had amassed an incredible $46,000 in one evening alone. Indeed, half of the article detailed the fact that the campaign had hired a "traveling money-raiser from New York" to perform the "amazing shake-down."[68] In another article the following day, Wallace was described as a "rabble-rouser, exhibitionist, common scold and twisted thinker." Accordingly, he and his Hollywood supporters had achieved a masterful fundraising feat. Wallace's "spectacle" was compared to the "means employed by Nazis and Fascists when Hitler and Mussolini were using the ladders of hatred and dissension to clamber toward power."[69] The *Times* also referred to Wallace as Joseph Stalin's "favorite candidate" and thus helped cast doubt on his qualifications for the job, his patriotism, and his moral compass.[70] The negative campaign appeared to be so successful that by the end of the month the newspaper could confidently print a story predicting that Wallace would quit the race before the November election.[71] But for IPP stalwarts, their attention remained focused on the primaries in June.

The primary election outcome turned out to be neither an outright victory for Chávez (who had cross-filed as a Democrat) nor a defeat. California election laws permitted candidates for any office to enter the primaries of as many parties as they wished.[72] The *Eastside Sun* boastfully reported that Chávez had "rolled up 5,167 votes, five times as many as he polled in 1946." A statement released by the Chávez campaign clarified the widely held misconception: "It is not true that Mr. Bennett has been reelected in the June 1st primaries. . . . On the contrary, Mr. Bennett will engage in a run-off in the November elections with Mr. Chavez."[73] Chávez, now running as the IPP candidate for the Fifty-First assembly seat, delineated his political program and positioned himself as a viable alternative to the Democratic incumbent. The campaign boastfully asserted:

> Thousands of voters remained away from the [June] polls because no opportunity was presented to vote for Henry A. Wallace, third party presidential candidate. These same thousands and those who voted want peace, retention of our Bill of Rights; jobs; an end to discrimination; low cost housing; adequate old age pension; child care centers; repeal of anti-labor legislation; protection of veterans from unscrupulous contractors; state bonus for veterans; protection of small business.[74]

Euphoric over the election results, the IPP campaign got into full swing in preparation for the November vote.

At a meeting of the Organizing Committee of the IPP in early July, Chávez and Cuarón assumed greater roles in the organization's formal leadership structure. Chávez, for example, was elected vice chair of the Los Angeles County Central Committee.[75] In fact, he was selected to represent the Nineteenth Congressional District at the founding convention of the IPP in Philadelphia, scheduled for late July 1948.

Convention participants felt nothing short of jubilation as they realized the significance of their endeavor to form a major third party in the country. Mexican Americans, of course, were also present among the throng of idealists hoping to chart a new course for the country. As Cuarón remembered, "I had a feeling of freedom as if someone had taken a tremendous load off my back."

> There were Mexican people there from Arizona, New Mexico, Colorado, Texas, Indiana and California. . . . Many of the delegates were candidates and leaders of the Progressive [P]arty. I felt that here truly was a democratic party, here at last my people from the mines, the agricultural fields, the schools, shops and cities were represented. . . . I looked for my people to express themselves and be part of this movement for freedom. . . . All of this made me feel strong and happy I was part of this beautiful party.[76]

The *Daily People's World* proudly featured a photograph of Cuarón and Bernardo Zermeño, who was selected to represent Amigos de Wallace at the convention. The IPP convention proved exceedingly popular, with 3,240 delegates and alternates having made the trip to Philadelphia. "That alone," explain Culver and Hayde, "was different: triple the number of delegates at the Republican convention, double the attendance at the Democratic convention. Almost half of them—46 percent—belonged to trade unions; more than a quarter were military veterans."[77] As the deadline neared to register voters for the November election, the IPP and Amigos de Wallace initiated another campaign effort to get out the vote in the Mexican American community.

Amigos de Wallace employed various cultural avenues, including icons of historical significance, to reach out to the Mexican American community. A flyer announcing September 23 as the deadline to register to vote, for example, prominently displayed the image of Father Miguel Hidalgo with the title "El Grito de Dolores," in celebration of Mexican independence. Translated

They're all for Wallame

Ralph Cuarón, left, above, and Bernardo Zermeno, who went to Philadelphia as Los Angeles representatives to the Progressive party convention, are shown deep in plans for the CIO-sponsored Freedom Fiesta to be held this weekend celebrating the birth of the Republic of Mexico. Inset shows Connie Contreras, CIO Warehouse Local 26 candidate for Queen of the Fiesta. Camillo Comacho, right, president of the Mexican Chamber of Commerce and a firm backer of Henry Wallace, reads a copy of Jose Chavez' election platform. Chavez is candidate for 51st district assemblyman. Guillermo Gallegos, inset, another third party supporter, has a new, happier outlook on life since progressive forces rallied to his support when he was persecuted for testifying against the policeman who murdered his friend, Augustin Salcido.

FIGURE 6 Ralph Cuarón working on Henry Wallace presidential campaign, 1948. Courtesy of the CRC Collection, Southern California Library.

from Spanish, the flyer read: *"The Hour Of Action Has Arrived. We Can No Longer Take The Abuses And Humiliations To Our Community."* Amigos de Wallace drew on Mexican nationalism to boost pride in the hope of securing a high voter turnout. *"Honor Your Parents, Your Family, Your People, By Supporting This Program For Independence, For Peace, For Wallace and Chavez,"* the flyer asserted. Frank López's name was prominently displayed as the coordinator for Amigos de Wallace.[78] During this outreach effort, Cuarón paid a visit to the local office of the Young Progressives of America. It was here that he and Sylvia Lucas met for the first time.

Sylvia remembered vividly the day that Ralph came to see her, seeking the organization's help. In late September, Young Progressives of America had been formed from an amalgamation of three youth groups—Youth for Wallace,

FIGURE 7 Ralph Cuarón and Sylvia Lucas with fellow Young Progressives, 1948.
Cuarón Family Collection.

Students for Wallace, and Young Amigos de Wallace.[79] The local chapter of the
Young Progressives in Boyle Heights had a total membership of not more than
twenty. The mostly Jewish contingent had recently selected Sylvia to be their
president when Cuarón approached her to solicit their help on the Chávez campaign. Sylvia instantly remembered Ralph from an earlier community meeting
and, without hesitation, accepted the invitation. As she recalled, the campaign
work was exhilarating and she learned a great deal. "[Ralph] would come in and
do poster work . . . beautifully. I learned how to do silkscreen from him. We used
to knock them out like quarters and dimes."[80] They began to see more of each
other outside of work as the campaign wore on, but they kept their relationship
a secret from friends and relatives. They had agreed to be discreet so as to avoid
disturbing racial sensibilities, especially during the campaign.

Amigos de Wallace staged one last event before the November vote. On
October 1, 1948, *El Expectador* announced: "Henry A. Wallace Will Speak

Before the Patriotic Monument."[81] Julia Luna Mount recalled that thousands of people walked to the Five Points intersection on the Eastside (near the corner of Lorena and Brooklyn Streets), the site of the monument to the fallen heroes, to hear Wallace speak one last time in their community.[82] This was a stop in Wallace's final nine-day campaign tour of the West Coast. On this day, Wallace addressed an audience of approximately three thousand in this largely working-class area. The *Eastside Sun* prominently featured a photograph of the throngs of supporters who came out to see Wallace, but also José Chávez, Frank López, and a host of other activists.[83] Sylvia proudly recalled that Cuarón spoke out that day on the issues of police brutality, discrimination, and military conscription. And yet, despite the large crowd that had gathered, it was smaller than earlier rallies. Indeed, according to Curtis MacDougall, the rally held the next day at Gilmore Stadium proved to be not only the climax of Wallace's Los Angeles trip, but also of his campaign tours.[84]

The downward spiral of the IPP's campaign became evident to some as early as the organization's convention in July. Along with the continual attacks by newspapers and dirty tactics used by the opposition such as phony leaflets, picketing, heckling, physical intimidation, and denial of hotel accommodations, the campaign suffered from a host of internal weaknesses.[85] MacDougall focuses on three principal problems: a movement built around, and dependent on, a single personality; a support base (largely middle-class professionals) not willing to perform the difficult day-to-day work necessary to sustain a third-party movement; and the participation of Communists. Most historians agree that the Communists performed an important role. "Communists and fellow travelers, as seasoned political workers," writes MacDougall, "did a disproportionate amount of the practical administrative and street-level work of the Progressive Party," but their participation could not counter the lethargy of the "amateurish liberals" and the "smear" tactics of the anti-Communist forces.[86] Dorothy Healey conceded that she and CP leaders were surprised by the outcome of the elections:

> Like everyone else I was misled by the size and the enthusiasm of the crowds that Wallace was attracting across the country. . . . In the California primaries in June, about a half million people cast ballots for candidates who had filed or cross-filed as Progressives, one fifth of the total primary vote. It was a very energizing campaign, and no one in the Party thought that Wallace could possibly end up with less than five million votes nationwide.[87]

The pre-election punditry that anticipated a major third-party defeat proved prescient. Henry Wallace garnered only a surprising 2.4 percent of the popular vote (1,156,103).[88] The IPP reasoned that the overall results were due, in part, to bad planning in a number of districts. However, IPP stalwarts believed, and rightly so, that they had not only provided the electorate with an alternative choice, they had also helped push the political discourse further to the left and forced progressive issues onto the national agenda.[89] For some Mexican Americans activists, the experience had made clear the necessity of forming a new kind of organization—a leftist version of LULAC and one that would focus greater attention on national issues affecting this community.

The exhilaration created around the campaigns of José Chávez and Richard Ibañez, as well as Edward Roybal's campaign a year earlier, raised the level of activism and political awareness to new heights on the Eastside. Carey McWilliams described this activism as flowing beyond the confines of Los Angeles: part of a "new consciousness" among Mexican Americans throughout the nation.[90] The Communist Party in Los Angeles, and in particular Mexican American members on the Eastside, looked back on this period and recalled how, prior to 1949, there existed no organization that could weather the reactionary political storm sweeping the nation. As the Los Angeles CP further explained: "Consequently, we began to raise the demand for such an organization. This organization we insisted would merge both the cultural and heritage [sic] of the Mexican people with the struggles for first class citizenship within the framework of the general political activity in the community."[91] This clamor within the party, Cuarón proudly explained, led to the passage of a resolution on the Mexican people that he helped draft and ultimately presented at the party's national convention in August 1948.[92] "The convention endorsed our work," Cuarón asserted. "The position on the Mexican question changed to our favor." Indeed, the party endorsed the idea of "a national organization for the Mexican people."[93] In early February 1949, a small group of fifty delegates assembled in Phoenix, Arizona, and organized the Asociación Nacional México-Americana (ANMA)—the Mexican American National Association.[94] Nonetheless, the principal thrust of and financial support for the formation of the association came from organized labor.

The International Union of Mine, Mill and Smelter Workers was instrumental in fulfilling the aspirations of progressive and radical Mexican Americans in forming a national organization. Mine-Mill provided the funding and volunteers from its ranks to help organize the fledgling organization. According to Bert Corona, ANMA would have formed without the direct participation of Mine-Mill, "but it might not have been so strongly oriented toward *mexicano* workers and toward helping to stimulate trade unionism among them."[95] Cuarón and members of the Mexican Commission of the CP in Los Angeles also played an important role during this formative period. Cuarón, Frances Lym, and Ramón M. Welch served as delegates to the organizing meetings held on February 12 and 13, 1949. Before leaving Arizona, Cuarón had been selected as the *director juvenil* (youth director) of ANMA's executive board. The other provisional officers on the national board included: Alfredo C. Montoya, president; Virginia X. Ruiz, executive secretary; Bebe Grijalva, treasurer; Carlos Salgado, director of education; Ramón Welch, publicity director; and Chris Ruiz, cultural director.[96] Activists in Los Angeles soon moved to establish their own chapter.

In October of that same year, the East Los Angeles chapter of ANMA held its founding convention at the Alianza Hall located on West Venice Boulevard. In an article in the *Eastside Sun*, Cuarón explained that ANMA was organized, "in order to bring an end to the long series of abuses and discrimination which we, the Mexican people, have suffered down through the years, and for the purpose of defending our economic, political and social rights as well as developing our cultural and democratic traditions." Furthermore, he argued that Mexican Americans were "strangers in their own historic homeland." Cuarón went on to explain that Mexican Americans were the only group that had not formed a "national organization."[97] Whether by design or not, his remark clearly ignored the long history of LULAC and other groups doing similar work in Latino communities. Despite this overgeneralization, excitement built and activists poured their energies into this new organization.

The list of individuals and organizations sponsoring the convention indicated that Los Angeles would play an important role in the national association. A partial list of sponsors included a number of leading progressives with a long history of political activism on behalf of civil liberties:

Carey McWilliams, noted writer and authority on Mexican problems; former State Attorney General Robert W. Kenney; Reverend Oscar Lizarraga; James Daugherty, state CIO President; Aaron A. Heist, American Civil Liberties Union leader; Charlotta Bass, publisher of the California Eagle; William Elkonin, International Field Organizer, United Electrical Workers, CIO; Eleanor Raymond, California Legislative Conference secretary; and many prominent fraternal and trade union leaders.[98]

While ANMA would function as a civil rights organization on behalf of Mexican Americans, its support base included an ecumenical coalition of forces.[99] The newly elected officers of the Southern California regional chapter of ANMA included a number of longtime leading Mexican American activists in labor, civil rights, and progressive causes: Armando Dávila, president; María Galloway, vice president; Julia Luna Mount, secretary-treasurer; Mauricio Terrazas, organizational secretary; Carlos Salgado, recording secretary; Rene Di Maestri, educational director; and José Ramón Chávez and Eduardo García as trustees.[100] In his capacity as a member of the National Executive Board, Cuarón worked diligently to strengthen the organization.

In its invitation to all chapters to converge in Los Angeles for ANMA's national founding convention, the leadership asserted that Mexican Americans stood "on the eve of a new half-century" and "on the brink of a new life."[101] The lofty goals of the organization were proudly displayed on its letterhead: *"To Protect Civil, Economic and Political Rights and Encourage the Education, Culture and Advancement of the Mexican-American People of the United States."*[102]

> We cannot erase the letters of blood with which our history has been written in this country; we cannot forget the years and entire generations of violence and lynchings against our people, first in Texas and California and later in Arizona. Nor are we unaware of the monumental work done by the Mexican people in the Southwest, who have made the desert blossom and have girded it with steel rails and concrete highways. We know that from the mines of New Mexico, Arizona and Colorado we have dug out treasures worth ten times the mines of "Potosi." We still see our sugar-beet workers doing their penance on their knees like the humble pilgrims of yesteryear. We see our youth, the guardian of our people's future, abused, beaten and assassinated by racist police officers in dozens of Southwestern cities.[103]

The group clearly placed ANMA's mission within a larger historical context and appealed to its members, and potential members, with a sense of urgency to challenge and rectify these injustices. Significantly, ANMA appeared to ignore the contributions made by organizations like LULAC, El Congreso, CSO, and the GI Forum. They envisioned ANMA as breaking new ground and transcending the mistakes of past organizations. "This was not the first time that an effort had been made. But this time one obstacle was being eliminated: the former isolation between the Mexican communities throughout the Southwest as well as between the Mexican communities and other minority groups and organized labor was being bridged."[104]

Soon, ANMA chapters were being established throughout the state and across the Southwest with great enthusiasm and fanfare. Alfredo Montoya and Francisca Flores captured some of this enthusiasm in a pamphlet they co-wrote titled *Toward the Unity of the Mexican People in the United States*. In this pamphlet, printed in 1950, the authors spoke of "a new Spirit" gathering among the Mexican people. "It is a spirit tempered in the crucible of struggle and bitter experience. It is a spirit accompanied by a more mature social and political consciousness." According to Montoya and Flores, the increasing "resistance . . . to discrimination in any form, against police abuse, deportations, etc." was a sign that this population had shed its isolation. Montoya and Flores recognized that a new "aggressive, enlightened and intelligent young leadership" had emerged from all areas of community life, forging new relationships, and creating "progressive organizations with roots in the communities."[105]

ANMA proved to be a great catalyst for organizing around national as well as local issues. In its first year, the organization reached a membership of fifteen hundred.[106] By the next year, ANMA "reported a membership of 4,000 in more than 30 locals." As Mario T. García explains, local chapters "sprang up in six regions: Arizona, northern California, southern California, Colorado, New Mexico, and Texas. These locals included Phoenix, Tucson, East Los Angeles, Denver, Albuquerque, El Paso, San Antonio, and Chicago." ANMA chapters rallied around a variety of issues, including rent control, segregated housing, anti-immigrant federal legislation (i.e., the 1950 McCarran Act), educational equity, political representation, and police brutality. Nothing seemed to galvanize the organization more than the last of these. For example, in Downey, a city located southeast of Los Angeles, Alfonso Venegas and other residents rallied to organize a local chapter of ANMA after the death of a young Mexican American in that community. Similarly, the local chapter in Estrada Courts, located in East Los Angeles, was organized as "a result of an incident of police brutality."[107] Cuarón became especially concerned with this incessant problem and, as the youth director of ANMA's national provisional board, advocated for extensive outreach and the organizing of youth.

Cuarón worked diligently to mentor and train young Mexican Americans for leadership roles. According to García, "ANMA observed that young veterans, in particular, welcomed the opportunity for political work, since after returning from the battlefields they discovered that American society had little to

FIGURE 8   Ralph Cuarón, participating in the national convention of the Asociación Nacional México-Americana, El Paso, Texas, 1953. Some of those present were (1) Art Flores, (2) Clinton Jenks, (3) Maclovio Barraza, (4) Rito G. Valencia, (5) Bennie Flores, (6) Lorenzo Torrez, (7) Ralph Cuarón, (8) Angel Flores, (9) Ray Marufo. Courtesy of Lorenzo and Anita Torrez.

offer them."[108] Indeed, Cuarón was very proud of those he had helped mentor, including Felix Padilla, Robert Sambrano, Maclovio Barraza, and Rito Valencia. He recalled with great pride how he had advised Alfredo Montoya before he became president of ANMA. "[Alfredo Montoya] was one of my students who lived in my house and I was teaching [*sic*] him about unionism and how to function as a union leader."[109] He recalls how he had helped Montoya obtain employment first with the meatpackers union in Los Angeles and then later as a business agent for Mine-Mill in El Paso, Texas. Cuarón's work on ANMA's national board, as well as his activities with the Southern California regional office and his position as an organizer for Furniture Workers Local 576, kept him on the road, as he made frequent trips throughout the Southwest. It was during these excursions that he was introduced to the struggles of the Mine-Mill workers in Bayard, New Mexico, as well as the Hollywood crew that would produce the film *Salt of the Earth*.

In 1951, Cuarón and Montoya traveled together to New Mexico and "visited all the little communities." Cuarón came away from the trip convinced more than ever of the need to organize "these people [Mexican Americans] into ANMA." During this period, he also became closely acquainted with Juan Chacón, a key leader in Mine-Mill Local 890, and its struggle with the Empire Zinc Company.

> I was doing other trade union work up and down the Southwest with the Mine, Mill and Smelter workers. I used to travel up and down from El Paso to L.A. I was doing educational work. I used to work with new union elected officials. . . . I would help educate them into the union and union leadership. . . . I don't know if you remember the movie, *Salt of the Earth*; I was very instrumental in working with that group.[110]

Indeed, Sylvia vividly recalls the day that Ralph first became involved with the making of the film.

> One evening [Ralph] was invited to attend a meeting in Hollywood where Mike Wilson and Herb Biberman[111] were getting together to do this screenplay for a strike out in Bayard, New Mexico. . . . They wanted the input from a Mexican American . . . [about] how to approach writing the script so that it would show the true issues involved which were not only the strike. There was man, woman issues, women taking over the strike, etcetera.[112]

Sylvia remembers the excitement that she and Ralph felt about the project: that finally there would be a film depicting the struggles of working-class people and, more importantly, that of Mexican Americans. So, when a group working on the screenplay for the film came and offered Sylvia the lead female role, no one was more surprised than she.

Heading this exploratory committee, Sylvia recalled, was Gale Sondergaard, an accomplished actor and wife to Herbert Biberman, a blacklisted Hollywood screenwriter and director. Although Mike Wilson, also blacklisted by the Hollywood film studios, had originally written the role of Esperanza Quintero for Sondergaard, the plan was scrapped in order to give the film more authenticity.[113] "She [Sondergaard] came over and asked if I would be interested to play the role of Esperanza. At that time I was, maybe . . . what? . . . thirty years old. And, so, I told her, 'Thank you, but I think you should look for a Mexican

FIGURE 9 Ralph Cuarón (wearing cap), background actor in the film *Salt of the Earth*, ca. 1954.

FIGURE 10 Rito Valencia (wearing miner's helmet), background actor in the film *Salt of the Earth*, ca. 1954. Ralph Cuarón stands behind Valencia.

FIGURE 11 Lorenzo Torrez (in background smiling with beer in hand), background actor in the film *Salt of the Earth*, ca. 1954.

American to do the role, not me. I'm not.' And she was flabbergasted." Indeed, Sondergaard seemed unaware that Sylvia was Jewish, and of Ukrainian descent. The lead role would eventually be given to Rosaura Revueltas, an acclaimed Mexican actor. And both Sylvia and Ralph Cuarón would be cast as extras in the famous eviction scene. As Sylvia remembers, "And there's a shot there when there is a freeze. . . . There is a shot of Ralph's face that you cannot [forget]. . . . Just beautiful."[114] Casting issues aside, Biberman and the production crew would struggle against the tremendous pressure of conservative politicians, commentators, studio executives, and labor leaders.

By the time *Salt of the Earth* began production in 1953, Hollywood had long fallen under the penetrating gaze of conservative groups. Beginning in 1938, and in the wake of rising labor activism, the House Un-American Activities Committee (HUAC), led by Texas Democrat Martin Dies, sought to investigate "un-American" activities by radicals—supposedly of the Right and the Left. As historians of the period have noted, however, the actual effort was intended to suppress the growing militancy of the labor unions and radicals. With a profound paranoia, this conservative movement demonized its enemies as atheistic Communists—foreign agents of repression and chaos. "Projecting their own fears and insecurities onto a demonized 'Other,'" writes Ellen Schrecker, "many Americans have found convenient scapegoats among the powerless minorities within their midst. Native Americans, African Americans, Catholics, immigrants—all, at one time or another, embodied the threat of internal subversion."[115] Many of these Red-hunters also had their own self-interests in mind. The business community, for example, used anti-Communism as a tool to weaken organized labor and to delegitimize their grievances. A number of organizations, such as private detective companies, local and state police, and federal agencies, exaggerated the danger of internal subversion out of bureaucratic self-interest, to legitimize their roles as protectors of the community. Ambitious politicians and others in positions of power used anti-Communism as a tool to advance personal or group objectives. Increasingly recognized for its ability to influence social and political values, the film industry became an important testing ground to see who would control the stories and the messaging.[116]

The Communist Party USA did not wield control or have an overbearing influence on the film industry as the cold warriors so vociferously asserted. As Deborah Silverton Rosenfelt argues, if egalitarian values such as equality for women and ethnic minorities, and greater control over their lives by the working class, were inserted into *Salt of the Earth*, it is because Communists, as artists, "believed deeply in these principles," not because they were members of the CP.[117] Nevertheless, in 1947, when HUAC renewed its attack on the film industry, Hollywood inevitably succumbed to the pressures.

Eager to appease the inquisitors—and to dispel any notions of unpatriotic activities—industry leaders, and some within labor, agreed to work with HUAC to purge Communists from their ranks. Roy Brewer of the International Alliance of Theatrical Stage Employees union (IATSE) eagerly jumped into the fray. However, the anti-Communist and conformist atmosphere that spread over Hollywood arose not as a direct result of HUAC, but as a consequence of a conflict between two rival unions in the motion picture industry. The destruction of the upstart Conference of Studio Unions, by the avidly anti-Communist and corrupt IATSE, in effect laid the groundwork for Hollywood's weakened response to HUAC's red-baiting.[118] Brewer's collaboration with the Motion Picture Alliance for the Preservation of American Ideals, an organization of high-profile conservative filmmakers, and its supporters in the American Legion, the

Catholic Church, and elements in the press proved critical in helping to force studio executives and management to acquiesce to their demands for purging subversives. Consequently, when HUAC, led by J. Parnell Thomas (R-New Jersey), tried and convicted ten Hollywood notables (directors and screenwriters) for contempt of Congress for refusing to give testimony to the House Committee on Un-American Activities, the progressive forces shattered. The Hollywood Ten, which included Alvah Bessie, Herbert Biberman, Lester Cole, Edward Dmytryk, Ring Lardner, John Howard Lawson, Albert Maltz, Samuel Ornitz, Adrian Scott, and Dalton Trumbo, were subsequently blacklisted and unable to find work. The result of this and succeeding investigations would be the development of an expanded blacklist, which identified somewhere between three hundred and five hundred Communists, former Communists, and their sympathizers, with the intent of forcing them out of the industry altogether.[119]

When Herbert Biberman set out to make *Salt of the Earth*, his goal was not only to circumvent the industry's blacklist, but also to break through the static conventions that had developed after the war. With the end of World War II, some Americans yearned for a return to *normalcy*, which invariably meant a return to an emphasis on domesticity. Therefore, explains Elaine Tyler May, Hollywood obliged by elevating the "subservient homemaker" over the independent and emancipated heroine.[120] The struggle between Mine-Mill and Empire Zinc epitomized the kind of story that Biberman, producer Paul Jarrico, and writer Michael Wilson wanted to tell. *Salt of the Earth* would not only break with the highly restrictive and conservative genre imposed on Hollywood that exalted paternalism, but also with unfettered individualism and consumerism. The script, Ellen Baker reminds us, was the product of a close collaboration between Wilson and the union families. "The script reflected their recent history and the leverage women had gained in representing their strike. In both settings—Hollywood and Grant County—left-wing women pressured Wilson to incorporate a feminist message." And this community would have a final say over the script.[121]

In *Salt of the Earth*, the female protagonists do not abandon their husbands and community for "freedom and money," as Lary May eloquently describes in his assessment of Hollywood's consumer ideal. Instead, they actively engage the source of their suffering.[122] They perceive themselves as individuals with depth and dignity—beyond the mainstream symbols of motherhood and domesticity. They clearly do not reject modernity; they embrace a form of it that reflects communal security, gender equality, and class solidarity. Refusing to be sidelined, the women see this struggle as representing more than fair wages and safety in the mines; they are also struggling for running water and indoor plumbing. The women also compel the men to recognize their organizational and creative leadership as well as their courage as they confront employer aggression. Consequently, the women succeed in carving out a space for themselves as leaders in the strike, and in the process they alter the relations between the sexes.[123]

Clinton Jencks, the international representative of Mine-Mill Local 890, was an organizer at the mine and directly involved in the Empire Zinc strike. Jencks and his wife, Virginia, believed that the struggle in Grant County represented more than a simple union conflict. As Jencks remarked, he and Virginia discovered a struggle of "a whole people" for self-determination and first-class citizenship.[124] In *Salt of the Earth*, the Jenckses proved quite adept at playing themselves in the characters of Frank and Ruth Barnes. And, as a couple in the film, the Barneses prove both politically and culturally sensitive to the desires of Mexican Americans for equality and justice.[125]

Cuarón had long expressed a strong sense of ethnic identity and pride as well as frustration with the apparent lack of progress in racial equality both inside and out of the union movement.[126] His position on this issue, for example, was no secret within the CP, a fact zealously recorded by the FBI. In Cuarón's activities organizing Mexican Americans into Mine-Mill, the FBI noted, "he is reported as having told these Mexicans whom he was attempting to organize that they were not to trust 'any Anglos,' and that all Mexicans had to unite, not against the boss, but against their own union leadership."[127] Although the FBI report exaggerated the point, Cuarón did routinely invoke cultural nationalism with rank-and-file Mexican American workers. Indeed, Cuarón's articulation of radical politics, class-consciousness, and cultural nationalism seemed to predate the Chicano Movement of the 1960s. Although he remained strongly committed to the unity of *all* workers, Cuarón articulated a very fundamental issue: the desire that Mexican Americans be central figures in their struggle for greater equality. The producers of the film were sensitive to these issues and made certain that these workers were directly engaged in telling *their* story, from critiquing and revising drafts to altering scenes they perceived to be false.[128]

The filmmakers were also keen to put forward another view of American society—a more egalitarian view—by exploring real possibilities within human relationships. However, the appearance of mixed racial groups, men and women, working together may have stretched some sensibilities too thin. Years later, at the end of IPC's antitrust suit against IATSE and the Hollywood corporate establishment, Biberman revealed the extent of these apprehensions. Pathe Laboratories, for example, had come to the conclusion that something was terribly wrong with *Salt of the Earth*. As they processed the film, the evidence became all too clear. They found that

> there were Mexicans [in the film], that they were living in poverty, that they had organized a strike and they were on picket lines, that the Sheriff's [*sic*] and the police were also involved and appeared to be lined up against them, and that there were women and children in jail banging their cups against the bars.[129]

Hollywood was targeted by HUAC, explains Victor Navasky, partly because of its image as "the dream factory."[130] *Salt of the Earth* seemed to unsettle the status quo by raising unrealistic expectations among Mexican Americans.[131] In what can only be described as a zealous spirit, Roy Brewer, chair of the Hollywood AFL Council in 1953, assured California Republican congressman Donald L. Jackson that his organization would do everything it could to "prevent the showing of the *Mexican* picture, Salt of the Earth" (my emphasis).[132] Biberman reveals that he understood early on that HUAC's investigations into the motion picture industry in search of "subversives" meant that "films were apparently too influential to be permitted to remain an oasis of popular expression."[133] *Salt of the Earth* represented more than a straightforward film depicting the struggle of a Mexican American community in a small town in New Mexico—important as this story was. Juan Chacón, who played the lead role of Ramón Quintero in the film, proudly asserted, "SALT OF THE EARTH shows that workers can get along regardless of religion, color, or politics. It shows the gains we have made through the work of our Union."[134] And it was this exact story that some inveterate executives and political ideologues hoped to control and manipulate.

The film became a source of great pride for those Mexican Americans directly involved in its production. Although the actors, film extras, and production crew members understood that they were engaged in a historic project, they also understood that this was part of a larger struggle. Joe T. Morales, a charter member of Mine-Mill, for example, explains, "This was nothing new."

> We have had the same names thrown at us every time we did something for the good of the people here. We got it when we organized the union, and when we abolished the 'dual' scale of wages. We are doing something here that unions

SHOULD do—tell the story in every way we can. I hope there will be a lot more union movies.[135]

Chacón echoed these same sentiments.

The union has just about as much right as RKO or MGM or any of the individual corporations that have made movies. These people are helping us to tell our story. That's our gain. We are confident that our movie will serve the best interests of our union, our community and our nation.[136]

The *Labor Herald*, a California CIO paper, reported in early 1953 that the film had suffered a series of attacks by employers, Hollywood producers, and Representative Donald L. Jackson. These attacks included "death threats against workers in the film, burning of the Mine-Mill union hall in Bayard, attempts to stir mob violence against the filming unit, and the deportation of the star of the film, Rosaura Revueltas."[137] The relentless persecution carried out by HUAC, the FBI, the Hollywood blacklist, as well as the myriad of "free-lance blacklisters" negatively affected the film's production and distribution and, hence, its overall message.[138]

Despite this escalation of opposition, Cuarón took *Salt of the Earth* on the road, screening it to as many workers as he could throughout the Southwest. Regardless of where he showed the film, the subversive story proved highly popular. This response allowed Cuarón to believe that most Americans, if given the opportunity, would see through the Cold War smoke screen. Still, he could not have realized at the time the sheer determination of the anti-Communist crusade to impose their script, their story, on a national narrative. As a result of being banned, *Salt of the Earth* opened in no more than a dozen commercial theatres nationwide by mid-decade and was never financially successful. Despite the heroic efforts by Biberman, including a long protracted legal battle against the IATSA, the film remained suppressed. Soon, the Mexican American National Association also became a victim of Cold War machinations.[139]

By mid-decade, ANMA was all but defunct in Southern California. It gained the dubious honor of being placed on the national House Un-American Activities Committee's list of disloyal organizations. Eager to implicate ANMA with the CP, explains Mario García, the FBI went beyond making the standard personal and institution connections; they were portrayed as ideologically one in the same. "Guilt by ideological association was likewise extracted from

comparison of stands on other issues such as racial discrimination, mass deportations, Mexican culture, the peace movement, the labor movement, the history
of the Southwest, and black-Mexican unity."[140] Cuarón dismissed the claims
that the CP dominated ANMA. Nevertheless, a culmination of factors led to
its demise, including the Cold War climate of distrust, fears of clandestine CP
intrigue, government infiltration and interference, internal divisions over goals
and objectives, and personal rivalries. Cuarón admitted that the party did at
times use a heavy hand as it attempted to recruit from ANMA's membership.
For example, some party activists, Cuarón recalled, did not "see ANMA as an
independent, autonomous organization for Mexican Americans." Consequently,
they came to believe that ANMA members represented legitimate targets for
recruitment into the party. On the other hand, Cuarón acknowledged, "most
of the activists [those doing much of the actual work] were party people. And
he [Alfredo Montoya] couldn't get anywhere without them." By mid-decade,
these conflicts were stretched to their limit, and, as Cuarón wistfully recalled,
Montoya had become avidly opposed to the Communist influence, and they
subsequently ended their friendship.[141]

The wildcat strikes, mass mobilizations, general strikes, shop-floor insurgen-
cies, and cultural creativity that had characterized the labor movement of the
1940s were now on the wane. As Ellen Schrecker explains, the massive government offensive, with its "Congressional hearings, contempt citations, Smith Act
prosecutions, deportations, SACB [Subversive Activities Control Board] proceedings, security clearance denials, income tax audits . . . forced these unions
and their top leaders to face several different attacks at one time." Jurisdictional
battles between unions and the successful expulsion of the left-wing unions by
the CIO in 1949 and 1950 left little doubt that a significant era in labor history
had come to an end.[142] However, Cuarón refused to be marginalized. Despite the
additional indignity of the Internal Security Act of 1950, he decided to remain
active within the UFWA and Local 576.

The CIO did not expel the UFWA, but it struggled to oust the Communists
from the local's ranks, especially from positions of leadership. The "Communist
576" (as its detractors referred to it) represented one of a handful of locals where
the international union had largely failed to marginalize the Communist leadership. Indeed, the radical leadership that included Gus Brown, Oscar Castro,
Jacob Lehman, Armando Dávila, and Laurence Turner proved to be exceptional organizers and highly successful at protecting wage scales and workers'
rights. While this leadership was popular among some workers, others opposed

their dogged pursuit of local autonomy, support of leftist causes, and, more importantly, their refusal to abide by UFWA and CIO policies that supported U.S. foreign operations. In the midst of this contentious atmosphere, Mexican Americans (approximately 60 percent of 576's workforce) found themselves pulled in all directions by the competing sides.[143]

Mexican Americans were certainly divided by the pressures to conform to the national mood against Communism and by the more local and immediate "bread and butter" issues affecting them at the workplace. The third-party movement had also divided loyalties, with some Mexican Americans questioning the political rationale for such support. Some workers, Luis Arroyo points out, "were convinced that Truman was the only hope to keep the country from falling into the hands of reactionaries and stave off the Soviet Union."[144] However, other workers like Cuarón believed that the "reactionaries" had already ascended to power.

Cuarón recalled how on more than one occasion he found himself having to struggle with these "cold war warriors" on the shop floor and in the picket lines. In 1950, in what was admitted to be an "extraordinary measure," the UFWA chartered a new local to compete and eventually destroy Local 576.[145] Leading this charge was Eppy Galván, another active Mexican American union member and popular shop steward. Cuarón identified Galván as avidly anti-Communist: "He was against progressive ideas. He was a Catholic involved in anti-Communism."[146] Indeed, as Arroyo explains, "perhaps most importantly, Galván had been at odds with [Gus] Brown for years. The conflict between them was personal and ideological: Galván coveted the business agent position and disliked Communism."[147] Not too long after the creation of Local 1010, Cuarón was embroiled in an effort to dislodge Local 576, Independent, from Crest Pacific.

The raid on Crest Pacific had been orchestrated jointly by the owners and by a group led by Galván. As Cuarón recalled, Galván had been allowed access to the shop during business hours and entered through a back door without the consent of the workers. When Cuarón protested these actions, the owner physically assaulted him—and in the ensuing altercation, Cuarón managed to knock him to the ground. In the melee that followed, the workers loyal to Cuarón shut down the plant. Cuarón proudly recalled the events of that day: "All of the people were behind me and ready to do anything I would ask [of] them. . . . Eppy Galván never got inside that plant. I resisted. All of the plants decided to follow our stand and keep Eppy Galván from coming into the plant."[148]

Although this incident represented a great personal triumph for Cuarón, the victory proved short lived. As the political intrigues and raids escalated—and the treasuries of each local were depleted—considerable animosity grew among the contending sides.

When Cuarón attempted to challenge his old mentor, Gus Brown, in 1955 for the position of business agent, personal rivalry marred the campaign and the election. Indeed, Cuarón's campaign to depose a fellow comrade and longtime labor activist earned him a negative reputation within party circles. Although Cuarón maintained that he had strong support among the largely Mexican American labor force of Local 576, Independent, it was not sufficient to oust the incumbent. As Sylvia recalls, the election was perceived by some as a contest between an old, entrenched power and a more youthful voice questioning authority. Cuarón felt Brown had not done enough to encourage a new generation of young Mexican American leadership in the union. On the other hand, members of the party increasingly perceived Cuarón as reckless, headstrong, and untrustworthy, a man prone to following his own agenda at the expense of the party. The election results illustrated Brown's political adeptness at retaining power and protecting his job.

The price for challenging Brown proved high. As Sylvia remembers, "When Ralph lost the election, Gus Brown saw to it that he [Ralph] was replaced by another organizer . . . and so, no one would hire him because he's the ex-organizer. He was a big trouble-maker according to the owners of the furniture industry."[149] That Cuarón's continual failure to secure work was more than a coincidence became glaringly clear after his dismissal from the Revere Ware Copper plant in Riverside. When Cuarón demanded an explanation for his early termination, the employer disclosed that he had been identified as a "rabid nationalist" and thus a high-risk employee. This label, according to Cuarón, was tantamount to being called a "terrorist"—a disruptive element in the world of employer and employee relations. When Cuarón next attempted to obtain employment at Abel's Sheet Metal shop on the Eastside, the rejection he received was shocking.[150]

It became clear, then, that Cuarón had been blacklisted in the furniture industry. Abel's Sheet Metal shop was well known on the Eastside for hiring "left-wingers who were in trouble." But when he could not get a job at this haven-of-last-resort, Cuarón, for the first time, felt the sheer depth of his ostracism. "I could have at that time become a very anti-Communist person. . . . I could have become a stool pigeon. But I fought these feelings. I didn't want to believe what I felt."[151] Hard pressed as he was, Cuarón remained dedicated to his convictions and to the party. Although he managed to survive by acquiring odd jobs for short periods of time, he never reclaimed his former leadership role in the local or the International. It also soon became apparent that his ostracism was not confined to the union.

Increasingly, the party, too, seemed to shy away from Cuarón. Repeated overtures for assistance in helping him find employment went unanswered. "There was nobody visiting me," Cuarón recalled with some acrimony, "nobody counseling me. Usually you had somebody from the party come and counsel you. I had no such counseling. My former party members, they stayed away from me. They were actually intimidated by me."[152] Sylvia also remembers this period vividly and added that the party's failure to provide employment counseling after Ralph had lost the election signified to them that the party had decided to discard one of their own: it was "not so much that Ralph left the party as much as the party left him. . . . After all, he [Ralph] was always the gadfly, the young whippersnapper, as far as the bureaucracy was concerned. So, it was a sense of, 'Well, he's out of our hair now.'"[153]

Cuarón remained highly critical of the new leadership in the union. The new political atmosphere, Cuarón maintained, was infested with "opportunists" who were motivated by personal ambitions and interested solely in protecting privileged positions of power. He considered Galván and those who followed him as "sellouts" because their ambitions superseded the larger interests of the Mexican American people in the United States. Cuarón believed that the leadership "vacuum" that ensued with the ouster of the Communists and other radicals allowed a "middle-class leadership" to ascend to union power.[154] And it was his belief that this leadership could never be sensitive to the true needs of the working class or aspire to anything more than accommodation.

Indeed, a powerful consensus had developed on the home front in the midst of the new economic prosperity of the 1950s. As May explains, large sectors of the American public fell idealistically into a conception of society that offered them domestic bliss and security from "the dangers of the outside world." The Cold War fueled the belief that dangers to American freedom and security were external, but also internal. This new domestic ideology fostered the idea of affluence through materialism, consumerism, bureaucratic conformity, and traditional gender roles—with the family as the linchpin of this belief system. As May further explains, all groups were expected to conform to white, middle-class values that shaped the dominant political and economic institutions, and those who did not were marginalized and stigmatized. Ralph and Sylvia, however, were opposed to this rising cold war ideology and instead remained firmly committed to the ideals of grassroots activism.[155]

By the end of 1955, the Cuarón family had grown considerably. After all, Sylvia remembered, the role of a good Communist was also to expand the proletariat by having children. The eldest, Margarita ("Mita"), was soon joined by Rafael Jr., born in 1955, and then by Adela, in 1958. Cuarón's erratic employment strained the family's resources and ultimately forced Sylvia to look for work outside the home. "I got a job in the Shoe Workers Union [in 1955] as a job dispatcher. From there I got another job in the clothing industry—the [International] Ladies' Garment Workers' Union [from 1957 to 1958]." The jobs were never permanent, but they managed to pick up "little jobs here and there" and got by as best they could. By the end of the decade, Ralph Cuarón's new skills as a carpenter would serve him well as the family moved ahead with new projects and a new stage in their activist careers.[156]

4

THE MEXICAN QUESTION

You see, the Party considered the Mexican part of the working class—no different, no better, no worse. . . . We were saying [that] the Mexicans are a[n oppressed] national minority and they need to be organized as a national group. This was the great contention.

—Ralph Cuarón, 1999

HE "MEXICAN QUESTION" WAS far more than a theoretical abstraction for the Communist Party of the United States; it was a practical and political problem. What role would Mexican Americans play in the larger scope of working-class struggle and revolution? For many Communists, Mexican Americans embodied a *national minority group*; that is, they were indistinguishable from the multitude of ethnic groups that have historically immigrated to this country. Consequently, Mexican Americans did not merit any special status or approach by the CP. In effect, they were recognized as workers first (transitory and unskilled), and Mexicans second. By comparison, however, African Americans merited a different tact altogether. They would be considered a special group—an *oppressed nation*. This status would place them at the apex of revolutionary struggle in the United States.

The origins of this distinctive status for African Americans within the party's overall work and mission dated back to the 1920s. The theoretical basis for this assessment reflected the writings of Karl Marx and Friedrich Engels, political philosophers of Communist theory, Vladimir Lenin, the first leader of Soviet Russia, and Joseph Stalin, general secretary of the Soviet Union until 1953.[1] Almost from its inception, the CP identified the struggle for black equality as essential, if not crucial, to the destruction of imperialism at home and abroad. In fact, the racism perpetuated against African Americans would be, as some expressed, the "Achilles' heel of American imperialism."[2] But this formulaic approach, Clarence E. Walker contends, reveals a simplistic understanding of the deep roots of race hatred in American history. Accordingly, Karl Marx failed to comprehend that racism in the United States was not an abstraction; it cut across class, ethnic, and sectional lines, and, consequently, remains a powerful force all its own.[3] In fact, Walker maintains, the historical record reveals that race privilege has often taken "precedence over class conflict." Indeed, rather than class war, the relations between African Americans (free or not) and Euro-Americans have been characterized by "race war." Therefore, the belief that black liberation represented a panacea obscured the deeper fissures of the color line.[4] Although the party believed strongly that the unity of interests of *all* workers, regardless of color, was pivotal to the defeat of exploitation and oppression, the "Negro question" became paramount.[5] But for party activists living and working in the American Southwest, the national question—that is, what defines a people as a nation—was not so clear.

As Sylvia Cuarón recalls, the CP on the East Coast (the national headquarters was located in New York) appeared to be largely oblivious to the Mexican question. The CP on the West Coast and the CP on the East Coast appeared at times to be wholly distinct organizations: divided not only by geographic distance, but by history, ethnic composition, and culture. Dorothy Healey, for example, recalled how the national CP leadership proved "very resistant" to any suggestion or movement to consider Mexican Americans "an oppressed national minority, the same way that we had traditionally regarded Blacks."[6] Thus, for the New York–based leadership, the Mexican question seemed largely amorphous, and certainly not as vital or as urgent as that of the Negro question. However, for activists in the Southwest, the disparities experienced by Mexican Americans certainly demanded immediate attention.

Indeed, Communists, almost uniformly, presumed that assimilation would be the ultimate fate of Mexican Americans in the United States. Communists contended that the oppression and discrimination experienced by this population would be fleeting. But this simplistic understanding of the Mexican experience may well have been predicated on another important perception: that of a vast and open western frontier, still teeming with opportunities for those willing to work hard. As such, Communists and radicals were not immune from popular images and beliefs in American folklore. "Very often," Paul Buhle and Edmund B. Sullivan argue, "artists adopted stylized versions of the American mythology from Pilgrim to proletarian, including the conquering of the West (with Indians and Mexican-Americans strangely absent)."[7] In this context, the Mexican question remained peripheral at best and obscured at worst. Thus, many on the Left, including those in the CP, often failed to include Mexican Americans in the broader context of the working-class movement. However, this assessment does not reveal a complete failure on the part of the CP to address this issue. Through fits and half starts, the party struggled to take full advantage of the true potential for organizing Mexican Americans—a community described as possessing its own radical tradition. Despite these shortcomings, individual Communists did work courageously to mobilize and develop leadership among this population.[8]

Mexican Americans and Mexican immigrants played a significant role in defining their place within the CP and within the larger labor movement. From the 1940s to 1960s, in the midst of a repressive Cold War climate, Mexican Americans, like Ralph Cuarón, would help lead national and local organizing efforts. As they strove to organize the most marginalized workers, these activists devised creative and engaging strategies that would help inspire the work of a new generation of leaders. As the party aimed to expand its organizing efforts and recruit new members in the period after World War II, a resolution of the Mexican question became increasingly imperative.

The *national question* embodied ideas and concepts revolving around nationalism, nation-states, national liberation, and self-determination. In the nineteenth century, Karl Marx and Friedrich Engels wrote extensively on this issue through their observations of German, Polish, Hungarian, Italian, and Irish national struggles. However, in their assessment, the class struggle took precedence over most considerations of the national question. Marx and Engels called on socialists to support only those struggles of national liberation that could deal a significant blow to the oppressor nation and, hence, could contribute to an international movement for working-class liberation.[9]

Lenin, like Marx and Engels before him, also argued that national struggle formed part of the class struggle.[10] Thus, Lenin supported secession of national groups into their own nations only in circumstances when national oppression and national friction made "joint life absolutely intolerable and hindered any and all economic intercourse."[11] Nevertheless, the danger was always that these movements could fall victim to "bourgeois ideology," that is, to the ideas of the ruling class.[12] Still, Lenin placed a high value on national struggles for liberation and gave them special status in the arsenal of anti-imperialist struggles.[13]

The status of ethnic groups in the United States within this framework appeared clear and unequivocal. According to the CP's California Educational Department:

> Differentiation must be made between an oppressed nation and a national minority. A national minority has only cultural attributes, and lacks the other essential characteristics of a nation. National minorities in the United States would include Mexican people, Irish, Italians, etc.[14]

Thus, the CP identified only one group in the United States that qualified as a viable *nation*—African Americans.

From early on in the history of the CP, African Americans maintained a unique position in the organization's overall work. In 1924, in a resolution titled *Project for Resolution on Negro Question*, J. Amter explained: "The Negroes' fight for equal rights under capitalism is a fight against capitalism itself. By supporting this fight, by battling shoulder to shoulder with the Negro and the worker of any color, the white worker facilitates the struggle against world imperialism."[15] Although the resolution clearly linked the black struggle with the struggle of all peoples of color, it did not hesitate to recommend organizing African Americans into their own organizations. Similar resolutions would subsequently demand, for example, the publication of regular newspapers and pamphlets for African Americans, the creation of special departments within the party, as well as education and training schools. The underlying goal, as one resolution would state, was not only to train "negro comrades" to work effectively as regular party cadres, but "to fit them for work among the people of their own race."[16] These demands formed, as Robin D. G. Kelley explains, a corpus of resolutions and reassessments on the Negro question that would precede the decision in 1928 to designate this group as an oppressed nation.[17] Although some African Americans certainly continued to experience racism and discrimination within the party, they had made their interests heard within the national organization. In contrast, the lack of information on and direct contact with Mexican Americans led some party leaders to conclude early on that this group had limited leadership potential.

In 1925, for example, James Dolsen, the state organizer of the thirteenth district of the Workers Party of America (precursor to the Communist Party USA) located in San Francisco, revealed the degree to which he dismissed Mexican American leadership. In a letter written to Charles E. Rothenberg, a high-ranking party leader on the Central Executive Committee, Dolsen wrote: "We have many Spanish-speaking workers but I have never been able to locate Communists among them who could do anything, nor been able to find any Spanish Communist language paper [*sic*]. It seems there ought to be one in Mexico that could be used here."[18] These dismissive comments as well as other aspects of Dolsen's leadership did not go unchallenged. In a letter to the Central Executive Committee of the party, Emanuel Levine, chair of the City Central Committee in Los Angeles, made an urgent request that Dolsen be removed from his post. "His absolute incompetence as an organizer has kept our organization back so long we now appeal to your committee to remove him immediately."[19]

Levine also expressed concern that the district office headquarters, located in San Francisco, paid scant attention to party issues outside of the Bay area.[20] Paradoxically, Levine repeated the request that material in Spanish be obtained in "Mexico," assuming that this material could not be produced in the United States. Nonetheless, Levine countered Dolsen's condescending and uninformed remarks by acknowledging that Mexican Americans were already a significant presence in the nation's workforce. "We have in the Southern part of California and in Arizona thousands of Mexican workers in all industries. We also have a tremendous colored population, especially in Oakland and Los Angeles." Regardless, the party's penchant for disregarding the Mexican American population in favor of African Americans remained entrenched.

The status of blacks would soon shift significantly with their official recognition as a certified *nation*. As Gerald Horne explains, the designation of African Americans as an "oppressed nation" by the Sixth World Congress of the Communist International (Comintern) in 1928 became a turning point for organizing within this group.[21] The resolution passed by the international body declared that "African Americans had the right to self-determination: political power, control over the economy, and the right to secede from the United States." By 1930, however, another resolution further clarified that not *all* blacks would receive this consideration. As Robin Kelley explains, "Northern blacks, the new resolution argued, sought integration and assimilation, and therefore the demand for self-determination was to be applied exclusively to the South." However, not all among the national leadership were of one mind regarding the revolutionary potential of southern blacks. Indeed, some felt that the extreme nature of race relations in the South had impinged on any radical tradition. Through fits and half starts, Kelley maintains, the party came to understand and appreciate the region's long history of working-class and rural radicalism as well as its deep religious traditions. Pragmatism, and not strict party doctrine, would leave a lasting legacy of oppositional politics in the South.[22] In 1928, the "Black Belt" region of the country, the "heart and center of the Negro Nation," became the new ground zero for the Communist Party.[23]

The African American question, for some in the party, would become synonymous with the overall struggle for democracy and civil rights in the United States—and, indeed, the world. In 1947, for example, Benjamin Davis, the highest ranking and best-known African American in the CP national leadership, asserted that the struggle for black rights was paramount.

> Its importance rests in the fact that the Negro question, the question of the Negro people as an oppressed nation, of their national liberation, is in the center of all the problems today facing the American working class and its allies.[24]

William Z. Foster, chair of the national leadership, similarly asserted that the Negro question remained politically "the Achilles heel of U.S. imperialism."[25] In fact, an FBI agent noted this apparent enthusiasm by the CP when he observed that far more printed material was devoted "to the American Negro [than to] any other segment of the American population."[26]

Ralph Cuarón was highly critical of this position, particularly given its implications for Mexican Americans. Although Cuarón understood the importance of the Negro question, he chafed at the dismissal of Mexican Americans given their heavy concentration and historical significance in the Southwest. If fascism was *around the corner*, as most Communists strongly believed, then the party, Cuarón maintained, had failed by privileging African Americans above other groups. Even if the party meant to use the "Black Belt thesis" largely as a "propaganda" tool, the result remained the same.[27] For example, *Political Affairs*, the preeminent voice of the party, and its predecessor, *The Communist*, devoted far more space to issues affecting African Americans than to those of Mexican communities. Nonetheless, in 1939 *The Communist* did carry an article that, to a significant degree, influenced the policy direction for organizing among Mexican Americans in the Southwest.

Emma Tenayuca and Homer Brooks led the way with their article "The Mexican Question in the Southwest." As state chair and state secretary, respectively, of the Communist Party in Texas, the co-authors laid out what they perceived was a practical framework for approaching this community. The husband and wife team argued that Mexican Americans in the United States exhibited many of the attributes of the African American nation (a common history, culture, language, and communal life) except for two: "territorial and economic community."[28] In their assessment, Mexican Americans were economically and politically "welded" to those of the "Anglo-American people of the South-west."[29] Tenayuca and Brooks had been closely involved in organizing Mexican workers during the 1938 pecan shellers' strike in San Antonio, Texas, and this experience certainly informed their outlook. As Zaragosa Vargas explains, Tenayuca's contributions were instrumental in convincing the striking workers of the importance of collective action in order to gain higher pay and better working conditions.[30] "The task now is to build the democratic front among the Mexican masses," wrote Tenayuca and Brooks, "by unifying them on the basis of specific needs and in support of the social and economic measures of the New Deal."[31] The future, they argued, would lie in supporting all struggles attempting to address economic discrimination, educational inequality, cultural deprivation, and social and political oppression. Furthermore, success would lie in "trade union organization among the Mexican workers."[32]

Equally, the authors warned against taking "sterile paths" toward addressing Mexican Americans. They specifically mentioned the League of United Latin American Citizens (LULAC), a largely middle-class organization that they believed stressed civil rights but from a limited standpoint that privileged the elite above immigrants and the working class. Tenayuca and Brooks were particularly critical of LULAC's historical "glorification of the English language and Anglo-American culture" and its tepid, at best, support for labor unions.[33]

In summary, Mexican American liberation would be, for the most part, linked to the popular front against fascism. Despite the important attempt by Tenayuca and Brooks to argue a party approach in regard to Mexican Americans, they did not advocate the creation of a permanent organizational structure that would deal exclusively with this community. The key issues they outlined fell under the purview of individual organizations to implement on their own. Although the status of the Mexican people could be compared to that of African Americans, the experiences of the two groups, according to many party leaders and theorists, remained distinct.[34]

Consequently, organizing Mexican Americans on the basis of "special needs" still failed to recognize the revolutionary potential of this population. As Monroy explains, the party ignored the "integral value of Mexican liberation itself."[35] In other words, *melding* Mexican liberation with that of workers in general downplayed the individual character, wants, needs, and desires of this group.

This made Mexican Americans indistinguishable from other groups. Despite these drawbacks, the article may have had the positive effect of educating the party about the Latino population of the region.[36] As Vargas explains, Tenayuca's participation in national party politics, the "only Mexican American who held this distinction in the 1930s," put her in a unique position to influence policy. Under the leadership of Earl Browder, the CP general secretary, a new consensus took shape between 1938 and 1944 that challenged not only the foundations of the party but how the Mexican question would be handled.

As Dorothy Healey recalled, Browder and some in the national leadership began to take a more conciliatory approach to the federal government, organized labor, and to capitalism in general. The 1930s had witnessed an extraordinary growth of radical Left and liberal progressive organizations—and a closer collaboration among them. The CP had also developed closer ties with high-ranking labor leaders, and according to Healey, Browder was rightly concerned with maintaining these important ties.[37] The invasion of the Soviet Union by Nazi Germany in June 1941, and the subsequent alliance between Roosevelt, Churchill, and Stalin in December 1943, signaled a new direction. The belief that a "new world" was forthcoming compelled some of the leadership within the CP to dissolve the party altogether in 1944. Consequently, the organization was renamed the Communist Political Association (CPA), and was now oriented to enthusiastically embrace electoral and representative democratic politics. In effect, the Communist Party had shed its role as a revolutionary vanguard—the bogeyman of conservative politicians.[38] Yet, this change was never fully accepted by party stalwarts; so the experiment did not last long. By 1945, comrade Browder was unceremoniously ousted from power and the American Communist Party was reinstated. According to some, Browderism had been nothing more than a grand illusion.[39]

Moreover, Browderism had revealed some disturbing trends within the party, specifically with respect to the issue of race. In the interest of cooperating fully within the parameters of electoral politics in the United States, the CPA had embarked on a program that de-emphasized its leadership role in the struggle for racial equality. Indeed, as Horne explains, Browderism's "more conciliatory approach to racial matters" forced party activists such as Benjamin Davis to tread a fine line as they placed labor unity above civil rights.[40] For the activists that had long been on the forefront of race struggle, this new policy raised considerable concerns and questions. Was this new world on the horizon going to embody a racial utopia as well as a class one? The answer proved to be a resounding "no" on both scores. The racial violence that erupted during and after the war was an ominous sign.[41] For Mexican Americans, Browderism had further marginalized their status. Nevertheless, by war's end, a change in policy was in the offing.

In 1945, the party in Los Angeles established the Mexican Commission, specifically charged with overseeing the party's work within the Mexican American community.[42] Indeed, approximately 272,000 Mexicans out of a city population of 1,970,368 could not easily be ignored.[43] In the following year, the commission produced a report titled *Report on Mexicans in the U.S.A.*, in which it reviewed the history of Mexican Americans, their contributions and struggles, and concluded by outlining concrete policy directions for the CP vis-à-vis this community. The report minced few words in its assessment of the meaning of Browderism for Mexican Americans in the party.

> Revisionism liquidated the Mexican Section. Over the protests of the most developed comrades, and of most of the membership, all the work in the Spanish language was stopped; nearly all consideration of the Mexican people as a minority with special problems in the war effort was halted. All Mexican branches were dissolved and the comrades who did not know sufficient English were left politically homeless. Moreover, there was no progressive organizational channel through which the Mexican people might speak, not only in behalf of their own rights, but even in behalf of victory itself.[44]

With branches now established in San Diego and Chicago, commission members realized a clear role for themselves amid a new future. They would distance their mission from the older "Consul-organized 'Comision Honorifica'"–type organizations, which limited themselves to addressing minor "local grievances." Commission members, clearly, saw little value in what they deemed "bourgeois" organizing, which, in their estimation, also characterized organizations like LULAC. Although this characterization of LULAC was overdrawn, the commission envisioned itself playing a leadership role in advancing cultural and linguistic integrity and preparing the Mexican community against the increasing assault of "assimilation in an era of imperialism."[45] Immediately following his departure from the Merchant Marine, Cuarón became immersed in this political milieu and joined the Mexican Commission of the Communist Party.

The period after the war seemed ripe for opportunity within the party, and Cuarón wasted little time jumping in. He remembered with enormous pride and nostalgia when fellow activists like Frances Lym, Joe (José) Gastelum,[46] and many others reconstituted a "communist club with nothing but Mexicans." Although they fully understood that this "was not allowed" within the party, they formed the new organization anyway; they named it the Zapata Club of East Los Angeles. Choosing to name their club after Emiliano Zapata, the Mexican Revolution's most iconic figure, is telling. Revered by most Mexicans, Zapata embodied national honor, tragic hero, indigenous resistance, and cultural pride. "We developed the theory," Cuarón explained, "that Mexicans should have their own identity and have their own club." The club agitated for the creation of a national commission to reevaluate the national question. The group called for the CP to do more to recognize Mexican Americans as a national entity and also to recognize that Mexicans "had a right to autonomy."[47]

In the summer of 1947, the activists had an opportunity to bring their agenda to the fore. In June, the Los Angeles County Communist Party held their Party Building Conference, at which time the Panel on Mexican Work produced a special report on the problems and solutions to organizing in the Mexican American community.[48] Although the archival records do not place Cuarón at these specific proceedings, he recalled having participated in similar gatherings around Los Angeles and surrounding region. While the panel reported important gains made by particular clubs in recruiting and engaging Mexican Americans on local issues, they also reported the need to "organize the Mexican people into their own organizations." The two principal reasons for this recommendation had to do with "language difficulties and by the attitude of certain comrades that the work has to be done slowly" in these communities. The report was clearly critical of persistent ethnocentric attitudes within the party. In addition, the panel criticized the continuing problems faced by the party in organizing this group within the trade unions, which the report observed "amounted to nothing so far." "It seems not to have occurred to some of the union leaders," the report admonished, "that the mobilization of the thousands of Mexican members of the Los Angeles trade unions could constitute an important part of their job and would make their task more effective."[49]

The conference ended with different panel groups having submitted their formal proposals to the party's County Board for implementation. The following eight recommendations were included by the Panel on Mexican Work: outreach and recruiting activities in Mexican communities must be the responsibility of the entire party, and not just that of Mexican American members; more attention must be given to the weekly Spanish column in the *Daily People's World* and to the paper's distribution in Mexican communities; more education must take place among the membership on the history and issues affecting the Mexican people in the United States; a full-time education program must be organized for the Mexican community, with classes in Marxist fundamentals; conferences must be set up to address employment conditions and organizational strategies regarding Mexican workers in various industries; the party must be cognizant of any negative consequences to local community leadership and activism resulting from its promotion of Mexican American members to new responsibilities; efforts must be made to organize party clubs targeted at young people; and finally, greater attention must be paid by local clubs to promote civic education in Mexican communities. In this last recommendation, for example, the party called on county officials to provide greater voter information and targeted voter registration campaigns in Mexican American communities.[50] From the historical record, it is not clear what became of these proposals. Nonetheless, communities in other parts of the country raised similar concerns.

In October of that year, Isabel González, an activist from Denver, Colorado, produced a report detailing the conditions of Mexican immigrants in the United States. The report soon gained wide circulation among progressive circles.[51] In the report, titled *Step-Children of a Nation*, González addressed some of the problems faced by Mexican immigrants in becoming U.S. citizens.[52] The report was presented before a conference organized by the American Committee for Protection of Foreign Born that took place in Cleveland, Ohio. Interestingly, González echoed many of the concerns expressed by another activist, Luisa Moreno, who had presented a similar report seven years earlier to the American Committee titled "Caravans of Sorrow." Both authors highlighted the extreme alienation experienced by citizens and noncitizens alike as well as the systematic nature of the federal government's indiscriminate deportation drives.[53] In a critical study of the social construction of race, Natalia Molina illustrates how Mexican immigrants and Mexican Americans were regularly identified as outsiders and threats to the nation. Through "racial scripts," described as "attitudes, practices, customs, policies, and laws," U.S. administrators defined a clear racial hierarchy that identified Mexicans—legal or not—as undesirables and unfit to be Americans.[54]

Isabel González had been a longtime activist in Denver and operated a nonprofit agency that provided social service assistance to Mexican communities. According to Curtis D. MacDougall, she was "a firebrand" and would soon be involved in organizing the Independent Progressive Party within Mexican communities in Colorado.[55] González's report presented a damning account of the conditions under which Mexicans lived.

> Let me repeat that no distinction is made between citizens and non-citizens when it comes to the treatment accorded to the Mexican people. As a matter of fact, even among migratory workers, who are, generally speaking, the latest arrivals from Mexico, more than 90 percent of the children are, by birth, citizens of the United States; yet they too are regarded as "foreigners."[56]

González placed the Mexican experience outside that of other immigrant groups such as the "Italians or Irish or Jews" by stressing this community's status as "a conquered people." The "Mexican problem," she asserted, had resulted from expansionist policies pursued by both Northern and Southern economic interests. Keeping this population in "a constant state of impoverishment, hunger and misery," she declared, was a deliberate policy to secure a flexible, docile workforce. González concluded her report with a series of recommendations to address the barriers to citizenship, including the establishment of a formal congressional committee to investigate and expose the conditions under which Mexicans lived and worked.[57]

Although the party announced that it would allow greater local autonomy, the leaders in New York retained significant control. Party leaders on the West Coast as well as the rank and file often felt, and rightfully so, that they were stepchildren to the national office. As Sylvia Cuarón remembered, the West Coast section of the party appeared to be an "offshoot" of the larger organization.[58] Indeed, Mexican Americans often felt alienated from the CP because, as Cuarón succinctly explained, "they didn't know what the hell the party was talking about." The party often conducted its discussions and business utilizing Marxist lexicon unfamiliar to most community members. The local clubs, the nucleus of organization and recruitment, were not always successful in explaining party ideologies. As Cuarón recalled, most Mexican Americans who came to club meetings did so out of an interest in civil rights cases and issues that affected the community. As a result, party activists often failed to successfully recruit community activists into the organizational fold. When they did succeed in recruitment, retaining these members proved difficult.[59]

Frank López echoed these same sentiments when he criticized the CP for regularly failing to address Mexican American and immigrant interests. The party's rigid approach to class analysis, for example, failed to realize how nationalism could be a compelling force used to organize Mexican workers.[60] Though López made his comments in reference to the popular front period, these same weaknesses carried over after the war. As the 1948 presidential campaign approached, some Mexican American activists became increasingly vocal in party affairs. One opportunity presented itself in June 1948, within the pages of the party's *Pre-Convention Discussion Bulletin*.

In a prelude to the Los Angeles County Convention scheduled for July, the party produced a series of special bulletins in which members discussed and debated a number of pertinent issues. These discussions were meant to raise awareness and engage members on issues of policy, organizational structure, leadership, and vision. For example, in an article titled "Party Must Carry Out Policy on Mexican Work," an anonymous author, "F. L.," wrote that the party's failure to carry out the recommendations from its 1947 National Conference on Mexican Work had "severely" affected the organization's "education work on the Mexican question."[61] The author reiterated the importance of these recommendations, which ranged from creating a "Mexican training school" for the development of party "cadres" to translating into Spanish the constitution of the CP.[62] The county convention did make a strong effort to address the concerns of its Mexican American members, though not without controversy.

In July 1948, the party in Los Angeles held its county convention where it discussed and consolidated its platform in preparation for the upcoming national assembly. Healey's report to the convention floor revealed renewed concerns about the party's work among Mexican Americans. In her words:

> There is still not enough concern for the growth of the Party among the Mexican-American people. . . . During the height of the mass campaigns among the Mexican-American people, our two Spanish-speaking clubs did not meet. . . . Our concentration policy must include the selection of maybe just a few blocks in the Mexican-American community where systematic sales of the PW [*People's World*], our literature, and the distribution of leaflets take place, and where new Party clubs can be established.[63]

Differences of opinion among the top party leaders about increasing the presence of Mexican American workers in certain industries and shops became more apparent. Ben Dobbs, county labor secretary, supported a more cautious approach to this community. Nevertheless, though Dobbs agreed that the labor movement, and the party specifically, had not focused enough on blacks and Mexican

Americans, he maintained that the "fight . . . must be a sustained fight with gaining results as its objective and over a long period of time if necessary."[64] It was precisely this last point that concerned Cuarón most, and which he felt was self-defeating. In other words, this slow and deliberate approach had not achieved, in his estimation, any significant inroads among Mexican Americans. Cuarón felt that this fixation on *patience* and *long-term* work was precisely what allowed many in the party to relax into complacency and to neglect Mexican work.[65]

On the other hand, Nemmy Sparks, county chair of the party, maintained that "rapid recruitment" of Mexican Americans was a preferred strategy along with more concerted efforts at fighting "chauvinism." Interestingly, Sparks highlighted another concern that Cuarón often voiced: "[the] overcoming of sectarian tendencies to place excessive demands on Mexican workers before taking them into the Party."[66] The Communist Party state convention held in July did manage to produce a resolution on Mexican American work, but no substantive discussion about this community appeared in its official report.[67] One last opportunity to voice the issues affecting Mexican Americans before the meeting of the national convention came in the pages of *Political Affairs*.[68]

In his article titled "National Group Work in California," Pettis Perry, the chair of the Nationalities Commission of the Los Angeles Communist Party—and an African American—pointed out the need to work more closely with the state's large minority population in forming any "democratic coalition." With over 450,000 Mexican Americans, 258,000 Jewish people, and close to 225,000 "Negroes" in Los Angeles County alone in 1948, it was imperative, Perry urged, that the party examine "the unity of interests that offers the possibility for unification of these groups on the side of the labor and progressive movement." Perry outlined a number of major social ills affecting Mexican Americans but reminded his readers that the "resistance of the Mexican American people to these conditions is finally beginning to take shape in the fight for civil rights and the response to the Wallace movement." While admonishing his comrades that the new mobilization should be "led, organized, and developed by the Mexican-Americans themselves, with the cooperation of all progressive forces," he admitted that labor and progressives, "including the Communists," had not done enough to address the problems affecting this group. Although the CP had not coordinated any national effort, some Communists had already taken on that responsibility.[69]

By summer 1948, Cuarón was fully engaged in organizing for the Henry Wallace campaign for president. He had taken an official leave from his union activities with the United Furniture Workers of America in order to work full-time on the presidential race. His principal work involved organizing among Mexican American workers and potential voters. In fact, Cuarón had been a key organizer in forming Amigos de Wallace, which in turn helped mobilize many on the Eastside.[70] Soon after attending the founding convention of the Independent Progressive Party in Philadelphia in late July, Cuarón also took part in the CP's national convention, held in New York for a week in August.[71] Cuarón, and a number of other delegates, delivered a resolution that addressed important issues concerning Mexican Americans.

The policy measure titled *Resolution on Party Work Among the Mexican People* represented the culmination of the combined efforts of a number of activists. Prominent among them were Frances Lym, Ramón Welch, and Cuarón, all of whom belonged to the Mexican American Commission of the CP in Los Angeles.[72] The resolution read, in part: "The special historical development of the Mexican people in the United States as a conquered people, victims of American imperialist expansion, with close ties to Latin America, requires a new and special approach by our Party to the Mexican problem." The national party affirmed that it would carry through the following: devise a final scientific formulation of the Mexican question; print party material in Spanish; develop leadership training schools for Mexican Americans; push for a one dollar minimum wage for migratory workers; pledge full support for development of the Amigos de Wallace movement; coordinate on a national level for effective work among the Mexican people; campaign effectively to combat racist attacks against Mexicans; integrate and promote Mexican American leadership in the trade unions; and, finally, increase the struggle in all facets of civil rights work, including police brutality and deportations.[73] The legislative action was bold and progressive, and the activists were encouraged to submit a second resolution.

The second policy measure was titled *Resolution on the Conditions of the Mexican People*, a general condemnation of the economic, political, and social disenfranchisement experienced by this community. The resolution also outlined the party's pledge to struggle alongside Mexican Americans to overcome these circumstances. Interestingly, the resolution's acknowledgement of the Augustino Salcido murder case, in 1948, showed the influence that the Mexican Commission in Los Angeles had on the wording of the measure.[74]

The introduction and final passage of the resolutions before the body of the national convention served as a high point in Cuarón's political life inside the party. He felt confident that significant changes would come from these organization platforms. More importantly, he now had the endorsement of the

FIGURE 12 Freedom Fiesta, 1948. Cuarón would use the event to highlight issues affecting Mexican Americans in Los Angeles. *Daily People's World*, courtesy of Southern California Library.

party to continue, if not accelerate, his organizing activities among Mexican Americans, not only in Los Angeles but throughout the Southwest. Organizing could now take place on a national scale: to formulate, as he understood it, a radical organization exclusively for Mexican Americans. As Cuarón explained, these efforts were the first stirrings of what would culminate in the formation of ANMA. Despite the defeat of Wallace in November, the energy that had generated so much enthusiasm around his campaign remained. As a result, Cuarón and a group of young workers and political activists embarked on an ambitious plan to establish cross-border ties with their neighbor to the south.

FIGURE 13 Ralph Cuarón, visiting a higher education institution in Tijuana, Mexico, 1948. Cuarón Family Collection.

The "hands-across-the-border" project, as Cuarón remembered, represented far more than mere fanciful dreams by a handful of idealist Angelenos. Nationally, young progressives strove to reach out to like-minded individuals—*to the workers of the world*—in hopes of influencing an alternative international order. Henry Wallace had been critical of Cold War policies, and his campaign had been premised on the need to turn toward a more cooperative and multilateral approach to world affairs. He had rejected the growing rivalry between and unilateralism of the two remaining superpowers. For Wallace, Latin America

remained essential—not solely for hemispheric security and trade considerations, but also as nations that shared cultural, linguistic, and historic ties with
the United States. The Los Angeles CIO Council, already a strong advocate of
civil rights and supporter of its Mexican American members, helped initiate the
first cross-border event—dubbed "Freedom Fiesta." The celebration to bring
attention to the countries' shared history of labor solidarity was in part motivated by the recent success of the Amigos de Wallace rally in East Los Angeles.[75]

The Freedom Fiesta gala, which took place in September 1948, in honor
of Mexican independence, drew wide attention, giving Mexican American
activists in Los Angeles a platform to highlight local issues. The announced
visit of Mexico's top labor leader—Vicente Lombardo Toledano—established
this event as a true binational affair. Cuarón used this opportunity to spotlight
issues affecting Mexican American youth in the city, such as police brutality,
discrimination, and poor education. He also stressed the need to develop new
leadership and broaden cultural and political ties with Mexico. The speech was
so well received, Cuarón recalled, that he was invited by a Mexican legislator
attending the event to visit a civil engineering polytechnic institute located in
Tijuana, Mexico. Enthused by the prospect of working with youth across the
border, Cuarón accepted the invitation.

Three months later, a small contingent of young progressives finally made
their way to Tijuana. As Sylvia recalled, "We all met at Brooklyn and Soto
[Street] at about 4 o'clock in the morning . . . at Irving's Café."[76] This particular corner on the Eastside was popularly known as "Red Square," the loca-
tion where radical groups gathered for political, cultural, and social events. The
group of about a dozen or so piled into a chartered bus, accompanied by a local
musical group, and headed off to meet their counterparts in Mexico. Students
and administrators at the institute greeted the enthusiastic contingent from
Los Angeles with great fanfare. As Cuarón recalled, the institute had been a
prized educational project organized and supported by labor groups since the
1930s.[77] The hope on both sides of the border was that the students as well as the
school would benefit from a relationship with labor groups in the United States
by sharing technical and managerial innovations and alerting the students to
job opportunities in the United States. Before ending their three-day visit to
Tijuana, the group traveled to Ensenada, where they met with Rafael Estrada,
the mayor of the city. Sylvia remembered the three-day event fondly. The day
ended with a great celebration in which young people, Mexicans and Jews, came
together in a way she had never experienced.

Well, it was just a beautiful, youthful endeavor; dancing, eating, sharing experiences across the border. It was an unheard-of thing. It was organized by Ralph; the whole thing. He charted the bus; we gathered money for an orchestra. It was just beautiful. It was a prelude to our marriage.[78]

By the end of the trip, some friends and relatives became aware that Sylvia and Ralph were more than mere acquaintances. Before their jaunt across the border, the Lucas family appeared to be unaware that the two had become a couple. Only Sylvia's sister, Rose, knew of their "secret" relationship. Sylvia recognized her family's misgivings about such mixed unions and the agitation this news would cause. As Sylvia recalled, she preferred to "shield them" from her *transgression*. Despite the increased racial tolerance within the most liberal circles, these kinds of relationships were often met with mixed approval.[79] Sylvia and Ralph could recall that relationships of mixed ethnicities were not uncommon. Indeed, within their circle of acquaintances, they could point to a number of such unions during this period. These included Robert and Lillian Sambrano, Harold Dunn and Dorothy Salazar, Julia Luna and George Mount, Frank González and Joy Sands, Bill and Shirley Taylor, Julia and Jimmy Gray, Art Jones (he was Puerto Rican and his spouse Italian American), and Bert and Blanche Corona.

Nevertheless, these marriages exemplified, for some within the conservative Right, the degree to which social degradation was already underway in the nation. For them, there was no doubt that the Communist Party was a contributor to this aberrant behavior. State Senator Jack B. Tenney, for example, the leading anti-Communist crusader in California, was taken aback by the views of intermarriage expressed by Carey McWilliams during his testimony before a senate committee in 1941. "McWilliam's[sic] views on racial intermarriage are identical with Communist Party ideology," wrote Tenney in his highly vituperative book *Red Fascism: Boring from Within . . . By the Subversive Forces of Communism*. Challenges to the belief of racial exclusivity within the institution of matrimony, however, did not come only from the Communist Party. Indeed, in 1948, the California State Supreme Court ended the ban on interracial couples in its decision in *Pérez v. Sharp*. The sections of the civil code that had provided that "all marriages of white persons with negroes, Mongolians, members of the Malay race, or mulattoes are illegal and void" were found by the court to be arbitrary and discriminatory beyond reason.[80] But as Dara Orenstein reminds us, the state did not act from a concerted effort to end its anti-miscegenation statute; it acted because Mexicans "destabilized the legal apparatus of de jure segregation."[81] That is, "Mexicans' hybridity rendered the state's miscegenation statutes 'too vague and uncertain to be enforceable regulations of a fundamental right." And unlike earlier periods when scientific racialism was readily admissible in court, it was now increasingly challenged as pseudo-science by cultural anthropology. Concern by the dissenting judges about the dangers of crossing distinctive races failed to win the day.[82]

The incidence of exogenous marriages, as Frank G. Mittelbach and Joan W. Moore would reveal in their work a decade later, represented a growing and inevitable trend. In fact, Los Angeles may have offered these unions a distinctive milieu to thrive. The "relatively open opportunity structure" that characterized the city, wrote Mittelbach and Moore, coupled with such factors as gender and generational differences, occupational status, and age at marriage, helped weaken ethnic solidarity and allowed for increased exogenous unions. Indeed, in regard to Mexican Americans, the study revealed not a population distinctly inassimilable and isolated, as a number of previous studies had shown, but one increasingly open to intermarriage across race and class. As second- and third-generation Mexican Americans increased their contact with American society, and especially as these contacts allowed for social and economic upward mobility—and political integration—the more readily they engaged that environment.[83]

For Cuarón, too, the accumulation of experiences had afforded him a unique view of the world he inhabited—and his place in it. His participation in the Civilian Conservation Corps, the Merchant Marine, the Congress of Industrial Organizations, and the Communist Party, as well as his involvement with the IPP, Amigos de Wallace, and civil rights activism, helped shape his identity, allowing him to pursue goals and objectives beyond the Eastside barrio. In a very similar way, Sylvia's experiences led her to reexamine her own identity. For example, the family's move from New York to Los Angeles, the death of her father, her work with Mexican American youth, and her involvement with progressive groups allowed her to peer beyond her ethnic community for social relations. Marriage outside one's group was one avenue by which an individual could challenge old barriers. Sylvia had to navigate carefully the racial stereotypes and fears that influenced some members of her family, especially her mother.

The Lucases had gravitated closer to the matron of the family, Adel Lucas, after the death of Sylvia's father, Samuel, in 1945. As she recalled, broaching the issue of marriage with her mother was complicated.

FIGURE 14 Sylvia and Ralph Cuarón, recently married, 1949. Cuarón Family Collection.

I was trying to get my mother to understand why I was in love with Ralph. . . .
And she did ask, "But why him?" We would speak to each other in Yiddish and
I didn't know how to explain to her that we were lovers and that he was very
much a part of my life and I of his. I had already met his mother and his sisters
and knew the neighborhood so very well. "Because he loves me mom." . . . I just
did not know how to explain to her that on other dates that I had had it was just
dating, it was doing things that were expected of you—it didn't have the warmth;
it didn't have the excitement that Ralph was giving me. So, she kind of shrugged
her shoulders . . . and, you know, I realized that mom wasn't going to actually say,
"You have my blessings."[84]

With little money and last-minute planning, Sylvia and Ralph married in July
1949.

The ceremony brought together many of the activists who had worked on the Augustino Salcido case and the Henry Wallace campaign. Judge Stanley Moffatt officiated the civil ceremony that took place at his home in the city of Southgate. Frank González, a good friend of the couple, served as the best man, and Rose, Sylvia's sister, was maid of honor. Ben Cruz topped off the wedding celebration with his solo performance of "Mi Casita," a song he had composed for the newlyweds. Sylvia did not inform her mother about the marriage until sometime later.

> Until one day, I told her, "Mom, I have to tell you that we did get married." And she said, "Sylvia, I know, I know. . . . I have two thousand [dollars] at hand. I'm going to give this to you and Ralph." That was my mother from the old country: who was not a communist, who was hardly what you would call a socialist, just a warm giving Jewish mother. And with that two thousand dollars . . . we bought a brand-new Chevy.[85]

The Cuaróns moved into a modest apartment next to Ralph's mother's home in the Maravilla district of East Los Angeles. His family soon became, as Sylvia described, her "surrogate family." The extended kin provided the support the new couple needed to sustain their busy schedules. Indeed, the Cuarón clan even went so far as to tolerate the fact that Ralph and Sylvia were avowed atheists. But when Mita and Ralph Jr. were born, family members, led by Ralph's older sister, Marjorie, intervened to secretly get the children baptized. Ralph and Sylvia were out of town at the time; so all they could do was feign ignorance and tolerate the backdoor sacrament. However, some local Jewish and Catholic institutions proved less indulgent to this accommodation.

The first rebuff by a religious organization came soon after the couple had married. As Sylvia remembered, she approached a Jewish community center located in the city of Monterey Park in an attempt to join a club for recently married couples, to see if she could "relate to Judaism." Her attempt at rapprochement was also a sincere gesture to placate her mother. But she never got that opportunity. Even before she could complete the application, the rabbi administering the program rejected the couple outright: her marriage to a Catholic disqualified them immediately. "Very crudely, without any gentility, he said, 'We cannot accept you. We are within the bounds of Judaism.'" In effect, the rabbi let Sylvia understand that "outsiders were not welcome."[86] On some level, Sylvia's attempt at reconciliation with her religion disappointed her. And her mother's hope that she might one day return to the family's faith never came to pass.

Then three years later they were summarily rejected as godparents in the Catholic Church. In this instance, the local parish of Our Lady of Lourdes, located at East Third Street and Rowan Avenue, concluded that Ralph's marriage to a Jew was inappropriate for raising a *good Christian*.[87] Having now been rebuffed by two significant religious organizations, the Cuaróns were not deterred; they still had the CP. But soon the issue of ethnicity revealed itself even in this unlikely place.

The Mexican American party cadre, and their supporters, would identify *chauvinism* as a persistent barrier to the full integration into the party. For example, Cuarón often complained of the refusal by some party leaders to allow club meetings to be conducted in Spanish or to allow for the translation of printed material. These problems were often discussed in numerous internal party documents produced for educational purposes. Some of these complaints were discussed in a party document titled *The Mexican Question in the United States*, which accused the leadership of allowing an atmosphere of disrespect to thrive within the organization. According to the document, the representation of the Mexican people as "lazy, dirty, slow-witted, and inefficient" was infused within the party. To further illustrate the point, the document continued: "Only recently a Mexican comrade, invited to the home of an Anglo progressive, was greeted as he came into the house with the statement, 'We cooked an awful lot of beans because we knew you were coming.'"[88] These insensitive comments and episodes notwithstanding, the CP remained an organization committed to advancing racial equality. And to demonstrate its commitment against racism, the party initiated a campaign against *white chauvinism* between 1949 and 1953.

The CP, certainly, had had a long and courageous tradition of combating intolerance within its ranks. As Dorothy Healey rightfully noted: "we [the Communist Party] were a working model of racial integration."[89] Nevertheless, the party was not immune to the pressures of the world around it. Racism, McCarthyism, and the Cold War, for example, placed unimaginable pressures on the organization and its membership such that legitimate concerns were sometimes turned on their head by obsessive behavior. According to Healey,

once an accusation of white chauvinism was thrown against a white Communist, there was no defense. Debate was over. By the very act of denying the validity of the charge, you only proved your own guilt. Thousands of people were caught up in this campaign—not only in the Party itself, but within the Progressive Party and some of the Left unions as well. In Los Angeles alone we must have expelled two hundred people on charges of white chauvinism, usually on the most trivial of pretexts. People would be expelled for serving coffee in a chipped coffee cup to a Black or serving watermelon at the end of dinner.[90]

Ben Davis, for example, supported the campaign and believed that "the proclaimed vanguard of the working class" had to set the example.[91] The excessive nature of the campaign may also reveal the degree to which internal party structures stifled debate and allowed an atmosphere of intimidation and berating. This cannibalizing environment raised few concerns among party leaders, as some believed that trimming the membership "to fighting shape" would strengthen the overall organization.[92] Ralph and Sylvia did not escape from this self-imposed witch hunt unscathed.

The challenge came one evening during a meeting of the Young Communist League, hosted by Sylvia and Ralph in their apartment. During a routine discussion, Sylvia unwittingly made a remark that prompted a challenge by a party member in the room. "And I said something like, 'So many times I'm mistaken for a Mexican.'" One CP member responded, "'I accuse you of chauvinism!'" Ralph immediately countered by challenging the accusation. "Little by little," Sylvia remembered, "this guy sat down very quietly." Ralph's ethnicity may have played an important part in quelling the entire incident.[93] Nevertheless, episodes such as these left behind confusion and unease. And in the midst of this senseless purging, the party now had to contend with a new growing menace outside of its fold: anti-immigration.

By the end of 1949 and early 1950, anti-Mexican and anti-immigrant sentiment in the country had begun to climb. That sentiment became cemented with the passage of the Internal Security Act of 1950 (McCarran Act) and the Immigration and Nationality Act of 1952 (McCarran-Walter Act)—the promulgation of what Jeffrey Garcílazo described as a new "Brown Scare." As Garcílazo explains, "In the same sense that the 'Red Scare' captures the anti-communist, anti-alien hysteria of the late teens and the early fifties, the 'Brown Scare' raises the intersection of political and racial oppression as it applied to Southern California."[94] The McCarran Act provisions not only required Communist organizations to register, it also barred persons from attaining naturalization and admission into the United States if they retained Communist or other totalitarian affiliations. The law also provided for the deportation of aliens affiliated with the CP and thus became a powerful tool for the political Right. The McCarran Act became, as Ellen Schrecker notes, "the most important anti-Communist law passed during the cold war."[95] Those on the political right were now poised to vigorously pursue their crusade to *save* the nation, not only from the *godless* Communists, but also from foreign provocateurs.

In 1950, the Los Angeles Committee for Protection of Foreign Born (LACPFB) was created to counter this growing assault on civil liberties as well as civil and human rights. The LACPFB argued that the provisions of the McCarran Act were contradictory to and out of step with the nation's democratic principles.[96] So repugnant was the new law that even General Dwight D. Eisenhower, the former supreme allied commander of Europe during World War II, was moved to declare it a "glaring example of failure of our national leadership to live up to high ideals." "A better law must be written," he asserted, "that will strike an intelligent, unbigoted balance between the immigration welfare of America and the prayerful hopes of the unhappy and the oppressed."[97] Eisenhower's fears were not unfounded, as Latinos of all political persuasions became targets as a result of this vacuum in leadership. Even the venerable League of United Latin American Citizens, with its strict anti-Communist position, did not escape the watchful eye of the government.[98] Ignacio López, newspaper editor and community activist, became the subject of investigation by the FBI for his stance on civil rights issues.[99] Labor organizer Luisa Moreno and other union members in the Food, Tobacco, Agricultural, and Allied Workers of America union were also red-baited and deported.[100] The Civil Rights Congress rallied much of its energy to support Armando Dávila, an organizer for the furniture workers and resident for forty years in the United States, who was also targeted for deportation.[101] Dorothy Healey also recalled the deportations of key Mexican American leaders such as Tony Salgado, a CP and AFL member, and Ramón Welch, another active member of the Communist Party.[102] The LACPFB stepped into this maelstrom, as the volume of deportations escalated and organizations like the CRC could no longer meet the need.

The CRC joined with representatives of "trade unions, the rank and file, nationality groups, cultural clubs, independent community and political organizations" to help found the LACPFB.[103] The LACPFB patterned its principles on those of the national organization, the American Committee for Protection of Foreign Born, chiefly centered on upholding and defending individual rights guaranteed by the Constitution and the Bill of Rights. Rose Chernin, longtime activist, assumed the responsibility for directing the LACPFB. Chernin understood the implications of the Cold War and McCarthyism for Mexican American and Mexican immigrant communities. "Under her leadership," writes Garcílazo, "the LACPFB identified the collusion between the federal government and agribusiness, and showed how they used deportations to terrorize Mexican-American workers into submission."[104] Chernin wasted little time in contacting leaders in the local Mexican American community, focusing her efforts first on the Eastside. In one of her initial outreach efforts to solicit support for the fledgling organization, she visited the offices of the furniture workers—located on Slauson Street and Avalon—near downtown Los Angeles. It was there that she sat down with Ralph Cuarón. "One day, I was in my office of the furniture workers union," Cuarón recalled, "and I had a visitor by the name of Rose Chernin. . . . She said, 'Well, I'm here to organize the Committee for Protection of Foreign Born in Los Angeles . . . and we have chosen you to be a member of this chapter and to help us organize.'"[105] Needing no further persuasion, he enthusiastically joined the new organization. Other activists such as Ben Cruz, Frank López, Rito Valencia, and Mauricio Terrazas also gave their support to the new organization, and soon the United Furniture Workers of America became an official sponsor. Not surprisingly, within a short period the LACPFB became branded as a subversive and parasitic organization.

Rose Chernin's membership in the Communist Party was well known and certainly affected the overall work and strategy of the fledgling organization.[106] In 1952, for example, the Associated Farmers of Orange County made certain to inform the readers of its bulletin of Chernin's past record of radical activism. "Mrs. Rose Chernin Kusnitz you will recall was one of the twelve top leaders of the Communist party arrested in July, 1951 and accused of advocating violent overthrow of the United States Government."[107] Her 1952 conviction, indeed, became part of a long litany of cases under the infamous Smith Act that prosecuted hundreds of Communists from 1941 to 1957. As if to add more fuel to an already raging fire, the Associated Farmers explained that "she was born in Vitebsk, Russia, September 14, 1902."[108] In their bid to further expose the activities of this *subversive*, and by implication *foreign* element, the group also placed under suspicion Lillian Durán, who served as the acting director of the LACPFB while Chernin was in jail. "In 1949 Lillian Duran [*sic*]," reported the bulletin, "was an employee of the Orange County Hospital . . . [and is] the sister of Mrs. Rose Chernin Kusnitz."[109] No stone was to be left unturned by the hardline Associated Farmers, even if revealing that information might compromise the safety and security of fellow citizens.

The Associated Farmers clearly regarded the activities of the LACPFB as dangerous and a threat to the bottom line of its membership. They were especially incensed that the LACPFB and its counterparts in Orange County were reaching out to Mexican immigrant communities—the source of their workforce—and exposing them to un-American ideas.[110] The bulletin published what they believed to be the radical agenda of these organizations, including, for example, organizing "the Mexican community into a left wing pressure group" and convincing "the Mexican community that the Independent Progressive Party is the only organization striving to protect the rights of and looking for the interests of 'oppressed' minority groups."[111] The Associated Farmers disparaged any issue related to racism and discrimination. In their minds, these issues were nonexistent, wholly contrived by radical rabble-rousers for the sole purpose of stirring up the masses. Given the profound domestic chill, the extent of the educational campaigns performed by the LACPFB seems surprising. While some organizations cut back their activism, the LACPFB increased its.

The LACPFB proved exceedingly adept, explains Garcílazo, at soliciting sponsorship and support from a broad spectrum of individuals and community organizations. Indeed, in the political atmosphere of McCarthyism, it became imperative that Chernin reach out to as many progressive contacts as possible.[112] The LACPFB opened branch offices in a number of communities, including the Bay area, Santa Ana, San Fernando, Harbor district, and East Los Angeles. Josephine Yañez, a longtime activist in the community, led the Eastside branch.[113] Sylvia recalled that during this early period Frank Amaro, another community advocate and close friend of the Cuaróns, served as chair of the Eastside branch. Delfino Varela, a close associate of Chernin, Yañez, and Dorothy Healey, worked directly with deportation cases.[114] Available records on the LACPFB reveal that the organization employed an array of creative strategies to educate the public about its cases as well as to discredit the McCarran Act, such as petition drives, targeted brochures, leafleting, "Know Your Rights" pamphlets, and press releases. In addition, the LACPFB held numerous press conferences; published *The Torch*, their regular monthly bulletin; and held annual conferences and testimonial dinners. The group also participated in delegations to Washington, D.C., and to the offices of the Naturalization and Immigration Service, organized marches, mass meetings, and picket lines.[115] The Cuaróns were intimately engaged in almost every aspect of this work.

The level of community involvement maintained by Sylvia and Ralph was impressive. For example, in addition to her regular employment at Mund Boilers

Incorporated,[116] Sylvia divided her volunteer time between the LACPFB and ANMA. Pregnant with their first child in 1952, she remained highly active and rarely gave a second thought to limiting her political work. Sylvia had also risen to some prominence within the ANMA network of regional offices, becoming the secretary of the Southern California office in 1953. Among her many responsibilities, she helped conduct public meetings to discuss the McCarran-Walter Act and its repercussions for members of the community.[117] This work had now reached new levels, as the number of noncitizens arrested and subjected to deportation hearings had increased significantly.[118]

Ralph's activism mirrored Sylvia's dizzying pace. Heavily involved with ANMA, Cuarón helped organize and lead a number of projects and organizations directly concerned with the exploitation of Mexican immigrants. He regularly helped lead LACPFB conference panels that discussed mass deportations, the state of the Mexican worker, and, of course, strategies for repealing the McCarran law.[119] As an organizer for the UFWA Local 576, Independent, at the time, he continually supported events and kept workers abreast of Smith Act defendant cases throughout the country.[120] Cuarón's activities did not go unnoticed. In a bulletin published by the Associated Farmers of Orange County in 1952, Cuarón was given prominent mention under the section titled "Subversive Activities."

A new front organization has been formed in Los Angeles. Known as the Trade Union Defense Committee, its purpose will be two-fold. (1) Repeal of the McCarran and Smith Acts. (2) Opposition to the government's deportation drive against the foreign born, particularly as it effects Mexican workers. Meeting was held at the CIO building. Ralph Cuaron of the Furniture Workers was elected provisional chairman.[121]

The bulletin also identified Elsie Monjar as the "chosen" provisional secretary and cited the participation of twenty-seven "rank and filers" (read: Communists) as having formed the committee. In addition, the bulletin provided the names of the new provisional executive board: Bessie Reback, Robert Sambrano, Olive Thompson, Felix Padilla, and Morris Rubin. The Associated Farmers was exhibiting a significant level of anxiety over any efforts to organize agricultural workers. Despite this heavy scrutiny, the LACPFB kept its public profile largely intact. In addition to its impressive list of activities, the LACPFB's cultural events were one of its most successful outreach strategies.

One of the LACPFB's most popular events was the Festival of Nationalities.[122] The festival became a venue through which different ethnic groups exhibited cultural arts, foods, music, and dances. The success of the events "reflected the committee's pluralistic ideology and served to create and reinforce solidarity between ethnic groups, deportees, the committee organizers, and the Left community in general."[123] The Eastside branch organized similar cultural events. The yearly Cinco de Mayo celebration, for example, combined cultural pride with a strong political message. As one flyer declared,

> Cinco de Mayo is a holiday that can and should be understood by the people of the United States, whose day of triumphant struggle for independence is similar in important respects. It also has great meaning for the entire foreign-born, who are struggling in the face of the racist, hateful Walter-McCarran Law to keep alive the traditions of freedom.[124]

On this occasion, as on so many others, the Eastside branch celebrated with Mexican regional dances, folk music, and bands. The Eastside branch also coordinated festivities for September in honor of Mexico's independence.

A key component of the community outreach was the showing of the banned film *Salt of the Earth*. "Salt of the Earth has been hailed by all who have seen it," explained Chernin, "as an epoch-making production. Unfortunately, it has not been able to draw the audiences it deserves because of the advertising black-out by all the local commercial newspapers (except the Daily News)." Chernin added,

> Our Committee feels that this picture must be seen by the widest possible audiences. Peoples from all walks of life must be given the opportunity to see a film, which portrays with dignity the struggles of the Mexican-Americans for full equality.
>
> Once this picture is seen by a vast audience, it will no longer be possible for the Justice Department to implement the racist aspects of the Walter-McCarran Law against foreign-born Americans. They will not permit the illegal mass roundups, illegal jailings, illegal mass deportations of Mexican nationals, and the establishment of a concentration camp in Elysian Park. They will regard this treatment of the members of the Mexican-American community as an insult to all democratic-spirited, fair-minded Americans.[125]

However, despite the committee's best efforts, they could not stem the tide of anti-immigrant sentiment that followed a national recession from 1953 to

1955, brought on by the end of the Korean conflict.[126] Indeed, calls to reduce the nation's reliance on Mexican migrant labor also came from some within Mexican American communities.

In the aftermath of World War II, the Bracero Program, the contract labor agreement between the United States and Mexico, became a target of scrutiny among many American citizens, including Mexican Americans. This community viewed the presence of hundreds of thousands of temporarily employed Mexican nationals as a threat to their limited economic, social, and political opportunities. Organizations such as LULAC, the GI Forum, and the National Agricultural Workers Union actively sought to bring an end to the program and quell illegal immigration. Despite the strong opposition of these national organizations, some Mexican Americans expressed ambivalence about the presence of resident aliens within their midst. In fact, the links between citizen and noncitizen were stronger than most realized.

The accommodation between Mexican Americans and Mexican nationals remained complicated. Despite the efforts by some Mexican Americans to identify Mexican nationals as "eternal outsiders," writes Matt Garcia, the reality was that their destinies were too intertwined. Indeed, they shared similar employment opportunities, lived in the same neighborhoods, and engaged closely in intra-ethnic dating and marriages.[127] And as Mae M. Ngai reminds us, the racialized concept of Mexicans as *foreigners*, imposed by Euro-Americans, created little space for distinction. For individuals of Mexican descent, "American citizenship, whether by native-birth or by naturalization, accrued few benefits."[128]

In the summer of 1954, the Immigration and Naturalization Service and the Border Patrol initiated a highly publicized solution to the large influx of undocumented workers. They dubbed their deportation program Operation Wetback. Clearly, federal authorities felt no compunction in using the term "wetback," a word that was clearly and historically disparaging to Mexicans. The LACPFB more accurately labeled the expansive deportation sweeps as Operation Terror.[129] Members mailed and passed out leaflets, gathered signatures on petitions addressed to Attorney General Herbert Brownell, formed picket lines at a temporary holding facility set up at Elysian Park and INS offices downtown, and held mass meetings throughout the city.[130] But the national roundups continued unabated.

Whether arriving as braceros or as undocumented immigrants, Mexicans were largely viewed as belonging outside the range of a *normal* immigrant experience. As such, writes Juan García, these immigrants were often described as being devoid of "needs, desires, and dreams."[131] The Mexican immigrant seemed to represent, instead, a pestilence that blighted the American landscape as they contended for jobs, placed demands on social services, and brazenly violated the nation's laws—a perception that has not markedly changed even today.[132] The undocumented migrants, disparagingly referred to as "wetbacks," were subjected to intense vitriol. According to Ngai, "The construction of the 'wetback' as a dangerous and criminal social pathogen fed the general racial stereotype 'Mexican.'"[133] And Mexico was not immune from these negative attitudes. As the roundups would eventually reveal, Mexican deportees received nominal support from their own government.

Although some Mexican officials expressed sincere concern over the plight of their compatriots in the United States, not enough was done to intervene on their behalf. Indeed, as García explains, the Mexican government, although aware of the impending deportation drive (the Mexican government publicly supported the operation), found itself unprepared and, surprisingly, unwilling to provide necessary aid to the deportees.[134] Enrique Buelna Echeverria, a Mexican immigration officer who worked in Nogales, Sonora, at the time, confirmed his government's inability to adequately process the large volume of people entering via this relatively small border crossing.

> They [U.S. agents] would drop them [the deportees] off on the American side, they would walk across on foot, and as they arrived we would escort them to another location where we handed them five pesos per head, for every person regardless of whether they were man, woman or child. From there, we would take them to another location where various agents would document the complaints of each deportee; the manner in which they were apprehended, the manner in which they were deported. Some were not allowed to cash their wages, their checks. Many were due many months of wages from companies or private employees, farmers. Many were given checks . . . many of the checks would turn out to be worthless. . . . There were people that had not been given an opportunity by [U.S.] immigration agents to recover personal belongings, therefore they were coming with nothing but what they had when they were apprehended. We would then give them five pesos so they could eat and then we would place them on a train. Eight or ten trains would leave [Nogales] daily. Ten buses would arrive [from the U.S. side] daily.[135]

Legal residents and American citizens were also caught up in the deportation roundups.[136] U.S. authorities regularly failed to ascertain the legal status of those they apprehended. As Buelna recalled with dismay, "Many of them [the deportees] would tell us that they had papers, others that they were American citizens. They [U.S. immigration officials] did not care." These unfortunate individuals would often remain in Nogales under what must have been desperate and stressful circumstances as they attempted to contact the American consulate as well as families and friends to arrange for their return home. Despite Buelna's attempt to perform his duties with utmost care and to follow procedures as instructed, the processing of the deported proved to be a colossal failure.

The trains leaving Nogales for the interior were regularly filled to capacity with deportees. As Buelna recalled, between five hundred and a thousand deportees were placed on the Sur Pacifico rail line destined for Guadalajara in the state of Jalisco. Mexican officials escorted the deportees to the cities of Magdalena, 75 miles away, and to Hermosillo, some 250 miles from Nogales. After that, Mexican immigration officials made no efforts to track them.

> Many would begin their return [to the U.S.] immediately. . . . Some of the deportees would disembark and then try to get back on the train. But we could not force them at that point to get off or force them to get on again. That wasn't within our power to do and nor was it within our mandate to act in that manner.[137]

As Buelna readily admitted, his office was not prepared to provide such basic necessities as food, clothing, and shelter. Once the deportees had spent their *ration* of five pesos (approximately 55 cents), they were largely on their own.

Despite the general public alarm over unsanctioned Mexican immigration, the reality is that this labor was, and remains, critical to agricultural operations in the United States. Operation Wetback of 1954, as Kelly Lytle Hernandez chronicles, was, at its core, a struggle for control over that labor. Many agricultural employers were not supportive of the Bracero Program and were indignant over the limited rights and protections accorded these workers under that system. Moreover, these growers "had built empires based upon controlling land, water, and the mobility of Mexican workers," and they resented any action by the federal government that placed limits on their power.[138] This cross-border cooperation between the United States and Mexico, initiated in the mid-1940s, aggravated a prevailing delicate balance—especially so along the Texas-Mexico border—that privileged local customs in dealing with migration issues. The rebellion in south Texas by ranchers and farmers in the 1950s was in response to "their loss of influence" over the control of migration. Therefore, Operation

Wetback was, in effect, a federal campaign to reassert and reaffirm its policing powers and control over immigration, while also placating the concerns of growers along the Texas border.[139] What ensued, writes Hernandez, was a highly publicized show of force that never reached its intended goals, but played well in the public eye. Nevertheless, Mexican immigrants as well as many Mexican Americans were forced to endure the Border Patrol's expanded net of surveillance and invasive law enforcement. By fiscal year 1954, starting July 1, 1953, and ending June 30, 1954, the Border Patrol had recorded over one million apprehensions through a process of indiscriminate interrogations, intimidation, roadblocks, raids, and roundups. This aggressive border enforcement was part and parcel of a long-standing practice that supported the notion that this population was socially suspect and could be legitimately targeted for policing.[140]

In September 1954, the LACPFB released a document titled *Shame of a Nation: A Documented Story of Police-State Terror Against Mexican-Americans in the U.S.A.* The report highlighted the wholesale disregard for civil and human rights in regard to this community across the southwest. *Shame of a Nation* opened with a quote from President Franklin Delano Roosevelt—"We are all descendants of immigrants"—and then proceeded to delineate how far the nation had moved away from this central ideal. Indeed, Mexican immigrants had come to be regarded by the general public with such disdain and suspicion that the nation's top immigration officials openly characterized their work in militaristic terms. It was not uncommon for these officials to identify this population as *enemy aliens* that needed to be ferreted out, captured, and herded over the border.[141] Most significant was how the Department of Justice seemed to disregard and violate the rights of American citizens. Josephine Yañez from the Eastside branch of the LACPFB described this threat succinctly.

> The role of the immigration authorities—their dragnet operations wherein they swoop down upon fields, factories and entire communities—is so well-known and feared in any Mexican community that the word "Los Federales" (the Federals) strikes terror not alone to the noncitizen but to Mexican-American citizens of the first, second and third generation.[142]

The end of Operation Wetback did not signify an end to deportations. The LACPFB continued to defend victims of arrests and detentions and into the next decade remained committed to changing the nation's immigration laws. The Communist Party, too, supported these efforts, but some Mexican

American Communists remained critical of the party's continued lack of substantive policies with respect to their community.

In 1956, members of the Eastside division of the CP in Los Angeles convened a special conference to address these persistent disparities.[143] Longtime activist Isabel González summarized the report in the October issue of the *Party Forum*. In the first paragraph, she compared the Mexican experience to that of African Americans and admonished the party for having paid so "little attention on a national level" to this population. This was no time for "token discussions on Cinco de Mayo and the 16th of September," González insisted to her readers. Instead, she maintained, the party should be at the forefront of activism demanding education reforms, an end to discrimination, and access to the political arena. Mexican Americans represented a major political force in the Southwest but remained largely obscured even within progressive circles. "If this was common knowledge, the People's World, for example, would not restrict a Spanish column to the Los Angeles page of the paper, but would be aware that such a column will find readers in Oakland, San Jose, Salinas, the entire San Joaquin Valley, as well as Colorado and Arizona."[144] As important as the public airing of grievances was, they were preempted by Soviet premier Nikita Khrushchev's revelations about Joseph Stalin's atrocities.[145] Made in 1956, they would have a profound effect on the Communist Party USA.

As Dorothy Healey recalled, "Nothing had prepared me for the magnitude of what we were hearing."[146] For Ralph and Sylvia, the revelations were nothing less than devastating. As Ralph remembered, "It tore me to pieces. I never was the same [again]. It took me years to recoup. I never could regain my faith in the party." Many felt a deep sense of betrayal. "Some friends were going one way, others another way . . . anti-Russian, pro-Russian." According to Sylvia, "The split gave people the opportunity to be more critical of their beliefs."[147] Nevertheless, the party remained largely intact even during this very difficult period. Despite the Cold War climate and Khrushchev's revelations, Ralph recalled that many longtime members decided to stay and try to change the organization from within. Indeed, some tried to reform the party to make it more independent and pragmatic.[148] But as Healey explained, this became increasingly difficult as the CP began to lose many members. "By the end of the 1950s, the Party, nationally, would be reduced to about three thousand, considerably fewer than we had had in Los Angeles alone a decade earlier. In Los Angeles, by 1959, we could count fewer than five hundred members left."[149] This precipitous decline in membership, Healey observed, significantly affected the party's ability to carry out its regular functions. Still, the CP continued to ignore the needs and desires of some of its Mexican American cadre.

Party documents reveal that Mexican Americans remained critical of the organization's work within this community.[150] Although the Mexican Commission had been reestablished in the latter half of the decade, there is little indication that the party initiated any major policy shift in regard to the status of Mexican American work. Though some party members did recognize the importance of developing Mexican leadership, actual implementation fell short of the official rhetoric. Nevertheless, despite the glaring contradictions, and now the devastating news from Khrushchev, Cuarón was determined that the CP had to change—even if that meant ruffling some feathers along the way.

Cuarón saw the CP as the principal agent for social change, and he was resolved to do his part to steer it back to its original course—in the service of the working class. With the party now in turmoil, Cuarón saw an opportunity to fill a void and chart his own agenda, even as the FBI continued to maintain surveillance of his activities. In 1957, the agency ascertained that Cuarón was actively involved "on his own initiative" visiting various parts of the Southwest, "principally in the west Texas area." According to an informant, Cuarón "considers himself to be the leading Mexican comrade in the southwest and looks upon himself as sort of a commissar." The FBI noted that "these activities on the part of CUARON have been criticized by the Communist Party in this regard and CUARON is not in good graces with local functionaries because of his attitude and activities." In addition, the FBI also reported on "rumored" information suggesting that Cuarón was using a front group, the Communist Service Organization, to sow dissension within the CP in Los Angeles. Although the FBI report concluded that the CSO was "a legitimate Mexican American group," they also took note of the fact that the Communist Party leadership was actively engaged in trying to infiltrate this new organization.[151] It was clear that Cuarón's activities were not appreciated within the highest echelons of the party bureaucracy.

During this period, Cuarón remained actively involved with the Cuauhtémoc Club, located in East Los Angeles. The club was an affiliate of the Eastern Division of the Los Angeles Communist Party and had a large Mexican American membership. Here, he retained a significant following and was regularly elected and appointed to positions of responsibility. Despite his objections against the "party bourgeoisie" and his piercing criticism that the organization "had pulled away from the working class," Cuarón was selected by his club to attend the state CP Convention in 1957. Soon after the conclusion of the plenary event, he was nominated as a delegate to the Sixteenth National Convention of the CP, slated for February of that same year. According to the FBI, Cuarón arrived in New York City five days early and immediately took part in a number of activities. He met with like-minded state party representatives (similarly critical of the national leadership), interviewed with the *Daily Worker* (the party's newspaper), and attended the rules committee as it prepared for the final day of the convention. It was during the discussions over a draft resolution that Cuarón became irate with the Convention's National Committee. Cuarón chided the committee members for their weak and noncommittal stance with regards to minorities within the party. He criticized them for passing on these issues like "football[s]," delegating them "down to the lower Party levels to be decided on instead of making the decisions themselves."[152] After his return to Los Angeles, he reported his findings to a special party gathering, but not every party functionary appreciated his activism.

The meeting took place at the Hungarian Workmen's Home, located in the Mid-City neighborhood, almost one month after the National Convention.[153] At the meeting, Cuarón gave a scathing report and accused the national leadership of hiding behind closed doors and elevating "personal prestige" and "personal power" above party unity. According to an FBI informant, "After his lengthy remarks, CUARON stated that if the Party is to survive and accomplish its historical role, then the unhealthy elements within the Party now must be replaced by comrades who have contact with Party rank and filers as well as with the masses."[154] But Dorothy Healey was not impressed. She was still upset over Cuarón's poor participation at the state convention in San Francisco and his alleged "Trotskyite" activities. As the FBI reported, Healey was accusing Cuarón of collaborating with groups "actively devoted to eliminating the influence of the Soviet Union in the running of the affairs of the CP" and those engaged in "class collaborationism." It appears that Healey viewed these activities as having compromised "the positions of the CP with respect to truly revolutionary activities."[155] Cuarón viewed the situation differently, however. He remained frustrated with the party's lethargic response to demands for change and its penchant to react to exterior influences rather than to local conditions. Within the next few years, his participation in the CP waned as his life at home took precedence. In 1962, when the FBI attempted to interview Cuarón, he ignored their overtures and simply responded with: "RALPH CUARON died five years ago. You can find him in the graveyard."

By the end of the 1950s, Cuarón's view of the CP had changed. He no longer considered the organization as the infallible bulwark of the proletariat. The party had once been a living and breathing *human* institution, always alert and pragmatic to the changing conditions of the working class. However, now it no longer held Cuarón's binding loyalty. Yet, even in the midst of this bleak period, it was difficult to negate the long history of the unflagging CP. There was no doubt in his mind that the organization had been a key element in the struggle to give voice to the working class. The organization had achieved great successes in its pursuit of democracy and socialism.[156] But there was little that could erase the lingering doubt, disappointment, and even anger in the minds of the Cuaróns and other party activists in these final years of the 1950s. "In other words," Sylvia explained, "things weren't the same anymore . . . they could never be the same."[157]

By the close of the decade, there was no definitive answer to the question of what role Mexicans Americans would play in American society. The federal government's aggressive deportation policies seemed to indicate an attitude of grudging tolerance that ebbed and flowed with every economic and political crisis. Whether in the party or in society at large, this persistent attitude that viewed them as outsiders—as foreigners in their own land—undermined many an effort by Mexican Americans to be accepted as equals—as Americans. But for the indefatigable Cuaróns, and the many other activists, these struggles were par for the course. The Mexican question would be answered, ultimately, in the constant battles they would wage to lift up the community and to undermine these systems of oppression. As the Cuaróns moved into the 1960s, they would mount new challenges, devise bold experiments, and offer creative strategies to fulfill the promises of democracy. And the challenge of the Mexican question would be taken up by a new generation that would push the boundaries of identity and protest to new heights.

5

REVOLT ON
PRINCETON STREET

Our purpose is grander than simply guaranteeing every Mexican American the opportunity to achieve a decent American standard of living, even though that is a worthy goal. We are talking about providing a material basis on which a cultural tradition that is precious to America can grow and flourish.
—Hubert H. Humphrey, vice president of the United States, 1967

N JUNE 1964, the residents on the 3700 block of Princeton Street in East Los Angeles looked on with curiosity as one of their neighbors tore down his old bungalow. The atmosphere seemed festive as young and old participated in the demolition. Ralph and Sylvia Cuarón, the owners of the house at 3726 Princeton, had decided to embark on an innovative experiment in community housing and community building. They hoped that this converted living space would be the catalyst for social change, especially as a training ground for a new generation of local Mexican American leaders. Despite the obvious risks involved in such a speculative proposition, they plunged into their social experiment with great excitement and anticipation.

Why did the Cuaróns choose housing as an issue from which to launch their new activism? Housing in the East Los Angeles area during the sixties was in a state of crisis; the area was plagued with dilapidated homes with slumlike conditions and many public housing projects. "East LA's median family income," writes John R. Chavez, "of $4,800 compared poorly with the $13,000 of surrounding suburbs." Consequently, 45 percent of the area's population received some form of public assistance. For all males ages sixteen to twenty-four, the total unemployment rate in East LA stood at 30 percent.[1] But this housing crisis was also exacerbated by the fact that segregation remained firmly in place despite the Supreme Court decision in *Shelley v. Kraemer* (1948). Though the court declared that restrictive racially based covenants could not be enforced, exclusively white neighborhoods continued to thrive. This forced Mexican Americans to stay put, explains Jerry González, and "led to the expansion of Eastside barrios like Boyle Heights, Lincoln Heights, and East Los Angeles, with sharp increases of Spanish-surname residents that nearly doubled between 1950 and 1960." Some Mexican Americans would find creative ways to circumvent these housing restrictions and achieve the suburban dream, but many more would be left out of the expanding housing market.[2]

In October 1967, Peter Pérez, the executive director of the Ramona housing project, testified before a U.S. Cabinet Committee hearing that housing programs were sorely inadequate for Mexican American families.[3] "The needs for most Spanish-speaking people seem obvious and frustrating." Perez noted that houses in disrepair had increased from 10,905 to 14,730 in East Los Angeles between 1960 and 1965. Dilapidated apartments during the same five-year period had increased by 30 percent, from 2,792 to 3,630.[4] He went on to say that the federal government had a direct role to play in reversing these housing trends. Pérez urged the committee that "faith and imagination, dedication and boldness, perseverance and a sense of urgency" were required.[5] Other presenters from across the nation echoed these sentiments and made their pleas for increasing the number of demonstration projects and for developing innovative financing procedures to assist Mexican Americans. For the Cuaróns, however, the housing problem went beyond creative financing and the need for individual home ownership; they identified the home as a key site in a greater ideological struggle between capitalism and socialism.

The Cuaróns saw the home as a cradle of activism. It was from the home that the individual learned to understand and interpret the outside world and their relationship to it. The local neighborhood became a natural extension of the home, where individuals learned to engage, as Dana Cuff writes, with the "space of the city."[6] This interaction was central to the development of a positive, self-affirming confidence that could lead to constructive activism. The Cuaróns' sensibility viewed democracy as largely emanating from the laboring classes: democracy born and nurtured in the workplaces, by grassroots organizations, communities, neighborhoods, and *homes*. In their view, the corruption of democratic ideals seemed inevitable in bureaucratic structures (whether Communist or capitalist) and thus necessitated the watchful eye of the public. Certainly, Mexican American communities throughout the Southwest felt the sting of segregation, of being made to feel invisible before countless local, state, and federal institutions. Treated like second-class citizens, they were made to feel powerless to effect change. Nevertheless, the one institution that could galvanize them into action—despite a strong reticence to do so—was the educational system.[7]

Even though de jure discrimination against Mexican children was no longer in place by the end of the 1950s, de facto methods remained stubbornly there. Mexican American students and parents continued to perceive the educational system as an alienating and disconnected institution from their daily lives. As sociologist and educator Thomas P. Carter wrote during this period, the U.S. Census of 1950 and 1960 provided undeniable evidence of this population's neglect by American society. In terms of educational completion, the census data revealed that Mexican Americans ranked lower than any other ethnic group, except Native Americans. What accounted for this disparity? According to Carter,

> society and its schools produced an adult Mexican American population prepared for participation in the agricultural economy of the traditional Southwest. The school was, and in many geographic areas still is, "successful" in equipping most Mexican Americans with the knowledge and skills appropriate to low status: minimum English language ability, rudimentary reading and figuring skills, and the values necessary to a law-abiding, although nonparticipating and essentially disenfranchised, citizen.[8]

Despite the harsh conditions in the schools, Mexican Americans remained positive about education, albeit, "in the abstract."[9] Education was still perceived as the great equalizer—a way to overcome one's class and to achieve the American dream. However, the educational experience left much to be desired.

With the movement of largely white, middle-class Americans to the affluent suburbs during the 1960s, the poor and people of color became further concentrated—and isolated—in the central cities. "With whites gone," Rosales explains, "law-enforcement attitudes toward inner-city residents became uniformly less tolerant and, too often, police and media overreacted to minority crime." As tensions over unemployment, poverty, segregation, unjust treatment, and lack of opportunity rose, so, too, did resentment among the youth in the nation's barrios. "Their increasing ghettoization made Chicanos feel betrayed by the American Dream."[10] That feeling of betrayal burst onto the scene in a dramatic way in 1968.

In March of that year, thousands of Mexican American youth in East Los Angeles undertook what Carlos Muñoz referred to as "the first major mass protest explicitly against racism . . . by Mexican Americans in the history of the United States."[11] Indeed, the walkout of as many as twenty thousand students from the Eastside and from other areas of Los Angeles was also the largest of its kind and would leave an indelible mark on those who experienced these events. And in no small way, the house on Princeton Street became involved in those efforts, becoming a key site for organizing and raising the social and political consciousness of a number of future Chicana and Chicano leaders in Southern California.

The resurgent activism of the 1960s was not cut off from its earlier roots. On the contrary, those roots, those strands of memory, helped push the student activists and the Chicano Movement to new heights. For Ralph and Sylvia Cuarón, their radical history would be kept alive in the political activism of their children, particularly their eldest daughter Margarita (Mita) Cuarón. This chapter will explore how this radical thread added to a spirit of resistance against oppression and to a vision of a more inclusive America. The Cuaróns were instrumental in organizing the community response to protect their children during the student strikes and to support their efforts to bring about important changes to the local schools, and specifically to Garfield High School. This chapter discusses how the Cuaróns, in this small corner of East Los Angeles, contributed to a student-led civil rights movement that emerged from this Southern California Chicano community in the 1960s.

The idea that housing could be the catalyst for organizing and establishing stronger communities was not a novel one. This kind of social experimentation has a long history in California dating back to the nineteenth century. Robert V. Hines and Mike Davis provide fascinating examinations of these utopian societies. The long-defunct settlement of Llano del Rio, located in the Mojave Desert, for example, was built by a handful of members of the Young People's Socialist League in 1914. The social experiment thrived in virtual isolation for four years until 1918, when "creditors, draft boards, jealous neighbors, and the Los Angeles *Times*" targeted it, writes Davis. The loss of Llano's water rights in a lawsuit was a devastating blow to the community's irrigation infrastructure, which was instrumental to its economic success.[12] In contrast to these kinds of experimental societies that have periodically sprung to life, the Cuaróns opted for an experiment that could change living conditions from within established communities. Ralph Cuarón did not propose that a select group of pioneers set out to the nearest open space to build a new utopian society. Although the idea of forming a separate and cooperatively managed society away from the corrupting influences of the large metropolis seemed tempting, the Cuaróns' utopian dreams would be grounded in the built-out urban and overcrowded landscape of East Los Angeles. Thus, the Cuarón experiment could not technically be considered "utopian," as they did not "withdraw" themselves from the community at large.[13]

Nevertheless, the Cuaróns anticipated that this housing experiment would have transformative potential among the local populace and ignite a new movement for social change. They were eager to take action against what they saw as growing despair, poverty, and powerlessness within Mexican American communities. If the local citizens could be shown how to take greater control over their homes, there was no telling what other community institutions they could challenge. But this required that local citizens be exposed to an alternative vision for accomplishing change. Ultimately, they believed in a direct, communal democracy that would allow citizens to take greater command of their lives. And like the young activists of the 1960s, the Cuaróns also believed, as E. J. Dionne explains, that the federal government "could strengthen and 'empower' local communities to organize themselves and act on their own behalf, sometimes by fighting City Hall and the federal government itself on the streets and in the courts."[14] As Sylvia explained, they would begin a "pilot project so that people could see how it could be done."[15]

Early in the decade, Ralph Cuarón became closely involved with the Plaza Community Center. The center was located on Princeton and Indiana Streets, one half block away from where the Cuaróns lived. The center focused its energies on a number of social service programs, including a daycare center and several youth programs. According to Albert Ehrke, project director of the center, Cuarón was one of the first members of the community to volunteer and work closely with the youth at the center. As Ehrke explained,

> Mr. Cuaron frankly is one of the few neighbors on that block that displayed quite an ongoing interest in the problems of the community, quite often would go out of his way to try to hold meetings. I remember him in relation to young people coming over and borrowing our VW buses and taking some of the people out to the mountains.[16]

The center soon hosted community meetings to discuss and disseminate information regarding welfare programs, housing, education, and police abuse. These activities not only helped to inform local residents of important public resources, they also helped to foster greater sensitivity for local needs and pride in their community. Cuarón became a pivotal player in helping to develop this new direction at the center, and especially in educating neighbors on issues regarding housing.

In 1964, Cuarón proposed an alternative housing scheme—unlike large-scale housing projects—that emphasized communal housing arrangements in smaller units: organized, designed, and built by the local residents themselves. In other words, he envisioned an urban design plan with all the aesthetics of utopian modernism, but on a rational scale.[17] While Cuarón based some of his ideas loosely on the work of urban planners and social reformers of the 1930s and 1940s, his approach was a combination of these with a newer concept called *ekistics*.

Cuarón became acquainted with a book written by Constantinos A. Doxiadis titled *Architecture in Transition*, which advanced innovative ideas in architecture, urban design, and human development. Doxiadis proposed a new role for the architect that integrated this individual into all major aspects in the creation of new structures: from art and design to planning and construction. As the "master builder," the architect would be brought directly into the creative process of building neighborhoods and cities. But the master builder would be responsible for even more; this person also had to be the principal coordinator of "economics, social sciences, political and administrative sciences, technology and aesthetics." Indeed, the architect had to place all of these essential components into a coherent whole that would culminate in a "new type of human habitat."[18] Ekistics, then, was a holistic approach to concept, design, planning, and construction.

Doxiadis also conceived of the modern architect as an *activist*. In addition to being the master builder—"the coordinator of all forces"—the architect had to "expand his subject in size, so as not to include any longer just simple buildings but units which will better serve the new demands of his role; as well as to achieve architectural synthesis in the broader spaces created in the new type of expanding human settlements."[19] Therefore, the architect had to "proceed to all these activities," Doxiadis wrote, "in full knowledge that he is the scientist, the technician and the artist who is responsible for architectural creation. In order to achieve this, he has to gain a much broader education than at present." In effect, Doxiadis argued that elitists—disconnected from the lived experiences of the common folk—had usurped the creation of true living spaces. Which had clearly led to the dismal state of human settlement in modern times.[20] With this new understanding, Cuarón gained the confidence to undertake a bold experiment in urban planning. If vision and careful management were elements just as important as professional training in architecture and urban design, then there was no need to wait for change to come willy-nilly to East Los Angeles. He would take the initiative to make change happen immediately.

When asked why the family was willing to forgo privacy and the American dream of occupying their own detached, single-family home, Sylvia Cuarón responded without hesitation: "It never occurred to us."[21] Indeed, there was little about Ralph and Sylvia that could be labeled *traditional*—from their interethnic marriage to their rejection of the suburban ideal. They saw themselves, foremost, as conscious political actors engaged in a struggle to change the world, even if that meant one neighborhood at a time. Furthermore, they had contextualized their struggle as part of an international movement for democracy, justice, and peace. In 1964, when the Cuaróns contemplated this housing experiment on their property, they were still members of the Communist Party USA—and "in good standing."[22] But given their alienation from the Los Angeles CP, they increasingly became immersed in parenting their four children. Now their meetings and activism took them into the schools, particularly Rowan Avenue Elementary, where three of their children—Margarita (Mita), Rafael (Ralfie), and Adela (Adel)—attended. And yet, despite the ever-present economic challenges, the family found the wherewithal to move their experiment forward that same year.

Their vision for community renewal was given a boost from an unlikely source. In this period before their eldest daughter reached high school, Cuarón worked sporadically doing general carpentry work. It was Sylvia who gained full-time employment as a job dispatcher for Southern California Edison. In the breaks between jobs, Cuarón kept active by participating in community meetings and forums that discussed education, police relations, redevelopment, and housing. During these activities, he collaborated with community members of all political affiliations, including members of the local Democratic Party. Indeed, it was at a Democratic club meeting that Cuarón met Congressman George E. Brown. As Sylvia recalled, Brown took a liking to Cuarón and his bold ideas for development on the Eastside. And it was through this relationship that Brown intervened to help the Cuaróns with their housing project.[23] In 1965, Brown assisted Ralph and Sylvia in securing a low-interest loan through Monarch Savings and Loan that jump-started the project on Princeton Street. The demolition of the house and the construction of the apartment complex took place under Cuarón's direction and supervision. His skills as a carpenter served him well, and the new building was completed in January 1965.

FIGURE 15 Cuarón residence located on Princeton Street, East Los Angeles, 1965.
Cuarón Family Collection

Within a manner of months, a new community began to form in the Cuarón
family orbit. They had hoped to attract young people, especially college students,
to join their vision of community. They especially yearned for the youthful
energy and stimulating intellectual exchanges that such a group could provide.
So, they focused their advertising in the local paper associated with the East
Los Angeles Community College. Although young people answered their ads
and moved in, they did not always stay for very long. Between 1965 and 1968,
tenants came and went. Nevertheless, a stable community, of sorts, did emerge
on Princeton Street, but not in the form the Cuaróns had anticipated. Instead,
a number of local youths, mostly young teenagers, began to frequent the apartments. These visitors included friends of the Cuaróns' eldest daughter, Mita,
but others also gravitated to the apartments through word of mouth. It soon
became apparent to the Cuaróns that many of these youths belonged to single-
parent families—many of them struggling to survive economically.[24] A core
group formed, including Kenny Ortiz and his brother John, George Rodríguez,
Marti Rodríguez, Aurora Carreon, Cassandra Zacarias, Harry Gamboa, Steve
Valencia, George Reyes, and Moctesuma Esparza, to name a few. These young

Chicanas and Chicanos would become key actors in the political drama that would engulf East Los Angeles in 1968.

A sense of excitement and energy filled the apartment complex. Many of the youth were drawn there for a sense of belonging, and for the stimulating intellectual environment that Ralph and Sylvia provided. As Harry Gamboa remembered, these youths had an almost "idol worship" of Ralph.[25] They were especially impressed by the family's large collection of books located in the living room of their apartment. Thankfully, the Cuaróns had not destroyed their books as so many fellow Communists and radical activists had done during the height of the Cold War. The collection included such titles as Albert Memmi's *The Colonizer and the Colonized*, V. I. Lenin's *Imperialism* and *What Is to Be Done*, and a number of works by Karl Marx, Antonio Gramsci, and Maurice Cornforth. The Cuaróns also had a vast collection of fiction and poetry, including those of Pablo Neruda, Howard Fast, Thomas Mann, Leo Tolstoy, Thomas Wolfe, Jack London, Feodor Dostoyevsky, and Ethel L. Voynich. The Cuaróns freely shared their treasured collection and in the process helped instill in the youth a sense of literary curiosity not always present in their own homes.

Steve Valencia recalled how that collection of books—and the milieu of Princeton Street—changed his life. He arrived at the Cuarón home by way of his father, Rito Valencia, an old friend of Cuarón and a fellow comrade in the party. Valencia had experienced a racism and discrimination while attending Lynwood High School that left him bitter and confused. The largely white student body appeared to view the few Mexicans in their midst as interlopers, as threats to their racially exclusive enclave in southeast Los Angeles. Physical confrontations and regular threats of violence weighed heavily on the youth. Valencia was fifteen years old and suffering academically when his father introduced him to Cuarón, to whom Valencia was immediately drawn. "Ralph (Cuarón) became like a father . . . a mentor . . . a political mentor. He showed me that you don't have to just accept all of the conditions that are handed to you; you can do something about it. It was a different context of thinking." He recalled the "red books" kept separate from the regular books in the family library and how he read them whenever he could.[26] Mita recalled how Steve would take those books to Calvary Cemetery, located on Whittier Boulevard (one mile away from Princeton) so that he could "hang out and read" in the secluded burial grounds—a place to think in silence. The experiences on Princeton were so compelling that within a short time Valencia moved into the apartment complex.[27]

This natural inquisitiveness of the students allowed Cuarón the opportunity to form reading circles that the youths enthusiastically attended, sometimes up to four times per week. The students were also drawn by Cuarón's articulation of alternative ideas and novel ways of perceiving the world around them. For some, these regular discussions helped clarify their own experiences and provided them with alternative ways of coping and understanding. As Gamboa recalled, these small group discussions helped to explain "a few things in a couple of ways that I hadn't really understood. Previously . . . I had read a lot of different things, but I had never been instructed on organizing or, basically, socialist theory, communist theory, urban theory." Gamboa also remembered a time when Cuarón suggested that he read Dostoevsky's *The Idiot*. In retrospect, he believed that the book, whose principal character was an introspective observer, would later serve as a model for his own life's journey. Cuarón used his collection of literature, philosophy, theory, and history to engage and challenge the youth to reach new intellectual horizons.[28]

While the group dynamic proved to be a powerful forum, there may have been an undercurrent to these activities that was less benevolent. The numerous gatherings of the reading circles at some point became obligatory meetings. Thus, instead of participation being voluntary, Cuarón may have forced his will upon the group by using, as Gamboa explained, "new age psychology . . . to secure small group focus and cohesion." Gamboa instinctively steered away from these pressures of having to surrender his individuality; nonetheless, there was still something seductive about the whole experience. Indeed, Cuarón had recognized in these youths the need "to be a part of a group"—a part of something bigger and more meaningful. Although Gamboa disagreed at times with Cuarón about these methods, he learned a great deal from him. Gamboa compared Cuarón to Bert Corona as having a "hypnotic" quality that drew you in and "let you go when he was ready to let you go."[29] Despite these shortcomings, Gamboa stayed on, eager to learn more and exhilarated by the sense of possibilities.

These years before the student walkouts (or blowouts) proved pivotal in the psychological and ideological development of several future student leaders. Cuarón provided them with a training ground for activism and political consciousness. As Gamboa explained, what Cuarón and the other old radicals gave them was "the seeds of thought and the possibility of influencing people by certain activities."[30] As these seeds germinated on the Eastside, anger and frustration was seething in other parts of the city, especially among many African Americans.

Seven months after the completion of the apartments, the Watts riots broke out. "Watts forced acknowledgment of a new reality," write Thomas B. and Mary D. Edsall, "that passage of civil rights legislation was not adequate to either assuage black anger, nor to produce the relatively trouble-free integration of the races that had been anticipated by many liberals."[31] But *why* had passage of the historic legislation not been sufficient to achieve full racial equality and integration for African Americans and other people of color? The answer remained, in the eyes of some observers, *white supremacy*. Despite the landmark civil rights legislation, most white Americans were heavily invested—consciously or not—in an economic, political, and social system that privileged whiteness. This investment in whiteness, writes George Lipsitz, allowed European Americans opportunities for asset accumulation and upward mobility by denying these same opportunities to communities of color. White privilege manifested itself, for example, in white flight out to the suburbs, restrictions on Federal Housing Administration loans for minority residents (red-lining), restrictive housing covenants (despite being outlawed by *Shelley v. Kraemer*), highways and hazardous waste facilities constructed in minority communities, and a criminal justice system that disproportionately affected minority groups.[32] These manifestations of white privilege weakened communities of color—politically, economically, and socially, effectively casting them into second-class status. Of course, not all white Americans were complicit; there has always been "an element of choice," explains Lipsitz, in how we respond to life's challenges. That is, individuals can and do make a conscious choice to become antiracist.[33] For Mexican American activists during this period, the challenge was also having to confront the widespread belief that they were a regional population, largely disconnected from most aspects of American society and without relevant political power.

The events in Watts reverberated in Mexican American communities. By the mid- to late 1960s, communities on the Eastside, and elsewhere around the state, were powder kegs. The work of numerous organizations calling for reforms in education, political representation, health care, youth programs, and police relations began to attract greater attention and gain momentum. And as communities vied for limited financial resources, such as War on Poverty funds, interracial conflict and competition sometimes flared. Mexican Americans often felt that federal funding was too focused on African Americans, resulting in less investment in their own communities. As cooperation dwindled, and often failed, distrust led to open political battles between groups.[34] In addition, government bureaucracies continued to frustrate Mexican American attempts to effect change through policy mandates. On March 28, 1966, Mexican American representatives to the regional conference of the Equal Employment Opportunities Commission (EEOC) staged a protest during these proceedings in what was publicized as the "Albuquerque Walkout."[35]

The walkouts were orchestrated not only to protest the lack of inclusiveness by the EEOC conference, but also to publicize the sheer lack of respect and consideration Mexican Americans received from federal bureaucrats. The group of invited Mexican American leaders had not been given a role in the planning of a meeting designed to discuss employment issues affecting this community. According to Leo Grebler, director of the Mexican American Study Project at UCLA, the federal government showed an "astonishing ignorance, indifference, and insensitivity" toward Mexican Americans. More significantly, however, they appeared to be only concerned with African Americans. In a letter to the editor that circulated in a number of national papers, including the *Los Angeles Times*, Grebler continued his sharp criticism:

> If this was merely a federal "snafu" one could write it off as an unfortunate episode. But the problem is far more serious. Preoccupied by their concern over Negroes, federal agencies have yet to awaken to the presence of over 4 million Mexican-Americans in our midst. And they have yet to recognize that this group, despite its concentration in the Southwest, is emerging as a national minority.
>
> Its problems cannot be equated with those of Negroes, although both minorities share subordinate status, and action programs, which ignore its specific difficulties are doomed to failure.[36]

At the local level, young Mexican American students intimately involved in the civil rights movement also began to feel that their issues were ignored. "Some of those who had participated in SNCC [Student Non-Violent Coordinating Committee]," writes Carlos Muñoz, "and other organizations or who had been influenced by the civil rights movement came to the realization that Mexican Americans were not a concern of the Black civil rights leadership and its allies." The same was true of President Johnson's War on Poverty programs, which "did not initially address poverty in the barrios of the South and Midwest."[37]

These unresolved issues flared up in different parts of the country as the civil rights movement unfolded. In Denver, Colorado, for example, Democratic Party leader and community activist Rodolfo "Corky" Gonzales became highly critical of the War on Poverty programs as they concerned Mexican American communities.[38] Later in 1968, dissension arose when Gonzales joined the Southern Christian Leadership Conference (SCLC) in Washington, D.C., as a participant in the Poor People's Campaign. His decision to assert autonomy by keeping the Chicanos in his group outside Resurrection City did not sit well with the SCLC leadership. Time and again, Gonzales refused to move his contingent. His criticism, notes Ernesto B. Vigil, was that the leadership of SCLC did not view Mexican Americans as critical allies. Rather, they were viewed as a "regional minority with little impact on the national consciousness"; therefore, at best, Mexican Americans were considered a "minority-within-a-minority."[39] But as Rosales describes, Gonzales's personality may also have played a part. Gonzales had long shown a penchant for personal ambition, specifically by promoting a national *movimiento* united under his leadership.[40]

The walkout in Albuquerque and subsequent events elsewhere reverberated in East Los Angeles.[41] As for the Cuarón family, these events meant that they had to move with greater urgency to implement their housing initiative. In fact, the Cuaróns were pulled into the genesis of the Chicano student movement by the politicization of their eldest daughter, Mita, and the young people who lived and visited their small apartment complex.

At the start of 1966, Cuarón took part in three major undertakings: he founded and organized the East Los Angeles Improvement Council (ELAIC); he gained a seat on the Housing Committee of the Los Angeles County Commission on Human Relations; and he began rudimentary plans for the acquisition and construction of a second apartment complex.[42] In that same year, the Cuaróns identified a property on Hubbard Street that would be included in the next phase of their community building experiment. Indeed, the Hubbard Street property was located adjacent to the Cuaróns' property on Princeton. Cuarón converted one of the garage spaces in their apartment complex into a workshop where he and the neighborhood youths worked on the architectural plans for the proposed project. One year later, they had completed a scale model of the building.[43] As Mita recalls, they fashioned a miniature structure from wooden pegs that her father created using his woodworking machinery. The camaraderie that developed among the youths continued; in addition to the reading groups, Cuarón now began to introduce students to architectural design, urban planning, and, equally important, *theater*.

During this period, Cuarón familiarized his charges with protest strategies that elevated community organizing to a whole new level. As Gamboa recalled,

A POOR HOUSING PROTEST FROM EAST LOS ANGELES
Young Mexican - Americans from East Los An-   their community. A live "corpse" occupies box in
geles put on a demonstration in front of Federal   foreground. Demonstrators protested lack of funds
Building in protest against housing conditions in   granted low income families by Government.

FIGURE 16 Students protesting poor housing in East Los Angeles. Participants included (from left to right): John Ortiz (back to photo), George Reyes (holding up sign), Kenny Ortiz (in coffin), unidentified young female, Harry Gamboa (holding sign in background), and Mita Cuarón walking with sign. Courtesy of Hearst Communications Inc.

Cuarón's "notion of theatricality was rather interesting. I remember that we had a performance, [a] demonstration in front of the federal building [in downtown Los Angeles] in which we built a coffin. And we put Kenny Ortiz in the coffin and we carried it . . . it was the death of housing for East L.A."[44] In a photograph taken by the *Los Angeles Herald-Examiner*, Mita carried a sign that read "Mexican-American Young Peoples Demonstration" and George Reyes carried one that read "ELA [East Los Angeles] Is Dying." Gamboa can be

FIGURE 17 Ralph Cuarón with youth protesting poor housing, Federal Building on N. Los Angeles Boulevard. Cuarón Family Collection.

FIGURE 18 Kenny Ortiz and Mita Cuarón working on scale model of the Hubbard Street housing project, 1969. Cuarón Family Collection.

FIGURE 19 Steve Valencia (sitting atop table) talking with youth on Princeton Street, 1969. Cuarón Family Collection.

seen marching in the background, with Ortiz lying face-up in the coffin with a sign draped over him that read, "Here Lies East L.A. With Love We Mourn Our Dead."[45] The students had not only engaged in guerrilla theater to pub-licize housing problems; they had also laid the groundwork for the kind of leadership that would propel them onto the center stage of the school boycotts of March 1968.

The introduction of this kind of behavior on the streets—of combining protest and theater—changed how these youths perceived their lives in their neighborhoods and in society. For Gamboa, the experience helped launch his artistic career by providing him, and his friends, with "a kind of think tank training ground for young people. . . . The kind of place where we were intro-duced to quite a number of different theories that related to the power of words, the power of action, the power of leafleting."[46] They were, in effect, becoming organizers and activists with each new experience, gaining awareness of them-selves as important actors in an unfolding drama. Valencia recalled how crit-ical this period was for his own transformation. Despite being very quiet and self-conscious, Valencia was encouraged by Cuarón to confront this fear. After being selected to lead the youth section of ELAIC, he took part in a number of community meetings in which he stood up to address public audiences. "He [Ralph] would force me to talk in front of people. I guess that was part of

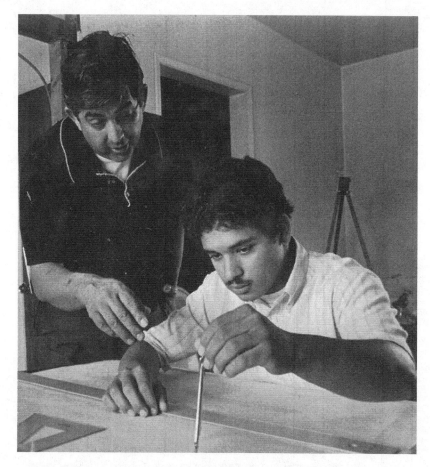

FIGURE 20 Ralph Cuarón and Kenny Ortiz working on the Hubbard Street project, 1969. Cuarón Family Collection.

the political education. But it was really scary." Nevertheless, Valencia could see how this work was changing the lives of his friends, how many of them were making new connections and realizing how small their world was. As he recalled, "those young people that came together around the East Los Angeles Improvement Council became the Garfield High School strike committee. They were already organized. That's the benefit of having organization."[47] But Cuarón was not the sole source of intellectual development. Francisca Flores (Frances Lym) also played a critical role in influencing and engaging the young minds on Princeton Street.

FIGURE 21   Cuarón family and neighborhood youth in front of the Princeton property, 1969. Cuarón Family Collection.

Most of the youth at the apartment complex knew Flores as "Francisca."
An old and dear friend of the Cuaróns for many years, Flores had been active
in the community for over two decades and a Communist Party member since
1939. She had worked with the Cuaróns on a myriad of issues, ranging from
immigration and discrimination to police brutality.[48] They had also struggled
together within the party in trying to advance the issue of equality for Mexican
Americans. In fact, Flores's activism dated back to the 1930s when, as a member
of Hermanas de la Revolucion (Sisters of the Revolution), a women's exclusive
organization, she encouraged social activism. In 1943, she joined the Sleepy
Lagoon Defense Committee formed to support twenty-two young Mexican
Americans placed on trial for the murder of a young man, José Díaz.[49] Later, in
1948, Flores worked on the Augustino Salcido murder case as a public relations
liaison with the Los Angeles Civil Rights Congress.[50] She joined the Cuarón
community in 1965 when the apartments opened. It was not long before she
became actively involved in mentoring and developing critical consciousness
among the neighborhood youth. As Gamboa recalled:

In the apartment complex there [on Princeton Street] was Francisca Flores, who was the editor of *Regeneración*, which I later became co-editor of. But she used to have a newsletter called *Carta Editorial*. . . . When I used to hang around there, I used to help her fold it so she could mail it out. And we'd sit and chat. And she had a very different understanding of what politics was supposed to be about. And she kind've had an understanding about media . . . and the idea about reaching out [to the community].[51]

Valencia remembered a time when he defiantly declared to Flores that he was no longer going to compromise "with the goddam system!" She responded patiently by explaining that his recent purchases of sunflower seeds at a local store and shoes at a mall were all examples of him doing just that—*compromising with the system*. As infuriated as she might make him feel, Valencia learned to appreciate her acumen and candidness. "What she was trying to do is get me to look at reality, . . . that it wasn't [about] idealism. That you had to look at the actual reality of the situation."[52] If the revolution was on its way, his mentors cautioned patience. Flores was there to help guide this youthful energy.

Francisca Flores was also an important catalyst for community-wide activism. She had already helped found the Mexican American Political Association and remained an astute observer of issues affecting Mexican Americans through *Carta Editorial*. Indeed, her newsletters were regularly filled with critical analyses of local and regional political campaigns, housing and education issues, as well as farmworker rights and race relations.[53] Unfortunately, Flores's activism and leadership, and that of many Mexican women, have often remained in the margins of printed historical narratives, relegated, as Vicki Ruiz describes, to "landscape roles." "The reader has a vague awareness of the presence of women, but only as scenery, not as actors . . . and even their celebrated maternal roles are sketched in muted shades."[54] Yet, Francisca Flores was anything but in the shadows; she remained at the epicenter of a growing movement. In her study of Chicana leadership during this period, Dolores Delgado Bernal notes that Flores exhibited a grassroots leadership style that focused on developing consciousness. This dimension of leadership helped "others gain awareness of school and social inequalities through discussion and print media." More importantly, this new awareness is what kept the "momentum" going and what sustained the student movement for the long haul. Traditional conceptions about leadership, with a focus on high positions in an organization, have tended to overlook "consciousness raising . . . as part of the dynamic process."[55] Later, in the 1970s, as editor for the magazine *Regeneración* (Regeneration), she became a leading force for Chicana feminism.[56] Flores, then, was part of a process that helped set the stage for a number of young Chicanas and Chicanos to develop a different understanding of power and history—and how to harness them.

In the years prior to the walkouts, a number of forums and informal gatherings were organized to channel the energy of the growing political awareness among Chicano youth in East Los Angeles. Community residents, students, and professionals took part in coordinating these efforts. For example, Mita Cuarón, Kenny and John Ortiz, Harry Gamboa, as well as Rachel Ochoa Cervera, Rosalinda Méndez González, and a number of other students, participated in various youth conferences arranged by the Los Angeles County Commission on Human Relations, where Cuarón was an active member.[57] As Gerald Rosen and Marguerite V. Marín confirm in their studies of the Chicano Movement, these conferences helped lay the groundwork for the blowouts.[58] A key figure in the success of these conferences was Sal Castro, a teacher at Lincoln High School.

Castro had grown up in East Los Angeles and was well aware of the devastating effects of discrimination on the lives of Mexican Americans. The bitter irony, Castro concluded, was that the schools themselves had become critical vectors in perpetuating shameful policies that hindered the intellectual development of young Chicanas and Chicanos. And, worse yet, these same institutions readily placed the responsibility for failures squarely on this population. As Castro recalled, administrators and teachers alike "blamed the Mexican American students, their parents, and their culture for the high drop-out rates, the low reading scores, and for not going on to college. They made the victims into the villains."[59] He also learned very quickly that this system would not tolerate change, let alone a direct challenge. Indeed, the simple act of encouraging Mexican American students to run for student government led to his eventual dismissal from his job at Belmont High School. The belief in a Mexican American pathology was so ingrained that many refused to believe this population was capable of anything meaningful. Despite his frustrations with Mexican Americans who seemed resigned to "hide their heads in the sand," Castro understood that any failings on the part of Mexican Americans were the direct result of systemic inequalities.[60] From his first assignment as a counselor at Camp Hess Kramer in 1963, Castro worked to develop youth leadership through critical consciousness. By 1967, as Castro recalled, "I was openly discussing with the students the possibility of a dramatic action in the schools."[61]

The summer conferences of 1966 and 1967 held at Camp Hess Cramer in Malibu, California, led directly to a number of new developments: the further coalescence of student relationships from throughout the East Los Angeles area; greater cohesion of organizational efforts; the formation of Young Citizens for Community Action (which by late 1967 became Young Chicanos for Community Action); and, finally, the formation of the Brown Berets (an organization formed to advocate on behalf of Mexican Americans on issues ranging from education equality, discrimination, and poor housing to protests against the Vietnam War and police brutality). In September 1967, the Piranya Coffee House opened, becoming a central meeting place for student activists.[62] The various public symposiums, such as the one held at UCLA in 1967, brought together Mexican American leaders from across the country and exposed local youth to the larger national struggles. "By the end of 1967," notes Carlos Muñoz, "the antiwar and Black Power movements had become other sources of growing militancy among some of the student leaders." Indeed, some Chicano students at colleges and universities even "joined with SDS [Students for a Democratic Society] and the Black student unions in planning campus protests."[63] For some of the high school students, the need to commit their thoughts and ideas to paper—to communicate with their community and to raise consciousness— became all too imperative.

A plethora of underground newspapers soon circulated on the Eastside and played an essential role in the developments leading to the walkouts.[64] "Newspapers, such as *La Raza, Inside Eastside,* and *The Chicano Student Movement*," writes Marin, "articulated specific grievances and helped spread student discontent." And just as important, the underground papers "promoted ethnic solidarity." "Poems and short stories were printed celebrating a pride in Chicano and Mexican history and culture. But perhaps more importantly, during the days immediately preceding the walkouts the newspapers actively supported student mobilization by openly promoting the walkouts."[65] A number of Chicanas, including Paula Crisostomo, Tanya Luna Mount (daughter of Julia and George Mount), Mita Cuarón, Celeste Baca, Cassandra Zacarias, Rosalinda Méndez González, Vicki Castro, and Rachael Ochoa Cervera, were integrally connected to the community newspapers. Luna Mount and Crisostomo, for example, wrote articles for *Inside Eastside* and *La Raza.* These students helped produce, distribute, and encourage their peers to read their articles and get involved.[66] Carlos Montes, a student activist and member of the Brown Berets, remembered passing out leaflets, including his organization's paper, *La Causa,* in front of the schools, at community meetings, on Whittier Boulevard, and to the local car clubs. These underground papers and pamphlets carried the life-blood of this youth movement.[67] Rather than being "smut sheets" encouraging "depravity and irresponsibility," as one member of the House Un-American Activities Committee would declare, they helped nurture a new self-awareness among Mexican American youth.[68]

When the walkouts finally erupted, Ralph Cuarón was not in East Los Angeles but in Washington, D.C., attending meetings related to federal housing programs. Sometime in late 1967, Congressman George Brown visited the apartment complex on Princeton Street and became impressed by the project. Sensitive to the housing problems and supportive of local community efforts, Brown hired Cuarón as a field deputy and funded his trip to Washington, D.C., to lobby federal officials. According to Cuarón, Brown wanted him

> to present our cases of the community and to go to the federal offices and try to give consultation in respect to this community to high government officials. . . . I took a delegation of young students from Garfield to speak on behalf of their community and their future, the relevance of federal programs to young people in this community.[69]

Kenny Ortiz and Steve Valencia accompanied Cuarón as members of a youth council affiliated with the Los Angeles County Commission on Human Relations.[70]

Although Cuarón was in Washington only a few days, he managed to speak directly with Vice President Hubert H. Humphrey. Gonzálo Cano, an employee with the Justice Department's Community Relations Service, remembered this meeting with Humphrey: "He [Cuarón] spoke very candidly with the vice president, and . . . the vice president . . . knew how to answer as opposed to some of the other fellows who he did not take serious. He took Cuarón pretty serious."[71] Cuarón participated in this lobbying activity in the wake of a significant effort by President Lyndon Johnson's administration to address the pressing needs of Mexican Americans throughout the country. On June 9, 1967, President Johnson established the Inter-Agency Committee on Mexican-American Affairs, a cabinet-level committee. The committee was charged with hearing solutions to problems, assuring that federal programs reached their targeted populations, and seeking out innovative approaches to meet the unique needs of Mexican American communities.

In October 1967, over fifty Mexican Americans delivered testimonies before a special hearing of the Committee on Mexican American Affairs held in El Paso, Texas.[72] The eclectic group of Latino experts, community activists, religious leaders, and elected officials included such notables as Dr. Ernesto Galarza and Dr. Julian Nava. The committee hearing was organized into six smaller presentations captioned under the following themes: "Economic and Social Development"; "Agriculture"; "Labor"; "Health, Education, and Welfare"; "Housing and Urban Development"; and "War on Poverty." In almost every presentation, the recommendations stressed the need for federal intervention, but with the caveat that communities should be allowed to develop local strategies: strategies that would allow some level of independence and self-direction. On the issue of housing, for example, recommendations included establishing a White House "National Citizens' Advisory Committee on housing needs for Mexican Americans"; authorizing research grants through the Department of Housing and Urban Development to study housing issues in Mexican American communities; establishing housing information centers charged with identifying and assessing problems, and "establishing 'workable programs'" in every barrio; building "four-to-six unit clusters of senior citizen homes" in every community to help maintain cohesion and historical memory rather than separating and institutionalizing this group; and prioritizing "the participation and involvement of the recipients in research, design, planning, and implementation" of these programs.[73]

Underlying the concerns of some of the presenters was the growing sense of disappointment and despair by Mexican Americans over the lack of attention given their communities by government agencies. Father Henry J. Casso, vicar of Urban Ministry for the Archdiocese of San Antonio, Texas, for example, quoted President Johnson from a 1965 speech: "The City is not an assembly of shops and buildings. . . . It is a community for the enrichment of the life of man."[74] Indeed, these words echoed the sentiment of the Cuarón project on Princeton Street. Cuarón had planned his trip to Washington not only to inform and educate, but to bring home the resources necessary to make an immediate impact on the housing needs in Los Angeles. However, the trip was cut short when he received word from Mita on March 5 that the students at Garfield High School had walked out.

For many students, the schools had lost their relevance, as these institutions appeared to be islands unto themselves—oblivious to the environment surrounding them. Kenny Ortiz recalled this atmosphere prior to the walkouts:

Well, I felt that there was a need. There was a need to have change. There was something wrong, lack of facilities, lack of textbooks. I had been noticing that my parents and friends in the community, . . . they speak of national crisis, and national unrest, and student disorders all over the country, and in my own little community and own home I have witnessed conflict and hostility, and I noticed it is very apparent to me in the high school that I attend at Garfield.[75]

The schools appeared static, unaffected, and indifferent. George Cole, a clergyman with the United Presbyterian Church and member of the East Los Angeles Improvement Council, observed:

Well, of course, one of the things that young people spoke about was the high dropout rate, the lack of communication that they felt with counselors in exploring the educational possibilities for them as Mexican American youths, the frustrations they sometimes felt in terms of communication with teachers who were not vitally involved in the community, but were living outside of the community and . . . found it difficult to relate effectively to the youth of East Los Angeles.[76]

Thomas P. Carter echoed these sentiments in his study at the time. He concluded that the schools were "inappropriate" for many Mexican American students and contributed directly to their low educational attainment. "Factors particularly disadvantageous are de facto segregation, isolation in its various forms, the dependence on English, and inadequate teachers. Less obvious factors include rigidity of school practices and policies, curricular irrelevancy, culture conflict, and the negative perceptions of educators."[77]

School administrators could not feign ignorance of community concerns, as a system of public outreach was already in place. The Los Angeles School District had direct communication with parents and students through their office of Urban Affairs and Community Relations. According to Vincent Villagran, who worked as a specialist in this office, he and his staff were responsible for helping parents and community leaders connect with school administrators, to share and resolve issues and concerns within the schools. As Villagran explained at the time:

Part of our function is to provide to school administrators feedback as to what people in the community feel about the schools, and also the secondary factor we assist by bringing in resource people to school administrators or ourselves talking to school faculty groups regarding the background of the East L.A. community and how best they can serve that community. . . .

Some of the problems that were developing at Garfield, probably no different than developing at most East L.A. schools, problems concerning regarding curriculum, treatment of Mexican-Americans in textbooks, teachers' attitudes toward the youngsters and community, and the facilities themselves.[78]

At Garfield High School, the students often felt overwhelmed by the large and impersonal bureaucracy. The tracking system the school used to divide its student body seemed draconian and arbitrary. Mita Cuarón's experience was representative of a large segment of the student population. Mita had been an honors student at Stevenson Junior High School (she had been a member of the Lamp Lighters Honor Society). But within her first semester at Garfield she had dropped to the bottom group.[79] As Mita vividly remembered:

And it became very clear that the schools of the sixties were the same schools of our parents, in the same community. The problems that they had been subjected to were the same problems years later that their children were being subjected to. . . . I remember being in a classroom where the walls were empty. I addressed the system of tracking. I remember an "A," "B," and "C" and, for some reason, I was placed in the "C." And I remember how stark, empty, [and] blank [it was]. . . . Materials were nil, if any. And I remember the "A" environment that had props and equipment and things on the wall, and a lot of photographs. In other words, there was a lot of stimulation.[80]

Once assigned to a particular track, it was difficult for students to transcend that status. The experience made Mita aware of the unequal and inferior education the students within this track received. Mita also recalled the alienation she felt from some of the teachers who appeared to have become resigned to this rigid tiered system. On one occasion, she approached a teacher to inquire why the "average" students could not participate in a particular program that offered exposure to the arts. The teacher responded in a terse manner. According to Mita:

She said, 'Well, in the first place, "A" and "B" students are already classified. They would appreciate such a program, but the "C" students, they wouldn't. Their minds wouldn't adapt to what they were seeing. They won't appreciate this.' This is what she told me.[81]

Mita and a number of students, including those from the apartments on Princeton, accelerated their informal discussions about school issues at Garfield; then in February 1968, they formed the Garfield Blowout Committee. Similar committees were organized at Lincoln, Roosevelt, Wilson, and Belmont high schools. As Dolores Bernal points out in her study, students such as Vicki Castro, Paula Crisostomo, Tanya Luna Mount, and Cassandra Zacarías played significant roles in forming and leading these committees. Soon, they began compiling lists of grievances and demands and circulated them among school board officials. What was most striking to Mita, when she looked back on this period, was the ease with which her aspirations were crushed by an arbitrary tracking system, and then having teachers and administrators provide little support in reversing that decision. Mita felt unprepared to navigate this maze alone. When it became apparent to the student activists that the board members were ignoring their demands, the students walked out.[82]

During the first week in March 1968, Wilson, Lincoln, Garfield, and Roosevelt high schools erupted in protest. By Friday, March 8, "more than fifteen thousand students had left their classes throughout the Los Angeles area."[83] When the strike erupted at Garfield on March 5, a contingent of parents mobilized immediately to provide protection for their children. The next morning, Sylvia Cuarón accompanied Mita and a number of students to the school where she met with other concerned parents, including Dora Esparza. As Mrs. Esparza explained: "I took it on my own to call some mothers and we went to school the following day because we understood there were going to be demonstrations, and I didn't want my daughter [Eva Esparza] getting hurt. So, we were there for that purpose."[84] Mrs. Esparza then notified the staff at the Plaza Community Center as well as religious leaders from the United Presbyterian Church, such as George Cole. Eager to have more community observers mediate the tense situation, parents also called Vahac Mardirosian, another Presbyterian minister and director of the ABC Project Headstart.[85] Mardirosian's participation would prove crucial, as he took a leading role in organizing parents and students in the aftermath of the walkouts. For many parents of the striking students, Principal Reginald Murphy's credibility was seriously damaged when Mita was attacked on school grounds and accused of being an "outside agitator."

The altercation occurred on March 6 as parents, student strike leaders, and Principal Murphy began gathering on the campus football field for a meeting. As students began arriving, two security guards, with the assistance of a teacher, approached Mita with the intention of apprehending her.[86] Arnold Rodríguez, the director of Community Relations for the Los Angeles City Schools, would later discover that individuals on his staff had identified Mita as the "ringleader" in the school disturbances and shared this information with campus security.[87] In the ensuing struggle, Mrs. Esparza attempted to free Mita from the guards but failed. "I felt very upset, and I went and grabbed the arm of Mr. Philips [one of two security guards on campus], and I asked him to release her, that she was one of the students. . . . He pushed me from him with his elbow and knocked me away."[88] Rodríguez immediately stepped in and ordered the guards to release Mita, and thus averted what could have erupted into a violent confrontation.

Ralph Cuarón arrived in Los Angeles early Saturday morning, March 9, to a full house, as over thirty students had taken shelter at the Princeton apartments. The Cuarón residence became a hub of activity, as planning meetings seemed to take place around the clock. As Cuarón recalled:

> My home became a little center of students and parents who came there and held many, many meetings to discuss complaints, and what they should do, asking us for counseling. I had one meeting there the night that I arrived. . . . I arrived about 2:00 o'clock on Saturday morning, and on that Friday night there must have been 50 people in that little apartment upstairs that I have, including Congressman Roybal and Judge Sánchez, and I don't know who else were counseling the people in respect to what they should do. So, yes, we were aware of, as I testified, very much aware of people coming to us and telling us their grievances, and in many respects, they were somewhat scared to go and present them.[89]

Also present that Friday night was Sal Castro. As Mita recalled, "Sal was in the apartment with other parents and other kids from the high schools. And there was a knock. So, we opened the door; there was Roybal, Judge [Leopoldo] Sánchez," as well as a representative of the Catholic Church and a member of the business community.[90] To Mita's surprise, they were insistent that Castro should bring a halt to the student protests. But as she remembered those heady days, the floodgates had already opened and the momentum was on the side of the students. The students were not going to give up the fight and, according to Mita, "Sal was not going to do that" either.[91]

Three days later, Cuarón was designated as the official representative by concerned parents and community leaders to deal directly with Principal Murphy. As Mrs. Esparza recalled, Cuarón was the natural choice for this role. "He has been active in the East L.A. Improvement Council out in the community. He has been looked up [to] as a leader. He has organized people, and he has many good ideas, and he has been acting as chairman."[92] As Cuarón remembered:

> So, I decided to, first of all, go to the principal by myself and ask for an explanation, number one, of what had happened to my daughter. Number two, to express my concerns that there was a very tense condition, feeling. . . . I saw that the measures that the school administration and the police were following were detrimental and were inciting the young into further disruptions and violence. I felt the young people had no one to intervene strongly [on their behalf]. The situation did not require soft spoken individuals to go in front of armed policemen and agitated principals with all of the laws on their side who were determined to punish young people one way or another.[93]

Mita recalled that several meetings took place that week with Principal Murphy, teachers, and students in preparation for a large community forum. Their efforts had gained the support of Dr. Julian Nava, recently elected member of the Board of Education and the first Mexican American in that capacity.[94]

FIGURE 22 Ralph Cuarón speaking at a community meeting regarding walkouts, 1968. Cuarón Family Collection.

FIGURE 23 Sylvia and Ralph Cuarón churning out pamphlets on a mimeograph machine located in their home. Cuarón Family Collection.

Though Nava supported Cuarón's right to be on campus and to make certain demands of administrators, he also cautioned him to be patient on some procedural matters and flexible with scheduling conflicts.[95] By Friday, March 15, when Cuarón, Dora Carreon (Cuarón's sister), Mita, and Kenny Ortiz entered the main office at Garfield High School, the administration was no longer willing to deal with parents and community leaders sympathetic with the walkouts.

The evening prior to Friday's meeting, Superintendent Stuart Stengel notified Cuarón at his home that he was no longer welcome on school grounds. Furthermore, he warned Cuarón that he would face arrest by school security or by the county sheriffs if he did not heed this warning. This decision was based on Cuarón's impromptu visit to a faculty meeting and his discussions with students on the campus earlier in the week. Principal Murphy evidently believed these actions contributed to the tense atmosphere at the school.[96] Cuarón, on the other hand, felt he had a right to be on campus as a parent and as a concerned member of the community. Moreover, he felt that he had to demonstrate

FIGURE 24 Peter Rodríguez, Wilson High School student, is at the microphone, waving his draft card to prove his participation in a student protest was not Communist inspired. Seated behind Rodríguez, over his left shoulder, are Steve Valencia (with glasses), Ralph Cuarón, and Harry Gamboa, 1968. Courtesy of the Los Angeles Public Library Photo Collection.

to his neighbors and to other parents that they had a right to access this public institution and should not fear school administrators. As Sylvia recalled, Ralph was "cracking the hierarchy of politics." He was going "to teach young people that it [the school bureaucracy] wasn't the monolith that it was."[97] The reason for the visit that Friday morning was to clarify Stengel's phone call and to finalize last-minute details for the public meeting scheduled for that evening. And it was that very morning that Cuarón and the group learned that their meeting had been canceled.

The news of the cancellation upset the group, as they had worked hard to organize in the community for this important forum. Within fifteen minutes of the group's arrival at the school, Murphy ordered the arrest of Cuarón and Dora. Approximately six to ten Los Angeles County sheriff's deputies arrived on the scene and, in the ensuing arrest, used mace and beat Cuarón. Both Cuarón and Dora would be charged with resisting arrest, and Cuarón was additionally charged with disturbing the peace on school grounds. On hearing the news of the arrests, Sylvia immediately contacted Rose Chernin, director of the Los Angeles Committee for Protection of Foreign Born. Chernin, another old friend and radical activist, immediately moved to inform community members about what had transpired and to provide the appropriate legal representation. In the end, Cuarón and Dora would pay a heavy price for their activism during the walkouts of 1968. The criminal court trial that ensued was evidence of the system's refusal to succumb to community pressures for change.[98]

The court proceedings that took place one year after the walkouts indicate that school administrators interpreted Cuarón's assertiveness and determination as aggressive and intrusive behavior. The judge's assessment that Cuarón's actions were "out of the realm of normal parent concern about the progress of his own child" is indicative of the court's posture.[99] Time and again, for example, the deputy district attorney, Reuben Ortega, questioned the credibility of Cuarón's assertions that parents and students felt intimidated by school officials. Instead, Ortega painted Cuarón as a "demanding person" bent on personal power and on having *his* way. Cuarón's ultimate goal in the trial, Ortega boasted, was "to put the police on trial, . . . to put the school on trial."[100] He refuted Cuarón's charge that he had been manhandled and subsequently beaten by deputy sheriffs during his arrest. Ortega declared those complaints "ludicrous" and "ridiculous," and nothing more that theatrics.

> Can you [the jury] imagine the kind of monsters we have going around in uniforms? He [Cuarón] is in the car, already they [deputy sheriffs] have accomplished their purpose. . . . I can imagine two teeth, maybe pointed ears. He [a deputy sheriff] is hitting the guy, beating him with the [night] stick, pouring mace, and he is giggling. Isn't that incredible? Can you really believe that? Doesn't that sound more like a bad dream or something? Can you actually imagine a person doing this?[101]

Ortega defended Garfield school administrators and the educational system with similar fervor.

Throughout the trial, Ortega belittled the student walkouts as well as the grievances put forward by Mita Cuarón and Kenny Ortiz in regard to their education. Indeed, he said Mita's experiences were no more than what a normal student encountered when transferring from middle school to high school. Going even further, he chided her for not being able to handle the pressure of more challenging course work. Ortega appeared to view the student protests in East Los Angeles as poor imitations of larger and more significant events occurring around the country. For example, during his cross-examination, he acerbically asked Kenny Ortiz the following: "After reading about this [national unrest and student protests around the country] and being a little unhappy with the situation at Garfield, did you feel that it was advisable to have your own little student unrest there at Garfield?" Kenny's absolute confidence in responding to this demeaning line of questioning so disconcerted Ortega that he dismissed the young man's testimony altogether. In fact, he was so incensed that he labeled Kenny a "smart aleck" with nothing more to contribute than "wisecrack" responses during the trial.[102] Obviously Principal Reginald Murphy and other school administrators and teachers did not appreciate the growing assertiveness by community members in the aftermath of the walkouts. On March 28, 1969, one year after the walkouts and at the end of a lengthy court trial, Cuarón was found guilty on both counts and sentenced to two weeks in the county jail and fined. Dora, too, was found guilty and sentenced to a short probation.

In the aftermath of the largest student walkout in U.S. history, lasting over a week, many students and community members felt disappointed with the pace of change in the schools. As Sylvia recalled, the school board and the various school bureaucracies seemed even more unwilling to admit to a failing system. Some teachers even resorted to mocking the student strike efforts as the work of ungrateful, irresponsible, and "dope-smoking" individuals. Mita then became a target in this caustic environment. Opinions within the student body were split. Several months after the walkouts, a bottle filled with gasoline and lit with a makeshift wick made of rags barely missed Mita, landing only a few feet away. Although the attack took place on school grounds, there was no significant investigation to ferret out the culprits.[103]

The Cuarón experience was certainly not unique. As other historians of this period have chronicled in some detail, school authorities took immediate and decisive action against perceived threats.[104] Although the board of education had gone on record a few days following the protests as opposing disciplinary action against students and teachers who had participated in the boycott, the intransigence of school authorities remained unchanged.[105] Sal Castro, too, became a target of school officials. His arrest in June, and that of twelve other individuals involved in the walkouts, illustrated for some the degree to which the school system would go to maintain order and discipline within its ranks.[106] Castro's subsequent ouster from his job only confirmed their suspicions. In addition to Castro, a Los Angeles grand jury ordered the arrest of David Sánchez, Carlos Montes, Ralph Ramírez, Fred López, Carlos Muñoz, Henry Gómez, Moctesuma Esparza, Eleazar Risco, Joe Razo, Patricio Sánchez, Gilberto Olmeda, and Richard Vigil on charges of conspiring to create riots, disrupting the functioning of public schools, and disturbing the peace. Although the charges were eventually dropped, the LA Thirteen, as they became known, fueled the growing student militancy.[107] While Castro eventually regained his employment, community activists involved in the group's defense were left exhausted and frustrated by the experience. Additionally, the infiltration and surveillance of high school and college student organizations and meetings by law enforcement agents, and their informants, only complicated matters and impeded progress on the issue of education reform. Despite these immediate setbacks, however, change was in the offing.

For Ralph and Sylvia Cuarón on Princeton Street in the late sixties, the walkouts and the court case certainly exhausted their energies, but this did not diminish their enthusiasm to tackle other pressing issues. As the excitement of the walkouts slowly diminished, Ralph moved ahead with his plans for Hubbard Street.

In 1968, Cuarón made plans with Esteban Torres and the fledgling East Los Angeles Community Union (TELACU) to help develop a second housing project.[108] The passage of the Economic Opportunity Act of 1964 by the federal government gave impetus to communities throughout the country to "take control of their own neighborhoods." In other words, Chávez explains, residents of poverty-stricken communities were encouraged to take the lead in achieving economic self-determination. However, conflicting interests among city officials and community activists as well as interracial conflicts (specifically between Mexican Americans and African Americans) led some to develop their own independent organizations to address community needs.[109] Hence, TELACU was born within this political context. Walter P. Reuther, president of United Automobile Workers (UAW), believed that labor had an important role to play.[110]

In May 1968, Torres, a one-time worker at a Chrysler auto assembly plant, became the executive director of the East Los Angeles Labor Community Action Committee (later renamed TELACU). Cuarón had known Torres for many years as he rose through the ranks of the UAW. Indeed, Cuarón often

FIGURE 25 Ralph Cuarón discussing the Hubbard Street project with Esteban Torres, Congressman George Brown, and others. Cuarón Family Collection.

spoke of Torres as one of his "students," as he helped guide him through the maze of labor politics and organizing. "Eddie Torres, who was a young man like ourselves," Sylvia recalled, lived next door to one of Ralph's sisters. He was an auto union worker. Ralph would counsel him and mentor him on the various aspects of bringing workers into that union.[111] Cuarón and local community members had very specific plans for the Hubbard Street experiment. Under Cuarón's leadership, the East Los Angeles Improvement Council submitted a proposal earlier that year to the Federal Housing Administration for a loan to build a five-unit demonstration housing project. The Episcopal Church and the East Los Angeles Junior Chamber of Commerce had also come to support the group in their efforts.[112]

In addition to envisioning a project "reflecting Mexican-American cultural values," ELAIC wanted the project to hire local laborers as a way of addressing the chronic unemployment in the community. They also wanted the project to hire youth as a way to get them off the streets and, more importantly, as a means of providing them with practical skills.[113] According to the *Los Angeles Times*,

FIGURE 26 Margaret Cuarón and her mother, Micaela, posing with Congressman George Brown, 1968. Cuarón Family Collection.

rather than simply rehabilitate old structures, the improvement council wants to rebuild from the ground up, temporarily moving inhabitants into a six-unit apartment center it already has, training those inhabitants as future home owners, or tenants who can solve their own problems.[114]

As Chávez describes, "The units, condominiums were to be purchased at low interest rates with low monthly payments by the families that resided in them. Furthermore, the buyers themselves would do the unskilled work on the project,

FIGURE 27 Esteban Torres and Ralph Cuarón discussing plans for the Hubbard Street project, 1968. Cuarón Family Collection.

thus cutting their mortgage payments through 'sweat equity.'"[115] But federal officials who perceived the project as too experimental and "economically unfeasible" stalled their proposal.[116]

ELAIC remained undeterred by this setback. According to Cuarón, "We rebelled. . . . We rejected their rejection." Hoping to revive their proposal, they reached out to other communities engaged in housing. The group changed its name to the Mexican-American Council for Better Housing in California to reflect a broader base of support, and Cuarón was installed as its president. The council soon opened an office in Washington, D.C., so that Cuarón could continue his efforts to educate authorities on the housing needs of Mexican Americans. Despite his efforts to obtain support for their proposal, he could not convince federal officials to release more funding.[117] The council soon realized that the project was in danger if they could not acquire outside financial support. Cuarón looked to Torres and TELACU to develop the project on Hubbard Street. TELACU had "embarked on an $80,000 project," notes Chávez, "when

FIGURE 28 Ralph Cuarón negotiating with Esteban Torres (Torres is at head of the table and Cuarón is to his right with outstretched arms), 1968–69. Cuarón Family Collection.

the Housing Division took over an effort launched three years earlier by residents of Hubbard Street in East LA. Despite the support of several other local organizations, the project had not received the approval of the Federal Housing Administration when the community union entered the picture."[118] Although the partnership seemed to function well in the beginning, it began to break apart as control issues and competing visions for the project led to increasing disagreements.

Although both men desired self-determination for Mexican Americans, their understandings of how to achieve this goal differed markedly. As Chávez explains, although Torres spoke of empowerment for Mexican Americans, he also "clearly indicated he sought independence through accommodation with the capitalist system and the larger society. He sought practical business solutions to community problems."[119] Cuarón, on the other hand, viewed capitalism as a transitory economic system that could be used to achieve important gains for the working classes, always with the long-term view of working toward an alternative social and monetary order. Cuarón believed in socialism, and his vision clashed directly with Torres's entrepreneurial and reformist views. Steve Valencia remembered this time vividly, as he had invested much energy to bring the project to fruition. "They [TELACU] took a community project and they converted it into a privatized, money-making operation. That's what stands out in my head. And I think it was very unprincipled. [TELACU] took the whole purpose of these programs into an entirely different direction."[120] Albert Valencia, Steve's older brother, was also disappointed, as he had been instrumental in writing the grant that got the project off the ground. He was nineteen years old and a student at Los Angeles City College when Cuarón recruited him. Albert had no prior experience in grant writing but believed in Cuarón's vision for community housing.[121] Cuarón's relationship with TEL-ACU did not last long.

Some of the neighbors in and around Hubbard Street had known Cuarón for many years and trusted his leadership. His consistent, assertive response to community issues had also gained him the respect and admiration of a new generation of Chicano activists. In contrast, as Carlos Muñoz explains, TEL-ACU had not appealed to many militant Chicano activists looking to pursue radical alternatives for self-determination and liberation. "In addition, TELA-CU's complex structure, intricate transactions, and connections to labor made its public image somewhat mysterious."[122] Cuarón played a key role in easing local suspicion. "Ralph became, through TELACU, the construction supervisor on the Hubbard Street project," Sylvia recalled, "which meant the first stage being the demolition of an existing building." In the existing structure on the property, a family had taken up residence illegally, and it became Cuarón's responsibility to notify them of the impending demolition and to make certain that all occupants were removed from the site. Sylvia's recollections were still raw even after many years:

> Well, the day came when I, as the job dispatcher [at the Southern California Edison Company], received a call from the supervisor on the job. That he was there by orders of TELACU to dismantle these lines of service because those were his orders. That call came from Ralph. . . . So I sent a crew out there to dismantle the lines of service. I can't remember how many days it was after that, it couldn't have been more than a week after that, I was called into the office and fired for being in collusion with my husband to dismantle lines of service where people are living.[123]

Within a month after Sylvia was dismissed from Edison, Ralph was fired from his position with TELACU. By this time, the relationship with Torres had become untenable and the management differences between them irreconcilable. Sylvia recalled a meeting at which she was asked by an individual associated with the project to persuade "Ralph to get out of this building [project] and away from Torres."[124]

Although Sylvia had filed a formal grievance with her union, the International Brotherhood of Electrical Workers Union Local 30, the process was stalled. "I never got a chance to have a hearing within my own union. I was repeatedly given excuses and postponements."[125] It appeared that her six years invested with Edison made little difference to company management, and to her union. The Cuaróns expected Torres to provide them with some support, despite their differences, but that support never came. The final insult, Sylvia recalled, was his refusal to listen to her plea to intervene on her behalf to recover her job.

Exhausted and feeling betrayed by those they had trusted, the Cuaróns decided to leave Los Angeles altogether in October 1970. The family had experienced ongoing financial problems and could not keep up with the mortgage payments on the Princeton property. Only days prior to Sylvia's dismissal from her job, Cuarón had been invited to speak at a meeting in Hemet, a small town in Riverside County. Community leaders on the Soboba Indian Reservation and activists in Hemet had heard of Cuarón's work with low-income housing. During that trip, a real estate agent, enthusiastic about his ideas, offered Cuarón a house at the top of the mountains of San Jacinto for fifty dollars. Cuarón gave him a down payment of twenty-five dollars (all the money he had in his pocket that night), and the deal was closed. At the end of October, the family reluctantly moved to this new house in the mountains. And for the next twelve years, the Cuaróns lived out a rugged existence atop a ridge overlooking the Hemet valley.

In July 1971, the *Los Angeles Times* ran an article announcing the opening of East Los Angeles's first "community-built apartments" at 3739 Hubbard Street. The article centered on the fact that the federally subsidized, low-income housing project was "designed and built by Mexican Americans" under the sponsorship of TELACU. Torres was quoted as saying, "It's kind of an emotional moment and I want to say 'gracias,' thank you, to each and every one of you." Those thanked for the completion of the project included the United Auto Workers, the Bank of America, and the "community people." Conspicuously

FIGURES 29A AND B Mita Cuarón presents Congressman Edward R. Roybal with an art piece she created depicting the walkouts. Her father, Ralph Cuarón, looks on, 1970. Cuarón Family Collection.

absent from the day's celebration was the Cuarón family. Just before cutting the ribbon to admit the first rental tenants, Leonard Woodcock, the UAW president, noted with great pride the name given to the project: the *Walter P. Reuther Villa.*[126]

The student protests of 1968 in East Los Angeles had a precedent almost four decades earlier. At the height of the Great Depression in 1931, several students at Roosevelt High School (approximately five miles from Garfield High School) decided to express views decidedly different from those held by the principal and other school administrators. The students were openly critical of school conditions and overcrowded classrooms, the quality of school equipment (or lack thereof), and poor cafeteria food. Some of these youths were also sympathetic to the plight of the working class, others admired the Soviet Union, and still others were quite critical of the attempts by the local government to deal with the Depression. School administrators felt compelled to crush this open rebellion. The penalty for these outbursts of "disloyal utterances," as some administrators perceived them, came swiftly: every student that expressed opinions antithetical to school spirit and, more importantly, that were *un-American*, was expelled.[127] The lesson learned was exceedingly clear—students would not be allowed to question authority.

In 1968, the students within this same community also protested a stagnant system of poor facilities and inferior instruction. This time, however, conditions were different. According to historian Abraham Hoffman, the Jewish militant students in 1931 did not have the community support that the Chicano students had in 1968; therefore, their protest was largely "brushed aside."[128] But something else may have been different about the Chicana/o student protests. There had been a long-established presence in the community—a historical memory—that reached back decades. Ralph and Sylvia Cuarón represented an important link to that past.

The opinions of the students of the 1930s and 1960s reflected their lived experiences and were in direct conflict with the sterile environment found in the schools. Noted neo-Marxist theorist and politician Antonio Gramsci once explained that children are the products of the communities from which they derive and each one reflects the sector of civil society from which they participate—society relations that are formed within their families, their neighborhoods, and towns. Children are not passive and "mechanical" receivers of abstract notions, Gramsci argued. "Education can only be realized by the living work of the teacher."[129] The teacher, then, has to function as a conduit—a bridge—to assist students in navigating the conflicts and contradictions imposed by society. Cuarón was a teacher, an *organic* intellectual. For him, Marxism was not merely a scholarly exercise in dialectical discourse, but a lived experience, steeped in the daily lives of the common man and woman. Cuarón was ultimately concerned with teaching his students critical thinking: in effect, to arm them with the intellectual (and practical) capacity to resist marginalization. The Cuaróns, and the many who supported the student protesters, had refused to be ignored; they were no longer going to be made to feel invisible. Mexican Americans, as Cuarón would explain, were charting the future of their community.

The apartment complex on Princeton Street provided an important anchor for the Cuaróns that kept alive the activism in this small corner of East Los Angeles. As intellectual, feminist, and social activist bell hooks describes, the home had become a sanctuary, a safe repository for those on the margins, a place from where to launch acts of resistance.[130] And like many utopian communities that have dotted the American landscape, the Cuarón experiment ultimately failed. Cuarón's ideas were certainly not conventional. As enthusiastic and energetic as he was, he could also be stubborn and domineering. For those activists who believed in working within the system, Cuarón was probably viewed as impractical, a doctrinaire leftist whose ideas harkened back to bygone days.

Like the ruins of those long-forgotten social experiments, the apartment complex on Princeton Street today stands as a pale shadow of the community that once thrived there. The endless buzz of activity that characterized the environment in and around the property is now gone. Today, tall iron fencing and a remote-controlled security gate flank the property. The Gold Medallion apartments, the one-time pride of the Cuaróns, no longer stands out, but simply blends into the landscape of East Los Angeles.[131] In the end, the only way to obtain true security is not by hiding behind heavy wrought iron but, as Cuarón would say, by organizing and reclaiming community.

CONCLUSION

Unbroken Threads

Behind a propaganda barrage of progress, reform and liberal slogans, the Communists steadily pursue a formal, dogmatic, organized program of infiltration into, and creation of, mass organizations, because they are studious, fanatical and single-minded in their service to Soviet foreign policy and the preparation for revolution in the country where they live.

—California Legislature, *Fourth Report of the Senate Fact-Finding Committee on Un-American Activities, Communist Front Organizations,* 1948

THE MEMBERS OF THE California Senate Fact-Finding Committee left little doubt that they regarded struggles for social justice in the United States as baseless and frivolous endeavors. Though the investigative committee admitted that racial discrimination and anti-Semitism existed in other parts of the country, California was, instead, a haven of impartiality. "The majority of the people of California," they maintained, "appears to be motivated by a high sense of tolerance, and the committee finds that racial intolerance is the exception rather than the rule. Very few vestiges of organized anti-Semitism, racial or religious bigotry remain in California."[1] How the committee arrived at this astonishing conclusion is unclear, especially given that they were not charged with investigating racism and discrimination in the state. What is clear, however, is that the committee held in contempt any criticism directed at government, law enforcement, the economic system, the nation's foreign policies—and their own grip on power. Therefore, by declaring the state free of racism, they apparently believed they could dismiss all condemnation; and better still, they could characterize such criticism as the machinations of outside and deviant forces.

The committee ultimately believed that the Communist Party of the United States was at the center of all trouble emanating from our workplaces, unions, politics, schools, Hollywood, poor communities, and communities of color. The communists were nothing more than professional agitators, "fomenting racial prejudices and antagonisms" while pretending to be champions of the victimized. As evidence, the committee pointed to the existence of countless "race-fronts"—facade organizations they believed were falsely representing the interests of communities of color. These organizations, they believed, were *fronts* for the CP, whose main purpose it was to charge police brutality or the specter of "'white supremacy' terror" at every confrontation with authority—charges that the committee members scornfully dismissed.[2] For many Mexican Americans, not only were the committee's conclusions disconnected from their lived experiences, they were clearly bigoted and condescending.

Despite the committee's treatment of Mexican Americans as largely invisible or as hapless victims of larger forces, this population was anything but. Those Mexican Americans who joined the Communist Party did so, some would say, out of sheer necessity. The grueling poverty of the Great Depression, miserable living conditions, discrimination, segregation, deportations, and empty stomachs led many to question the status quo, and others to ask: Was a different world possible? Therefore, Mexican Americans were not victims; these were folks who jumped into the political and social milieu of the times to take charge of their lives. They joined the CP because it provided them with a language— the ideological framework—to understand their oppression. In the process, they adopted new tools to strike back at a system that did not recognize them as legitimate citizens, let alone acknowledge their humanity. However, Mexican American communities did not wait for the Communist Party to act on their behalf; they already had a long history of militancy in defense of their rights. In many instances, it was only after communities were well entrenched in battles against employers and corrupt officials that they invited the Communists to join them—an invitation, no doubt, that could be rescinded at any moment.

Mexican Americans did not always accept the dictates of the party leadership. They often struggled for equal recognition within an organizational structure that at times marginalized their demands. Indeed, the party sometimes fell victim to the same racial beliefs and ignorance of history (which diminished the contributions of Mexican Americans) that permeated society at large. On numerous occasions, Mexican American activists urged party leaders to take a more proactive stance with outreach efforts and leadership development, especially in the Southwest where this population was mainly concentrated. Although many within the party acknowledged these demands, the greatest enemy appeared to be organizational apathy. This frustration often led Mexican American Communists to organize communities themselves, compelled, in other words, to move forward without party sanction. Yet, despite the formation of countless organizations and community actions—whether Communist-led or not—these efforts were often viewed with suspicion by society at large, and especially by the fanatical anti-Communists.

Under the Cold War microscope, these anti-Communists readily labeled community actions by people of color as subversive and un-American. Indeed, below this callous lens, even federal agencies such as the Fair Employment Practice Committee (FEPC), created under executive order by President Franklin D. Roosevelt, was identified as "Communist inspired."[3] While African Americans, Mexican Americans, and other groups saw in the FEPC a significant opportunity to end discriminatory practices (by companies engaged in war-related work), detractors viewed this agency as a fiendish plot by Communists to rally minority groups and get them to the polls. Regrettably, despite the FEPC's popularity in some circles, employers, elected officials, and many white workers opposed it. In this toxic environment, Mexican American organizations—including affiliated groups—such as El Congreso, Mexican American National Association, Mexican-American Civil Rights Congress, Amigos de Wallace, and the Los Angeles Committee for Protection of Foreign Born all fell under the unyielding gaze of the Communist hunters—marked for derision and probing, and ultimately targeted for destruction.

Although the CP seemed to weather most storms, nothing prepared it for the turmoil that came from the revelations of Soviet premier Nikita Khrushchev in 1956. The denouncement of the horrors of Joseph Stalin's rule was a blow for many American Communists, who were unaware of (or refused to acknowledge) this tragedy. As a result, many left the party during this period. But for those who remained, this time was punctuated by deep introspection and a reevaluation of their work ahead. The rationale for staying in the CP has to be understood from another perspective: for Ralph Cuarón as well as for many other steadfast comrades, their participation in the party had never been contingent on what happened in Moscow. Their activism was, first and foremost, informed by conditions at home and in their communities. Hence, despite the news from Moscow, Cuarón continued his activism and moved on to other projects, aggressively tackling housing, poverty, unemployment, civil rights, and educational issues in East Los Angeles.

Cuarón and other Mexican American Communists would continue to find relevance in the 1960s as a new generation rose up to make their own demands on the nation. The Chicano generation rejected not only the tenets of the Cold War, but also its accompanying domestic ideology, which fostered the idea of affluence through materialism, consumerism, bureaucratic conformity, and traditional gender roles. They stood up against obstinate authority to demand accountability and to reclaim their rights. But just as important, they endeavored to underscore the paralyzing effects of self-denigration and to overcome apathy. In this process, these young women and men transformed themselves by etching out a new identity—a Chicana and Chicano sensibility that demanded cultural pride, community service, consciousness-raising, and a commitment to social transformation. While credit must be given to the courageous voices that stood their ground against entrenched power, their struggle did not emerge from a vacuum.

As I have endeavored to argue in this book, the activism of Cuarón's generation helped lay the groundwork for the uprising in the 1960s. Mexican American Communists and their allies consistently pursued an aggressive course to help redefine democracy, equality, and self-determination. It was these activists who unabashedly called for a Mexican American agenda—an agenda that demanded a reevaluation of curricular content (that elevated Chicano collective memories), challenged their second-class status, and expected equality *on their terms*. In effect, the demand from these radicals was for a reevaluation of identity: What does it mean to be an American? Cuarón and his cohort worked diligently toward expanding that meaning. The audacity of this group of activists, therefore, is what rattled the emotions and deep-seated fears of those in power. For men like Jack B. Tenney, the chairman of the Senate Fact-Finding Committee, Cuarón was a "monster," who, in addition to disrespecting law and order, was a principal vector in the spread of a vicious disease—namely, "ethnic class consciousness." For Tenney, there could be no worse enemy of the state.[4] For Chicanas and Chicanos who rejected Tenney's worldview, the time for change was *now*—and there was no turning back. As Rosales reminds us, "The rise of the student movement in California and the walkouts were only the beginning of a continued Chicano militancy that spread throughout the state and even into other areas of the Southwest."[5] The threads of that legacy have not been broken.

In 2006, almost four decades after the East Los Angeles blowouts, over forty thousand students walked out of schools in Southern California in protest. Those student demonstrations were in response to proposed immigration legislation that would give police more power to enforce immigration laws and require up to seven hundred miles of additional fencing along the U.S.-Mexican border. According to then Los Angeles mayor Antonio Villaraigosa, the legislation was not friendly to immigrants and "it would criminalize 12 million people."[6] Coincidently, during the same month, the film *Walkout* premiered. Produced by Moctesuma Esparza (one of the L.A. Thirteen) and directed by Edward James Olmos, the film portrayed the 1968 walkouts and captured the spirit and intensity of the issues that compelled the youth to revolt. Though *Walkout* did not present the full complexity of those events, it delivered an engrossing story of courage and determination to make change against overwhelming odds. Indeed, the film helped situate these protests by Mexican American students within the context of the civil rights movement—one that helped raise the consciousness of a new generation. These activists became a driving force for social and political change in this community and an inspiration for future generations. "I'd be happy to take the credit," Esparza explained of the protests in 2006, "but students have been walking out for years on their own."[7] Just four years later, Mexican Americans were forced to take to the streets, yet again—this time, more poignantly, in defense of their history.

As the anti-immigrant pendulum swung toward Arizona, Mexican Americans and Mexican immigrants, not surprisingly, were caught in the crosshairs. Despite the passage of one of the nation's strictest anti-immigration measures at the time, conservatives in the state remained convinced that a tide of chaos—that is, Mexican immigration—was about to break on their shore.[8] In this overly charged atmosphere, and as other states moved to enact their own anti-immigrant measures, these advocates of stricter immigration laws were emboldened to move against another perceived danger: a threat not only to national security but to the very nature of American society itself. Their target was a successful academic program called Mexican American Studies (MAS). Implemented in 1998, the mission of this program was to reverse disturbing academic trends for Chicana/o students in the Tucson schools.

Though Mexican American Studies had received resounding support from parents, teachers, and administrators, the Republican Party leadership in the state (including the attorney general, state and local superintendents, and Tucson Unified School District governing board members) reacted differently.

Under House Bill 2281, they charged MAS with promoting the overthrow of the U.S. government, promoting race and class resentment, and advocating ethnic solidarity. Indeed, the wording and intent of this provision harkened back to the Cold War era when Republican senator Joseph McCarthy (Wisconsin) wielded enemy lists before the House Un-American Activities Committee in his witch hunt for Communist spies and public enemies. But this time, the community fought back immediately—and without fear.[9]

Scholars, artists, labor activists, and civil rights groups including TUSD teachers, parents, and students filed lawsuits, staged protests, sit-ins, media blitzes, and formed coalitions across ethnic, regional, and national boundaries to get their story out. And the effects of their activism were electrifying, as they helped generate multiple organizations and movements dedicated to supporting the spread of ethnic studies and campaigns to promote candidates for open school board seats. Rather than suppressing MAS and silencing the Mexican American community, and Latinos in general, the efforts of the right-wing, reactionary forces in Arizona helped to embolden a new generation of young Chicanos and Latinos to stand up for themselves and to demand first-class citizenship. More importantly, they challenged the highly offensive notion that they were somehow *minor characters* in American history and undeserving of attention. As students, parents, and community leaders made exceedingly clear, they mattered and the nation had to come to grips with that reality.[10] As Maria Theresa Mejia, a senior at Tucson Magnet High School stated succinctly, "For me, what I've learned through all this is that students and youth have a lot of voices that we don't get to express. . . . We're the ones who will be changed by this situation. We will be the ones who speak out and do marches, and we will be the ones making the future. And no matter what, we have the power to stand up for what we believe."[11] And just maybe, this is what conservatives in Arizona despaired over all along: a freethinking, critically minded, and independent populace that they have little connection with and whom they fear will be the future of Arizona.

Throughout his life, Ralph Cuarón remained committed to racial equality and first-class citizenship, especially for Mexican Americans. His experiences during the Great Depression and World War II ignited not only a passion for the working class and for social justice but also a biting critique of capitalism. So he joined the Communist Party and never turned back. Despite the inherent contradictions and risks of becoming involved with such an organization, he perceived the party as an important vehicle to pursue his goals. Nevertheless, he remained staunchly independent and did not subsume his ethnic identity. Through the CP he discovered a new language, a set of principles to comprehend race, class, and gender oppression. But did Cuarón represent a "studious, fanatical and single-minded" foot soldier in the service of the Soviet Union as the anti-Communists so readily charged?[12] Not at all. On the contrary, Cuarón envisioned his life's mission as in the service of the working class and did not advocate the violent overthrow of the U.S. government. However, if revolution was in the offing, he hoped to find it in the transformation of the hearts and minds of average citizens so that the nation might fulfill its promises of liberty, equality, and justice for all.

In the course of this research, I was often struck by the sheer determination and optimism shared by many activists in the midst of the Cold War. How was it possible that they were not overwhelmed or disheartened by the seemingly endless struggles? Howard Zinn's words are a partial response to this question:

> Human beings show a broad spectrum of qualities, but it is the worst of these that are usually emphasized, and the result, too often, is to dishearten us, diminish our spirit. And yet, historically, that spirit refuses to surrender. History is full of instances where people, against enormous odds, have come together to struggle for liberty and justice, and have *won*—not often enough, of course, but enough to suggest how much more is possible.[13]

The Cuaróns, and the many others who walked parallel paths, represented that spirit of hopeful resistance, and their journey recounted in this book is their contribution to the long road ahead.

EPILOGUE

Organic Intellectual

THE MOVE AWAY FROM East Los Angeles to the mountains of San Jacinto in Riverside County did not prove to be a respite from activism for the Cuarón family. Within a short time, Ralph went to work for Kingston Homes Incorporated, a mobile home manufacturer, in Mira Loma, and became a member of the Carpenters Union Local 3193.[1] Cuarón also began plans to convert their mountain home into a "worker school," hoping to create a community similar to that which they had left behind on Princeton Street.[2] Indeed, a sign was placed along the only road to the mountaintop: Cresta del Sol (Crest of the Sun). Within a short time, labor leaders like Lou Diskin, section organizer for the Communist Party's Southern California district, and other community activists paid frequent visits to the Cuarón home. Steve Valencia, who had joined the family in their move to the mountains, recalled countless meetings of the Young Workers Liberation League. The FBI, who were keeping surveillance on these activities, confirmed that members of the San Bernardino–Riverside County Communist Party were "helping" Cuarón and were actively engaged "in the indoctrination of Chicanos."[3] The environment around the house, Valencia recalled, was never dull, as young people from different walks of life and hailing from different points in the region came and went.

In addition to the intellectual stimulation, the mountaintop was also a refuge for Valencia and Kenny Ortiz, who were evading federal authorities. Their objection to the Vietnam War and refusal to be inducted into the military forced them to go into hiding. As authorities actively searched for their whereabouts,

Cuarón offered his home as a safe haven. Nevertheless, after a failed attempt to organize the workers at the Skyline Weekender travel trailer plant in Hemet, Steve was arrested for outstanding warrants and jailed. After breaking a deal with federal agents (he was released with the agreement that he would voluntarily report to a military induction center), he fled the state altogether.[4] For Cuarón, it was not long before he became immersed in labor struggles with his employer in Mira Loma.

In June 1971, the union at Kingston Homes rejected a contract that included a cut in starting pay by 15 cents an hour—from $2.75 to $2.60—and workers went out on strike. In addition, the local demanded a one-year contract, more holidays, an improved vacation plan, grievance procedures, group insurance, as well as higher pay. The strikers also pledged to demand "more opportunities for employment of minority groups and women." As the local newspaper reported, the women were not passive participants in this labor dispute. "The women hope to have a representative on the negotiating team to make certain their requests will not be overlooked. They have joined the union and plan to make themselves heard."[5]

About ten wives of the sixty striking workers took part in the work stoppage and some 125 additional workers walked off their jobs in support. The women began walking the picket lines along with the men and soon recognized that they should be paid as well as be represented on the strike committee. "We decided we were doing everything men were doing," explained Karen Nacsin, "so we should get strike pay too."[6] Nacsin, whose husband was on the picket line, became a member of the strike committee. After some months, the committee agreed to provide the women with the same strike pay the men received on the picket line—twenty-five dollars per week. According to Cuarón, who had subsequently become chair of the strike committee, the women helped to "solidify the strikers." More importantly, "they demanded to be recognized and we realized their value." By then, the strike had entered its sixth month and it was clear to Cuarón that "without the women, the strike probably couldn't have continued this long."[7]

Despite the objection of some of the men, the women remained active in the strike. Sylvia and her children—Mita, Adela, and Fernando—regularly walked the picket line along with the other strikers. According to Mita, some of the men were clearly intimidated by the women: "Some are afraid of emotional problems at home. They are afraid the wives will take over." Sylvia took a more stoic view of working families: "A worker's wife never has an easy life. This [strike] just makes us tighten our belts a little tighter." She also appreciated the educational value in the strike for the entire family. "It's educational for the children to be here. They are workers' children. They should have no illusions about life; there is no glamour, it's all hard work. But they're learning to strike back."[8] Despite the sacrifice of the workers and their families, the strike was lost. Their eight-month-long struggle cost most of the striking workers their jobs, including Cuarón. Nevertheless, the outcome had a silver lining. In 1974, Cuarón gained employment as a custodian at the University of California, Riverside (UCR), ushering in a new chapter in the family's life.

Within a few months, Cuarón was elected president of Local 3246 of the American Federation of State, County and Municipal Employees (AFSCME). The union represented a number of lower-paid workers, such as clerical staff, custodians, food service workers, cooks, bus drivers, and health care workers. In addition to the normal running of the union, Cuarón made connections with the broader campus community to engage them on issues of labor rights, political activism, and education reform. As Sylvia recalled, Ralph organized an intimate grouping of faculty and staff called the "radical circle" that met regularly to discuss these issues.[9] Jim Smith recalled many of these meetings. When he arrived at UC Riverside as a graduate student in 1974, it did not take long for him to become immersed in the politics of the union. It was here that he became acquainted with Cuarón.

"I can't remember the first time I met Ralph," said Smith, "but I remember hearing about this custodian who knew more Marxism than the professors. And he was kind of a legend on the campus." Though Smith had come to UC Riverside to pursue a doctorate degree in economics, the allure of organizing workers and graduate students led him to abandon those academic goals for the time being. He soon joined the Communist Party and became immersed in the radical political milieu of Riverside and San Bernardino. According to Smith, "the Communist Party was very active there at the time," and he honed his skills by organizing workers at the Kaiser Steel plant in Fontana. It was during this period that Smith also learned more about the influential janitor from other party activists. There was clearly some "ambivalent attitude" toward Cuarón, Smith recalled, especially because he had been an "ex" communist and had a reputation for being undisciplined. Others in the party considered Cuarón to be a "loose cannon" and "uncontrollable," but Smith guessed they were "harboring grudges from things that happened years ago." Having already met Cuarón, these descriptions appeared unwarranted. Smith saw in Cuarón a kindred spirit and believed that "he [Cuarón] was ideologically a communist or a socialist, but, like me, had an anarchist streak."[10]

What mattered most was that the rank and file supported Cuarón, and "they saw in him . . . somebody who would stand up to supervisors, the boss, or whatever. And they could count on him." Cuarón helped to bring on new employees, promoted both women and men to leadership positions, and invited folks to his home in the mountains. "I know in my case," Smith remembered, "he didn't just consider me a political ally, but for a while almost like one of the family. There wasn't anything he wouldn't do for you if he liked you." But for some the most endearing memory of Cuarón during his time on the campus of UC Riverside was his impromptu visits to the offices of the faculty. With a broom in one hand and a sharp knowledge of theory, he discussed and debated with some of the best minds in academia. The only complaint that Smith could muster about Cuarón was his resounding voice at meetings. "I got the impression that he was used to speaking to hundreds or thousands in a huge CIO hall. And, so, he would get up and project, so you could probably hear him all the way across the campus."[11] Cuarón's primary interest remained translating academic theory and philosophy into practical solutions in the streets and in the workplace. He also collaborated closely with faculty, such as Edna Bonacich, and taught several "teach-in" classes open to the campus community and the public at large.

Serving as president of her local faculty union (American Federation of Teachers Local 1966), Edna Bonacich fondly recalled working with Cuarón. Despite the fact that UC Riverside was a nonunion workplace at the time, AFT thrived because the district could not take away the right of faculty employees to assemble. Although AFT, and other units, were limited to "meet and confer," with no authority for binding agreements, Bonacich states that "AFT met regularly, discussed campus issues, passed resolutions regarding public events, and generally provided a community for the leftist faculty." It was in this capacity that she met Cuarón. "Ralph had been a Communist and trade union activist in Los Angeles," Bonacich recalled, "and, as a working-class Chicano, knew a lot about racism as well. Ralph had little formal education but was one of smartest people I ever met. I became Ralph's student, and he taught me a ton about teaching, philosophy, and trade unionism." After the state passed legislation in 1975 allowing collective bargaining rights, AFSCME International turned its attention to the leadership of Local 3246. As Bonacich recalls, "they decided the existing locals were 'too leftist,' and tried to do us in."

This was not a new experience for Ralph, who led the fight to try to stop this takeover, even as we fought for strong union representation. I remember sitting on the floor through the night at statewide meetings of the UC AFSCME locals as

FIGURE 30 Ralph Cuarón speaking as president of the American Federation of State, County and Municipal Employees Local 3246, UC Riverside, 1983. Cuarón Family Collection.

we passionately argued about how to counter the domination of the international and still have a successful organization drive. These learning experiences lay the ground for my moving to work with the ILG (International Ladies Garment Workers Union) when the opportunity arose.[12]

As the struggle to retain the local's autonomy heated up in the early 1980s, Cuarón remained at the helm, but not for long. In 1984, he suffered a heart attack. With his health in serious decline, Cuarón did not see the end of this internecine labor conflict. He decided to retire that same year.

FIGURE 31   Ralph and Sylvia Cuarón, Riverside, California, 2000. Enrique M. Buelna Personal Collection.

Ralph Cuarón's leadership had left an indelible mark for many at the university. Later that year, the members of Local 3246 presented him with this formal acknowledgement:

> *Certificate of Appreciation from the American Federation of State, County and Municipal Employees, Service Local 3246.*
>
> We present this to Ralph Cuaron a past President of our local, a leader in Unionism and a front line fighter for peoples' rights. You'll never know how much you're appreciated and thought about as an example to us in Local 3246.
>
> So this modest thanks for helping to bring this union to us here at UC Riverside. You were on the front line in establishing what we have today. Better wages, binding arbitration, good benefits and a say in our working conditions.[13]

From this period until his death in 2002, Cuarón became, as his family eloquently described, a "'sit-down' radical—dialoguing with friends, students, family, and writing notes on his life's struggles."[14]

NOTES

PREFACE

1. Celia Rodríguez, in discussion with author, February 17, 1999.
2. Frances Fox Piven and Richard A. Cloward, *Poor People's Movements: Why They Succeed, How They Fail* (New York: Vintage Books, 1979), 41–92.
3. Celia Luna, in discussion with author, February 17, 1999; Patricia Morgan, *Shame of a Nation: A Documented Story of Police-State Terror Against Mexican-Americans in the U.S.A.* (Los Angeles: Los Angeles Committee for Protection of Foreign Born, 1954), 42–43; List of deportation cases, undated, box 10, file 1, Los Angeles Committee for Protection of Foreign Born Collection, 1950s–1960s, Southern California Library for Social Studies and Research (hereafter abbreviated as SCLSSR).
4. County of Los Angeles v. Cuaron and Carreon, Municipal Court of East Los Angeles Judicial District, County of Los Angeles (1969), 512–23.
5. County of Los Angeles, 771.
6. County of Los Angeles, 775.
7. Matt A. Barreto, Sylvia Manzano, and Gary Segura, "The Impact of Media Stereotypes on Opinions and Attitudes Towards Latinos," Latino Decisions, September 2012, http://www.nhmc.org/wp-content/uploads/2014/01/LD_NHMC_Poll_Results_Sept.2012.pdf. See also Leo Chavez, *The Latino Threat: Constructing Immigrants, Citizens, and the Nation*, 2nd ed. (Stanford, Calif.: Stanford University Press, 2013); Otto Santa Ana, *Juan in a Hundred: The Representation of Latinos on Network News* (Austin: University of Texas Press, 2013).
8. Theodore Schleifer, "Univision Anchor Ejected from Trump News Conference," *CNN Politics*, August 26, 2015, http://www.cnn.com/2015/08/25/politics/donald-trump-megyn-kelly-iowa-rally/index.html; Jia Tolentino, "Trump and the Truth:

The 'Mexican' Judge," *New Yorker*, September 20, 2016, http://www.newyorker.com /news/news-desk/trump-and-the-truth-the-mexican-judge.

9.   "Transcript of Donald Trump's Immigration Speech," *New York Times*, September 1, 2016, https://www.nytimes.com/2016/09/02/us/politics/transcript-trump -immigration-speech.html.

10.   See Walter J. Nicholls, The *DREAMers: How the Undocumented Youth Movement Transformed the Immigrant Rights Debate* (Stanford, Calif.: Stanford University Press, 2013).

INTRODUCTION

1.   As quoted in Michael Denning, *The Cultural Front: The Laboring of American Culture in the Twentieth Century* (London: Verso, 1997), xiv.

2.   Ralph Cuarón, in discussion with author, June 9, 1998.

3.   Mario T. García, *Memories of Chicano History: The Life and Narrative of Bert Corona* (Berkeley: University of California Press, 1994), 3–4.

4.   Albert Camarillo, *Chicanos in a Changing Society: From Mexican Pueblos to American Barrios in Santa Barbara and Southern California, 1848–1930* (Cambridge: Harvard University Press, 1979), 205.

5.   See Douglas Monroy, "Anarquismo y Comunismo: Mexican Radicalism and the Communist Party in Los Angeles During the 1930s," *Labor History* 24 (Winter 1983): 53; García, *Memories of Chicano History*, 126.

6.   Monroy, "Anarquismo y Comunismo," 54.

7.   See Dorothy Healey and Maurice Isserman, *Dorothy Healey Remembers: A Life in the American Communist Party* (New York: Oxford University Press, 1990). Healey makes similar observations on the party's rigid and centralized organizational structure.

8.   Maurice Isserman, *Which Side Were You On? The American Communist Party During the Second World War* (1983; repr., Urbana: University of Illinois Press, 1993), xi.

9.   Theodore Draper, *The Roots of American Communism* (New York: Viking Press, 1957).

10.   John Earl Haynes and Harvey Klehr, *In Denial: Historians, Communism, and Espionage* (San Francisco: Encounter Books, 2003). In *Spies: The Rise and Fall of the KGB in America* (2009), Haynes, Klehr, and Alexander Vassiliev continue to create a narrative that seeks no nuanced view of the CPUSA, the popular front, and the countless activities by Americans hoping to bring about a better world. No doubt spying did occur, but to impose the charge of spying on the activities of some Americans without substantial evidence to support it is merely groping in the dark for imaginary enemies.

11.   Isserman, *Which Side Were You On?*, xi.

12.   Isserman, *Which Side Were You On?*, xii.

13.   Douglas Monroy, "Fence Cutters, Sediciosos, and First-Class Citizens: Mexican Radicalism in America," in *The Immigrant Left in the United States*, ed. Paul Buhle

and Dan Georgakas (New York: State University of New York Press, 1996), 33–34. See also Monroy, *Rebirth: Mexican Los Angeles from the Great Migration to the Great Depression* (Berkeley: University of California Press, 1999), 226.

14. George Sánchez, *Becoming Mexican American: Ethnicity, Culture, and Identity in Chicano Los Angeles, 1900–1945* (New York: Oxford University Press, 1993), 249.

15. Zaragosa Vargas, "Tejana Radical: Emma Tenayuca and the San Antonio Labor Movement During the Great Depression," *Pacific Historical Review* 66, no. 4 (November 1997): 553–80; and Vargas, *Labor Rights Are Civil Rights: Mexican American Workers in Twentieth-Century America* (Princeton, N.J.: Princeton University Press, 2005), 126–33. See also David G. Gutiérrez, *Walls and Mirrors: Mexican Americans, Mexican Immigrants, and the Politics of Ethnicity* (Berkeley: University of California Press, 1995), 107–10.

16. Vicki L. Ruiz, "Una Mujer sin Fronteras: Luisa Moreno and Latina Labor Activism," *Pacific Historical Review* 73, no. 1 (2004): 1–20.

17. Mario T. García, *Mexican Americans: Leadership, Ideology, and Identity, 1930–1960* (New Haven, Conn.: Yale University Press, 1989), 199–227.

18. Sylvia Cuarón, in discussion with author, June 9, 1998.

19. Marc Simon Rodriguez, *Rethinking the Chicano Movement* (New York: Routledge, 2015), 84.

20. Robert Bauman, *Race and the War on Poverty: From Watts to East L.A.* (Norman: University of Oklahoma Press, 2008), 3–9.

21. Robert Gottlieb, Mark Vallianatos, Regina M. Freer, and Peter Dreier, *The Next Los Angeles: The Struggle for a Livable City* (Berkeley: University of California Press, 2005), 49–64.

CHAPTER 1

1. Lizbeth Cohen, *Making a New Deal: Industrial Workers in Chicago, 1919–1939* (Cambridge: Cambridge University Press, 1990), 249.

2. George Sánchez, *Becoming Mexican American: Ethnicity, Culture, and Identity in Chicano Los Angeles, 1900–1945* (New York: Oxford University Press, 1993), 213–26.

3. Francisco E. Balderrama and Raymond Rodríguez, *Decade of Betrayal: Mexican Repatriation in the 1930s* (Albuquerque: University of New Mexico Press, 1995), 99–122.

4. Benjamin Márquez, *Constructing Identities in Mexican-American Political Organizations: Choosing Issues, Taking Sides* (Austin: University of Texas Press, 2003), 9. For a longer view of Mexican-Anglo race relations, see William D. Carrigan and Clive Webb, *Forgotten Dead: Mob Violence Against Mexicans in the United States, 1848–1928* (Oxford: Oxford University Press, 2013).

5. Sánchez, *Becoming Mexican American*, 249.

6. Márquez, *Constructing Identities*, 11.

7. Rodolfo F. Acuña, *Corridors of Migration, The Odyssey of Mexican Laborers, 1600–1933* (Tucson: University of Arizona Press, 2007), 36–40.

8.   Carol J. Adams-Ramos, in collaboration with Jamie Freitas, "Ramos Family History," August 1, 2002, document courtesy of Sylvia Cuarón. This genealogy is an ongoing project periodically updated.

9.   Acuña, *Corridors of Migration*, 102–5. See also Linda Gordon, *The Great Arizona Orphan Abduction* (Cambridge, Mass.: Harvard University Press, 1999), 122–29.

10.   Acuña, *Corridors of Migration*, 112–18. See also Gordon, *Great Arizona Orphan Abduction*. In 1903, Mexican miners went out on strike in Clifton-Morenci to protest a reduction in their wages. One of the leaders of that strike was Abrán Salcido, who is believed to have been the brother of Geronima Salcido Ramos. Salcido arrived in Morenci in the 1890s and was present at the time the Ramos family lived in town. Salcido spent two years in prison for his participation in the strike and continued to be involved in union activities after his release. By 1906, he was an officer in the Mutualista Obreros Libres in Douglas, Arizona, and involved with the Partido Liberal Mexicano. In that same year, Salcido was arrested for revolutionary activities against the Porfirio Díaz government in Mexico. U.S. officials turned him over to the Díaz government, who promptly placed him in prison.

11.   Gordon, *Great Arizona Orphan Abduction*, 62–64.

12.   Gordon, *Great Arizona Orphan Abduction*, 22–33. See also Carey McWilliams, *North from Mexico: The Spanish-Speaking People of the United States* (New York: Greenwood Press, 1968), 31–33, 196–99.

13.   Gordon, *Great Arizona Orphan Abduction*, 33. See also Don Lee, "A Copper Town Digs Out," *Los Angeles Times*, April 13, 2004, sec. A1, 14.

14.   Sánchez, *Becoming Mexican American*, 192; Antonio Ríos-Bustamante, "As Guilty as Hell: Mexican Copper Miners and Their Communities in Arizona, 1920–1950," in *Border Crossings: Mexican and Mexican American Workers*, ed. John Mason Hart (Wilmington, Del.: Scholarly Resources, 1998), 172.

15.   Manuel Gamio, *The American Immigrant Collection* (New York: Arno Press and the New York Times, 1969), 153–59. The early 1920s had brought little improvement to the family's economic status, and this led some to question the value of remaining in the state altogether. Gamio interviewed a number of immigrants who described the often overwhelming feeling of powerlessness to overcome economic obstacles. Nivardo del Rio, for example, who worked in the Miami mines, described the work as backbreaking and the wages as sorely inadequate to meet their daily needs. "In order to make a few cents extra I have to kill myself working. And I really mean kill myself. That is why all the *paisanos* [our compatriots] get sick with consumption and other diseases even when they don't have an accident." Although del Rio aspired to economic independence, he came to believe that in the United States barriers were set in place to block the progress of Mexicans. See also Ríos-Bustamante, "As Guilty as Hell," 167. Ríos-Bustamante describes the varying systems of control imposed by the mining companies on workers and surrounding communities in their blind pursuit of profits. Key to this control was adherence to a racial hierarchy that supported the following: a dual wage scale; segregated housing on the margins of towns (usually located on outlying hilltops);

limits on all business on or near company property; limits on civic participation (usually excluding Mexicans from holding public office); and maintenance of an informal segregation in all public services and amenities.

16. Sánchez, *Becoming Mexican American*, 191.

17. Ralph Cuarón, in discussion with Jeff Garcílazo, January 21, 1995. I am grateful to Professor Garcílazo for graciously sharing with me his oral history manuscripts.

18. Ricardo Romo, *East Los Angeles: History of a Barrio* (Austin: University of Texas Press, 1983), chap. 4.

19. Antonio Ríos-Bustamante and Pedro Castillo, *An Illustrated History of Mexican Los Angeles, 1781–1985* (Los Angeles: University of California, Chicano Studies Research Center Publications, 1986), 130–31. See also Robin F. Scott, "The Mexican-American in the Los Angeles Area, 1920–1950: From Acquiescence to Activity" (PhD diss., University of Southern California, 1971), 116.

20. Campbell Gibson and Kay Jung, "Historical Census Statistics on Population Totals by Race, 1790 to 1990, and by Hispanic Origin, 1970 to 1990, For the United States, Regions, Divisions, and States," Working Paper No. 56 (Washington, D.C.: Population Division, U.S. Census Bureau, 2002); Warren S. Thompson, *Growth and Changes in California's Population* (Los Angeles: Haynes Foundation, 1955), 83–84.

21. William Deverell, *Whitewashed Adobe: The Rise of Los Angeles and the Remaking of Its Mexican Past* (Berkeley: University of California Press, 2004), 132–66.

22. Natalia Molina, *Fit to Be Citizens? Public Health and Race in Los Angeles, 1879–1939* (Berkeley: University of California Press, 2006), 76–93. See also Stephanie Lewthwaite, *Race, Place, and Reform in Mexican Los Angeles: A Transnational Perspective, 1890–1940* (Tucson: University of Arizona Press, 2009).

23. Ralph Cuarón, in discussion with Garcílazo. Ralph recalled that his father secured the lot sometime before the family moved to Los Angeles. Jesús may have built the home in preparation for the move from Arizona.

24. Romo, *East Los Angeles*, 65. See also Sánchez, *Becoming Mexican American*, 74–75.

25. The cabinet shop was located across from the Los Angeles Orphan Asylum. See Sánchez, *Becoming Mexican American*, 168.

26. Luis Leobardo Arroyo, "Industrial Unionism and the Los Angeles Furniture Industry, 1918–1954" (PhD diss., University of California, Los Angeles, 1979), 5, 10–14.

27. Ríos-Bustamante and Castillo, *Illustrated History*, 134.

28. Monroy, *Rebirth: Mexican Los Angeles from the Great Migration to the Great Depression* (Berkeley: University of California Press, 1999), 121.

29. Balderrama and Rodríguez, *Decade of Betrayal*, 38; Sánchez, *Becoming Mexican American*, chaps. 8 and 9; Monroy, *Rebirth*, chap. 4; Ríos-Bustamante and Castillo, *Illustrated History*, 149; Scott, "Mexican-American," 148–54.

30. Ralph Cuarón, in discussion with Garcílazo.

31. Ríos-Bustamante and Castillo, *Illustrated History*, 135. See also Sánchez, *Becoming Mexican American*, chap. 8.

32. Sánchez, *Becoming Mexican American*, 187, 203.

33. Ralph Cuarón, in discussion with Garcílazo.

34. Julia and George Mount, in discussion with author, March 17, 1999.

35. Vicki L. Ruiz, *Cannery Women, Cannery Lives: Mexican Women, Unionization, and the California Food Processing Industry, 1930–1950* (Albuquerque: University of New Mexico Press, 1987), 14–16, chap. 2; Balderrama and Rodríguez, *Decade of Betrayal*, 43–45.

36. Sylvia Cuarón, in discussion with author, February 8, 2004.

37. Ralph Cuarón, in discussion with Garcílazo.

38. Ralph Cuarón, in discussion with author, May 19, 1998. The Grand Central Market, or "El Mercado Central," is located at 317 South Broadway.

39. Ralph Cuarón, in discussion with Garcílazo. Jesús Cuarón died in 1953 from complications associated with asthma. He never fully recovered from depression, which caused him to play a marginal role in the life of his children and family. He had become, toward the end of his life, a very reclusive man, isolated and unable to interact even with Micaela, who lived in the same house. See also Cohen, *Making a New Deal*, 246–49.

40. Sánchez, *Becoming Mexican American*, 75, 198.

41. Ralph Cuarón, May 19, 1998. Medina was not married at the time she became a new homeowner.

42. See Martha Menchaca, *The Mexican Outsiders: A Community History of Marginalization and Discrimination in California* (Austin: University of Texas Press, 1995), 54–58. Menchaca discusses how the Ku Klux Klan were supported by local Anglo-American communities in maintaining a system of segregation against Mexicans in the churches, theaters, restaurants, stores, and neighborhoods. The Klan regularly used threatening letters to intimidate Mexican families not only in the Santa Paula and Santa Barbara areas, but throughout Southern California.

43. Sánchez, *Becoming Mexican American*, 200; Romo, *East Los Angeles*, 85–88.

44. Ralph Cuarón, in discussion with Garcílazo. Cuarón also recalled befriending local business owners on Whittier Boulevard near Indiana Street, in particular the owners of the local drugstore. "I used to go in there and stand by the magazine rack and read the comic books and they would never throw me out."

45. Romo, *East Los Angeles*, 164. See also Scott, "Mexican-American," chap. 2; Sánchez, *Becoming Mexican American*, chap. 10.

46. Ralph Cuarón, in discussion with Garcílazo.

47. Balderrama and Rodríguez, *Decade of Betrayal*, 15–20. See also Romo, *East Los Angeles*, 163–65; David G. Gutiérrez, *Walls and Mirrors: Mexican Americans, Mexican Immigrants, and the Politics of Ethnicity* (Berkeley: University of California Press, 1995), 71–74; Gregory Rodriguez, *Mongrels, Bastards, Orphans, and Vagabonds: Mexican Immigration and the Future of Race in America* (New York: Pantheon Books, 2007), 159–200.

48. State of California, Department of Industrial Relations, Governor's Mexican Fact-Finding Committee, *Mexicans in California: Report of Governor C. C. Young's Mexican Fact-Finding Committee* (San Francisco: State Printing Office, 1930), 12.

49. McWilliams, *North from Mexico*, 206–7.

50. Nancy Leys Stepan, *"The Hour of Eugenics": Race, Gender, and Nation in Latin America* (Ithaca, N.Y.: Cornell University Press, 1991), 2. See also Alexandra Minna Stern, *Eugenic Nation: Faults and Frontiers of Better Breeding in Modern America* (Berkeley: University of California Press, 2005).

51. Stepan, *"Hour of Eugenics,"* 137, 145–53. See also Alexandra Minna Stern, "'The Hour of Eugenics' in Veracruz, Mexico: Radical Politics, Public Health, and Latin America's Only Sterilization Law," *Hispanic American Historical Review* 91, no. 3 (2011): 431–43. Though Mexico and other Latin American countries were influenced by neo-Lamarckian eugenics, which sought preventive policies to secure a fit population, no citizen was safe from the dangers of these ideas. In their effort to eradicate "threats" to the social order (in this case, sex workers), Veracruz became ground zero for a social experiment to use sterilization as a public health tool. It is not clear from available records that "any sterilizations were actually performed" in the state, but the fact that an entire legal framework was used to justify and implement policies that identified an *enemy within* is certainly sobering. The attempt to use eugenics as a tool to "control the lives and bodies" of citizens illuminates the dangers of eugenics even in a place that professed to have a more nuanced interpretation of these concepts.

52. U.S. Congress, House, Committee on Immigration and Naturalization, *Western Hemisphere Immigration*, H.R. 8523, H.R. 8530, H.R. 8702, 71st Cong., 2d Sess. (1930), 436, qtd. in Rodolfo Acuña, *Occupied America: A History of Chicanos*, 3rd ed. (New York: HarperCollins, 1988), 201.

53. Sánchez, *Becoming Mexican American*, 214. Here Sánchez describes in some detail the concerted campaign to respond to the economic downturn by attacking Mexican communities.

54. Stern, *Eugenic Nation*, 82–114. Stern writes that over twenty thousand Californians became victims of the state's sterilization regime.

55. For a discussion of the legal prohibitions put in place to restrict employing Mexicans in public jobs, see Scott, "Mexican-American," 110–12.

56. Gibson and Jung, "Historical Census Statistics."

57. Fifteenth Census of the United States: 1930, in Molina, *Fit to Be Citizens?*, 7.

58. Gilbert G. González, *Mexican Consuls and Labor Organizing: Imperial Politics in the American Southwest* (Austin: University of Texas Press, 1999), 90.

59. Balderrama and Rodríguez, *Decade of Betrayal*, 121–22.

60. Monroy, *Rebirth*, 150.

61. See Cohen, *Making a New Deal*, chap. 5.

62. Studs Terkel, *Hard Times: An Oral History of the Great Depression* (New York: Pantheon Books, 1986), 340. "A crisis in capitalist society doesn't necessarily produce revolutionary changes or even a sense of alternatives, unless people have an awareness of some other kind of social order in which disasters of this kind wouldn't happen."

63. William Z. Foster, *History of the Communist Party* (New York: International Publishers, 1952), 257–91.

64. Fraser M. Ottanelli, *The Communist Party of the United States: From Depression to World War II* (New Brunswick, N.J.: Rutgers University Press, 1991), 18. As Ottanelli explains, the stock market crash in October 1929 exceeded even the CP's own prophecy.

65. Foster, *History of the Communist Party*, 281.

66. Foster, *History of the Communist Party*, 282. See also Francis Fox Piven and Richard A. Cloward, *Poor People's Movements: Why They Succeed, How They Fail* (New York: Vintage Books, 1979), chap. 2.

67. Foster, *History of the Communist Party*, 282–83; Foster, "Twenty Years of Communist Trade Union Policy," *The Communist* 28, no. 9 (September 1939): 804–16. See also Dorothy Healey and Maurice Isserman, *Dorothy Healey Remembers: A Life in the American Communist Party* (New York: Oxford University Press, 1990), 31. According to Healey, "At the start of the depression many of the unemployed blamed themselves for having lost their jobs, thinking it was all their own fault. Watching the changes in consciousness that took place over the next few years taught me lessons I never forgot, as we moved from agitation to organization and began to form neighborhood-based unemployment councils."

68. Ottanelli, *Communist Party*, 28. See also Lizbeth Cohen, *Making a New Deal*, chap. 6.

69. Gerald Horne, *Black Liberation/Red Scare: Ben Davis and the Communist Party* (Newark, N.J.: University of Delaware Press, 1994), 92.

70. J. Edgar Hoover, *Masters of Deceit: The Story of Communism in America* (New York: Henry Holt, 1958), 201–3, chap. 18; *The Communist Party Line*, prepared by J. Edgar Hoover, Director of the Federal Bureau of Investigation, Subcommittee to Investigate the Administration of the Internal Security Act and Other Internal Security Laws, U.S. Senate (September 23, 1961) (Washington, D.C.: U.S. Government Printing Office, 1961), 3–4.

71. Foster, *History of the Communist Party*, 285–88.

72. Terkel, *Hard Times*, 295.

73. Horne, *Black Liberation/Red Scare*, 39.

74. Horne, *Black Liberation/Red Scare*, 51–53; Robin D. G. Kelley, *Hammer and Hoe: Alabama Communists During the Great Depression* (1990; repr., Chapel Hill: University of North Carolina Press, 2015).

75. Horne, *Black Liberation/Red Scare*, 40. The ILD provided legal defense for jailed union members and raised their bail. The ILD played a crucial role during the TUUL and later CIO period.

76. Douglas Monroy, "Anarquismo y Comunismo: Mexican Radicalism and the Communist Party in Los Angeles During the 1930s," *Labor History* 24 (Winter 1983): 42.

77. Monroy, "Anarquismo y Comunismo," 58. See also Juan Gomez-Quiñones, *Mexican American Labor, 1790–1990* (Albuquerque: University of New Mexico Press, 1994), 100.

78. Monroy, "Anarquismo y Comunismo," 53.

79. Mario T. García, *Memories of Chicano History: The Life and Narrative of Bert Corona* (Berkeley: University of California Press, 1994), 126.

80. Monroy, "Anarquismo y Comunismo," 56. Monroy writes, "In Los Angeles the Workers Alliance (WA) concerned itself primarily with organizing people on WPA projects to demand higher wages. It also organized people on relief to demonstrate for increased state relief appropriations. The WA attempted to build small organizations of people on WPA or home relief but suffered from the huge turnover of people in the local branches." See also Piven and Cloward, *Poor People's Movements*, 75–76.

81. Celia Rodríguez, in discussion with author, February 17, 1999. See also Healey and Isserman, *Dorothy Healey Remembers*, 40–54, and Terkel, *Hard Times*, 294. William Patterson recalled that activists often tolerated the dangers associated with participating in the unemployed councils, hunger marches, and demonstrations because of the profound personal rewards. "I recall men and women being shot, engaging in these activities. There were hundreds charged with sedition, conspiracy, on one pretext or another. But it was a period of great schooling." See also American League Against War and Fascism, *California's Brown Book* (Los Angeles: American League Against War and Fascism, Los Angeles Committee, 1934), Dorothy Healey Collection, California State University, Long Beach, University Library, Special Collections/University Archives (hereafter cited as Healey Collection). The bulletin reported the following conditions imperiling civil liberties in the state of California: "Here in California, strikes, protests and organization are being met with savage brutality. When profits are threatened, constitution rights are pushed aside and violence is used to maintain special privilege. This violence is that of the 'constituted authorities' and are called 'Vigilantes,' 'Silver Shirts,' 'Safety Committees' and perhaps a dozen other names. At times these bands and the police act openly together; again the vigilantes attack 'independently'—but conveniently without police interference.

The police in their capacity as servants to the privileged, function in the manner of Hitler's political police, against the leaders of those who fight for the people's rights. Hundreds of those who stand to the fore in this fight of the oppressed are taken into the jails of the State of California and tortured. This is a reversion to the coercive methods of the Dark Ages. *It is incipient fascism.*"

82. Celia Rodríguez, February 17, 1999; Monroy, "Anarquismo y Comunismo," 52.

83. Julia and George Mount, March 17, 1999.

84. Virginia Escalante, Nancy Rivera, and Victor Valle, "Inside the World of Latinas": "For many Latinas, there is a double burden of racism and sexism. Five Women talk about their experiences, their family relationships, their lives and their concerns," *Los Angeles Times*, August 7, 1983.

85. American League Against War and Fascism, *California's Brown Book*, 12. The conditions of workers in California's fields were some of the most deplorable that federal investigators had seen. In their bulletin titled *California's Brown Book*, the Los Angeles chapter of the American League Against War and Fascism published

some of the observations reported by members of a special federal investigative committee. The committee members found it shameful, for example, that many workers were unable to earn salaries sufficient to "maintain even a primitive or savage standard of living." In reviewing the average wage of 204 pea pickers, the committee discovered that the daily wage amounted to a dismal "fifty-six cents." According to one investigator, "The workers live in camps, to the wretchedness of which no photographs and no words possible could do justice—with filth, disease and misery on all sides." Committee members, it appears, concluded that these extreme conditions were part and parcel of a systemic repression that thwarted any efforts to improve the lives of these workers.

86.   Vicki L. Ruiz, *From Out of the Shadows: Mexican Women in Twentieth-Century America* (New York: Oxford University Press, 1998), 74.

87.   González, *Mexican Consuls*, 78–81.

88.   Healey and Isserman, *Dorothy Healey Remembers*, 44. See also Gutiérrez, *Walls and Mirrors*, 105–6. Healey led the CP from 1928 to 1973.

89.   Healey and Isserman, *Dorothy Healey Remembers*, 42–46. See also Bruce Nelson, *Workers on the Waterfront: Seamen, Longshoremen, and Unionism in the 1930s* (Urbana: University of Illinois Press, 1988), 86–87. Nelson makes similar observations about the CP's work and influence among the maritime workers. Though Communists were very influential in the National Maritime Union, they did not control or dominate the organization. Seamen and longshoremen were unwilling to commit to the strict and dogmatic approach often applied by party cadre. See also Monroy, *Rebirth*, 228–30, and Zaragosa Vargas, *Proletarians of the North: A History of Mexican Industrial Workers in Detroit and the Midwest, 1917–1933* (Berkeley: University of California Press, 1993), 179.

90.   Jacqueline Jones et al. *Created Equal: A Social and Political History of the United States*, vol. 2, *From 1865* (New York: Longman, 2003), 756–57.

91.   See Judith Stephan-Norris and Maurice Zeitlin, *Left Out: Reds and America's Industrial Unions* (Cambridge: Cambridge University Press, 2003). For yet another interpretation of the adversarial position to the scholarship above (and which views the CPUSA as an appendage of Moscow and thus subservient to its control), see Harvey Klehr, John Earl Haynes, and Fredrikh Igorevich Firsov, *The Secret World of American Communism* (New Haven, Conn.: Yale University Press, 1995).

92.   Ottanelli, *Communist Party*, 65–78.

93.   Foster, *History of the Communist Party*, 370–71.

94.   Ottanelli, *Communist Party*, 52–54. See also Healey and Isserman, *Dorothy Healey Remembers*, 57. As Dorothy Healey contends, many Communists gladly participated in antifascist activities not because of directives from Moscow, but because they realized, on their own, the dangers Nazism represented to democracy and to the rights of the working class at home and abroad. "Hitler's triumph made terribly clear the danger of our earlier notions," Healey explains, "as well as the very stark differences between a fascist regime and 'bourgeois democracy' as represented by

someone like Franklin Delano Roosevelt. By the mid-1930s the issue of anti-fascism permeated all our mass work. In countries like France and Spain where big socialist movements existed, Communists sought to unite the Left into antifascist united fronts. In the United States we sought to work with the socialists, and we also began to reevaluate our earlier, highly critical assessment of the New Deal." See also Nelson, *Workers on the Waterfront*, 86–87.

95. David Brody, *Workers in Industrial America: Essays on the Twentieth Century Struggle*, 2nd ed. (New York: Oxford University Press, 1993), 96–105. See also Cohen, *Making a New Deal*, chaps. 5 and 6. See also Gomez-Quiñones, *Mexican American Labor*, 104–6.

96. Gómez-Quiñones, *Mexican American Labor*, 101. As Gómez-Quiñones explains, the Mexican workforce was undergoing significant changes during this period. "In brief, the Mexican population was becoming more widely distributed, urban dwelling, and industrially employed. The work force was nearly equally divided between those who worked in agriculture (40 percent) and those who did not (45 percent), including manufacturing (26 percent) and transportation (19 percent). The demographic trend was in the direction of the distribution then current in the Midwest, where 88 percent of the population was urban, with 54 percent employed in manufacturing and 36 percent in transportation."

97. Ruiz, *Cannery Women, Cannery Lives*, 41–43.

98. Sánchez, *Becoming Mexican American*, 234.

99. Michael Denning, *The Cultural Front: The Laboring of American Culture in the Twentieth Century* (London: Verso, 1997), 3–37.

100. Cohen, *Making a New Deal*, 8, 283–86.

101. Sánchez, *Becoming Mexican American*, 239.

102. *Report on Mexicans in the U.S.A.*, folder 1946, CPUSA Collection, Southern California Library for Social Studies and Research (hereafter cited as SCLSSR), 6.

103. García, *Memories of Chicano History*, 110.

104. Gutiérrez, *Walls and Mirrors*, 110–12.

105. First National Congress of the Mexican and Spanish American People of the United States, April 28–30, 1939, Digest of Proceedings, box 13, folder 9, Ernesto Galarza Papers, Department of Special Collections, Stanford University Libraries, Stanford, California (hereafter cited as Galarza Papers).

106. García, *Memories of Chicano History*, 112.

107. Acuña, *Occupied America*, 3rd ed., 256.

108. Ruiz, *From Out of the Shadows*, 94–97; Ruiz, "Una Mujer sin Fronteras: Luisa Moreno and Latina Labor Activism," *Pacific Historical Review* 73, no. 1 (February 2004): 1–20.

109. Mario T. García, *Mexican Americans: Leadership, Ideology, and Identity, 1930–1960* (New Haven, Conn.: Yale University Press, 1989), chap. 6; Sánchez, *Becoming Mexican American*, 249.

110. Healey and Isserman, *Dorothy Healey Remembers*, 76.

111. "Resolution Adopted by the Second Convention of the Spanish Speaking People's Congress of California—English-Speaking Panel," December 9 and 10, 1939, box 13, folder 9, Galarza Papers. See also Gutiérrez, *Walls and Mirrors*, 112–13.

112. Healey and Isserman, *Dorothy Healey Remembers*, 76; García, *Memories of Chicano History*, 108–16. Corona states that Salgado worked for the Laborers Local 300. See also Acuña, *Occupied America*, 3rd ed., 238–39.

113. Sánchez, *Becoming Mexican American*, 245–46.

114. García, *Mexican Americans*, 155.

115. *Report on Mexicans in the U.S.A.*, 6.

116. *Report on Mexicans in the U.S.A.*, 249.

117. García, *Memories of Chicano History*, 116.

118. Margarita never married. As the eldest in the family, she took on a lifelong responsibility to maintain the economic stability of the family. According to Sylvia Cuarón, when Margarita passed away in 2000, the family recognized the incredible source of strength and stability that she represented.

119. Ralph Cuarón, in discussion with author, May 19, 1998.

120. Ríos-Bustamante and Castillo, *Illustrated History*, 151.

121. Acuña, *Occupied America*, 3rd ed., 229–31; Arroyo, "Industrial Unionism," chap. 3; García, *Memories of Chicano History*, 113.

122. Ralph Cuarón, in discussion with Garcílazo.

123. Ralph Cuarón, in discussion with author, May 19, 1998.

124. Scott, "Mexican-American," 137–43. As Scott explains in his study of the Mexican American community during this period, Cuarón's estrangement from education was not unique. Some school officials in Los Angeles had identified factors such as poverty, hunger, poor diet, and overfatigue as contributing to a lack of attendance and educational success by Mexican American children.

125. See Mark A. Weitz, *The Sleepy Lagoon Murder Case: Race Discrimination and Mexican-American Rights* (Lawrence: University Press of Kansas, 2010).

126. García, *Memories of Chicano History*, 103–5. See also Gutiérrez, *Walls and Mirrors*, 121–23.

127. Mauricio Mazon, *The Zoot-Suit Riots: The Psychology of Symbolic Annihilation* (Austin: University of Texas Press, 1984), 4. See also McWilliams, *North from Mexico*, 239.

128. F. Arturo Rosales, *Chicano!: The History of the Mexican American Civil Rights Movement* (Houston: Arte Público Press, 1996), 99.

129. María E. Montoya, "The Roots of Economic and Ethnic Divisions in Northern New Mexico: The Case of the Civilian Conservation Corps," *Western Historical Quarterly* 26, no. 1 (Spring 1995): 15–34.

130. Ralph Cuarón, self-interview, recording no. 3.

131. Ralph Cuarón, self-interview, recording nos. 3 and 4.

132. Ralph Cuarón, self-interview, recording nos. 3 and 4.

133. Ralph Cuarón, self-interview, recording no. 5. Gutiérrez, *Walls and Mirrors*, 117–26. Gutiérrez presents a compelling argument that questions the thesis that "Mexican

Americans and Mexican nationals uniformly developed a new collective mentality and that the political and cultural conflicts which had divided them as recently as 1939 had somehow been resolved." Although Cuarón certainly yearned for acceptance by American mainstream society, he continually ran into barriers that negated those aspirations. His decision to embrace his Mexican identity would bring him into continuous conflict with the contradictions of American life.

134. Cohen, *Making a New Deal*, 281. Cohen writes that participation in the CCC changed the lives of young men in Chicago by exposing them "to different kinds of people from all over the country" and "broadening their horizons beyond their families, neighborhoods, and even cities."

135. Montoya, "Roots of Economic and Ethnic Divisions," 27–32. See also Nan Elsasser, Kyle Mackenzie, and Yvonne Tixier y Vigil, *Las Mujeres: Conversations from a Hispano Community* (New York: Feminist Press, 1980), 36–41; Rita Kasch Chegin, *Survivors: Women of the Southwest* (Las Cruces, N.M.: Yucca Tree Press, 1991), 27–43.

136. Ralph Cuarón, in discussion with author, April 21, 1998.

137. See Maggie Rivas-Rodríguez, ed., *Mexican Americans and World War II* (Austin: University of Texas Press, 2005); Ralph Cuarón, self-interview, recording no. 5. See also García, *Memories of Chicano History*, chap. 7; Richard Griswold del Castillo and Arnoldo De León, *North to Aztlán: A History of Mexican Americans in the United States* (New York: Twayne, 1996), chap. 6.

138. National Maritime Union of America, AFL-CIO, *On a True Course: The Story of the National Maritime Union of America, AFL-CIO* (Washington, D.C.: Merkle Press, 1967), 63.

139. See Brody, *Workers in Industrial America*, 112–13.

140. NMU, *On a True Course*, 63–64, 67. According to the publication, 5,579 seamen perished and 733 American ships were lost by the war's end.

141. NMU, *On a True Course*, 63–64, 67.

142. William L. Standard, *Merchant Seamen: A Short History of Their Struggles* (New York: International Publishers, 1947), 201–5.

143. Ralph Cuarón, April 21 and May 19, 1998. See Nelson, *Workers on the Waterfront*, 246. "Between 1941 and 1945 the number of deep-sea jobs increased from fifty-five thousand to two hundred thousand. The War Shipping Administration operated training schools 'on a nondiscriminatory basis,' graduating more than a hundred thousand candidates for maritime employment."

144. Nelson, *Workers on the Waterfront*, 31. Ralph Cuarón, May 19, 1998.

145. Ralph Cuarón, self-interview, recording no. 7.

146. Nelson, *Workers on the Waterfront*, 228–33. See Howard Kimeldorf, *Reds or Rackets? The Making of Radical and Conservative Unions of the Waterfront* (Berkeley: University of California Press, 1988), 12. By the late 1940s, Curran would become a staunch opponent of ILWU president Harry Bridges and the Left.

147. Standard, *Merchant Seamen*, 195. See Kimeldorf, *Reds or Rackets?*, 1–19, 50, 180n10. In his comparative study of dockside labor on the West Coast and East Coast of

the United States, Kimeldorf presents an intriguing argument in explaining the emergence of radical and conservative working-class cultures on the docks after WWI. While the West Coast enjoyed a rank-and-file radical upsurge, the East Coast (and in particular New York docks) experienced a mass movement characterized by a conservative work culture that struggled for the "narrowest of wage demands." The factors that helped lead seamen, loggers, and longshoremen toward a radical orientation included geographic mobility, exposure to groups with a wide range of ideas, rapid labor turnover, economic independence, wide range of job-related experiences, and exposure to the syndicalism of the IWW.

148. Nelson, *Workers on the Waterfront*, 259.
149. Standard, *Merchant Seamen*, 198.
150. Bruce Nelson, *Divided We Stand: American Workers and the Struggle for Black Equality* (Princeton, N.J.: Princeton University Press, 2001), chap. 3. See also Michael Torigian, "National Unity on the Waterfront: Communist Politics and the ILWU During the Second World War," *Labor Herald* 30 (Summer 1989): 423–26.
151. Nelson, *Divided We Stand*, 122–25; Clete Daniel, *Chicano Workers and the Politics of Fairness: The FEPC in the Southwest, 1941–1945* (Austin: University of Texas Press, 1991), 9. Manuel Ruiz, Los Angeles attorney, community organizer, and activist discusses how racism had affected, indeed divided, the Mexican community between the unfortunate (the "dark Mexicans") and the "little more fortunate" (those with European physical attributes).
152. Daniel, *Chicano Workers*, 3, chap. 3. In his examination of the FEPC and employment practices in the United States during WWII, Daniel provides numerous examples of how Mexican workers described their inferior status in the workforce. The following is a description of Carlos Rivera, a veteran employee with the Phelps Dodge Corporation: "When Rivera asked why he was being replaced by an Anglo worker who, like himself, was classified as a laborer, the foreman explained that he was simply 'putting an American in the American job.' 'I told him,' Rivera stated, 'I was born and raised here in the United States of America and that I was an American. He said: 'I don't care if you were born in China, you are still a Mexican and I am putting a white man in the job.'" Investigators for the FEPC soon became aware (from European American workers) that the term "American" was reserved to mean "Anglo-American." See also Nelson, *Workers on the Waterfront*, 247–49.
153. Donald T. Critchlow, "Communist Unions and Racism: A Comparative Study of the Responses of United Electrical Radio and Machine Workers and the National Maritime Union to the Black Question During World War II," *Labor History* 17 (Spring 1976): 230–44.
154. Ralph Cuarón, self-interview, recording no. 8.
155. Ralph Cuarón, self-interview, recording no. 9. During his self-imposed layover in Chile, Cuarón discovered, to his surprise, that the gracious hosts who allowed him temporary refuge in their home exhibited a complex, disturbing mix of Pan-Latin American nationalism, virulent racism against indigenous peoples, and fas-

cist sympathies for the Axis powers, particularly Germany. See also Critchlow, "Communist Unions and Racism," 239. The author explains that the refusal to hire African Americans by many shipping lines and discrimination by crew members remained a constant barrier to the NMU's stated policy of racial integration. See also Stepan-Norris and Zeitlin, *Left Out*, 240–41.

156. Daniel, *Chicano Workers*, 19–21, 25, 142, 186; see also chap. 3. In May 1943, Executive Order 9349 replaced the earlier 8802, which, in effect, turned out to be a reaffirmation of the original order.

157. Elizabeth R. Escobedo, *From Coveralls to Zoot Suits: The Lives of Mexican Women on the World War II Home Front* (Chapel Hill: University of North Carolina Press, 2015), 72–76.

158. Daniel, *Chicano Workers*, 122, 172. According to Daniel, despite the incredible leadership and enthusiasm shown by activists of the Mine, Mill and Smelter Workers to change the conditions of Mexican workers, the union was limited by its commitment to "helping win the war." See also Sánchez, *Becoming Mexican American*, 249.

159. Ralph Cuarón, self-interview, recording no. 7. Indeed, according to Cuarón, the prevalent notion was "that unions were some kind of foreign organization that was working against the government."

160. Ralph Cuarón, self-interview, recording no. 7.

161. See Critchlow, "Communist Unions and Racism," 238.

162. Torigian, "National Unity on the Waterfront," 432. Torigian presents an insightful examination of Communist unionism in the ILWU. He argues that traditional Cold War historiography that hyper-politicized the CP agenda and the more recent New Labor historiography that has tended to de-politicize Communist unionism have not provided an accurate examination of this powerful influence in American labor. He argues, for example, that CP unionism was certainly motivated by political considerations, but that these actions were more complex than an organization blindly following the dictates of a foreign government or narrowly concerned with bread and butter issues. American Communists held to steadfast convictions about class, power, and race as well as to a grand vision of the future that awaited the working man and woman of the world—and they acted on these convictions in their daily work and organizing activities.

163. NMU, *On a True Course*, 56. Ironically, this argument regarding the prioritization by the CP may not be too far off the mark. The party certainly had placed unity (no-strike pledge) at the forefront of its wartime agenda (after the invasion of the USSR by Nazi Germany in 1941). However, it must also be said that Communist activists time and again ran into incredible resistance against their efforts to end discrimination and advance workers of color. When these efforts were met with violent resistance, they often abandoned or toned down their aims in order to salvage their overall organizing program. See Critchlow, "Communist Unions and Racism," 239.

164. Gutiérrez, *Walls and Mirrors*, 121–38. As Gutiérrez describes, throughout this period Latinos in the United States had been denouncing the attacks on their

communities as violations of the Good Neighbor Policy, as hypocritical actions by a nation professing a high moral ground, as infringements on the rights of American citizens, and as actions that were counterproductive to the war effort. See also Daniel, *Chicano Workers*, 39, 131–32. In the same month that the riots broke out in Los Angeles, the Mexican government canceled its agreement with the United States to send contract workers to help with manpower shortages in the copper industry. As Daniel contends, the Mexican government made its decision apparently out of fear of a public uproar over the arrangement and because of "the copper industry's continuing discrimination against workers of Mexican ancestry." See Edward J. Escobar, *Race, Police, and the Making of a Political Identity: Mexican Americans and the Los Angeles Police Department, 1900–1945* (Berkeley: University of California Press, 1999), 210.

165. Interview with Celia Rodríguez, February 17, 1999.
166. Chester B. Himes, "Zoot Riots Are Race Riots," *The Crisis*, July 1943, 201, 222; Mazon, *Zoot-Suit Riots*, 64–65.
167. García, *Memories of Chicano History*, 143–44.
168. Mazon, *Zoot-Suit Riots*, 111–13.
169. Escobar, *Race, Police*, 186–203.
170. Márquez, *Constructing Identities*, 14–16.
171. Ralph Cuarón to Margaret Cuarón, written during World War II while Cuarón was on board a Liberty ship, [undated], letter graciously provided by Sylvia Cuarón. His reference to "babies" was in regards to his younger siblings, Dora and Irene, whom he viewed as his and Margaret's responsibilities to raise and nurture.
172. Nelson, *Workers on the Waterfront*, 2, chap. 4. See Nelson, *Divided We Stand*, 67, and Kimeldorf, *Reds or Rackets?*, 146–47. Nelson describes how in 1943 the ILWU introduced new recruits to the progressive traditions of the union through their mandatory education program. African American recruits, for example, often expressed their political awakening, their new consciousness, as deeply transforming. They often used religious imagery to describe this profound experience.
173. See Kimeldorf, *Reds or Rackets?*, 147.
174. Foster, *History of the Communist Party*, 371. Foster expressed great pride, as did many Communists and non-Communists, in the participation of fellow comrades in this memorable struggle of working-class people against fascist oppression. "The Communist parties gave all possible assistance to the embattled Spanish Republic. Most importantly, they organized the International Brigades, which were made up of communists and other antifascist fighters from all over Europe—France, Poland, Italy, Germany, Bulgaria, Great Britain, and elsewhere, and also from many countries of the Americas. Fifty-four nations were represented. All told, the International Brigades were estimated to number up to about 30,000 men."
175. Ralph Cuarón, April 21, 1998.
176. Healey and Isserman, *Dorothy Healey Remembers*, 63.
177. Ralph Cuarón, self-interview, recording no. 7.
178. Nelson Lichtenstein, Susan Strasser, and Roy Rosenzweig, *Who Built America? Working People and the Nation's Economy, Politics, and Society*, vol. 2 (New York:

Worth, 2000), 534–56; Nelson Lichtenstein, *Labor's War at Home: The CIO in World War II* (Cambridge: Cambridge University Press, 1982), 203–20.

179. Lichtenstein, *Labor's War at Home*, 207; George Lipsitz, *Rainbow at Midnight: Labor and Culture in the 1940s* (Urbana: University of Illinois Press, 1994), 121. Immediately following V-J Day in August 1945 and through 1946, workers in nearly all major sectors of the economy struck back with wildcat strikes, mass demonstrations, and general work stoppages reaching across the nation.

180. Lipsitz, *Rainbow at Midnight*, 116, 133; Lichtenstein, *Labor's War at Home*, 221–22.

181. Standard, *Merchant Seamen*, 179–81, 212; Nelson, *Workers on the Waterfront*, 91–92, 292n31.

182. Lipsitz, *Rainbow at Midnight*, 103–5.

183. California Legislature, *Report of Joint Fact-Finding Committee on Un-American Activities* (Sacramento: The Senate, 1947), 146, 161.

184. NMU, *On a True Course*, 56. California Legislature, *Report of Joint Fact-Finding Committee*, 162.

185. Kimeldorf, *Reds or Rackets?*, 9–10; Stepan-Norris and Zeitlin, *Left Out*, 28–29, 273–74.

186. George Lipsitz, *Rainbow at Midnight*, 158, 176–79.

187. Ellen Schrecker, *The Age of McCarthyism: A Brief History with Documents* (Boston: Bedford Books, 1994), 51–52.

188. Stepan-Norris and Zeitlin, *Left Out*, 273.

189. Ralph Cuarón, in discussion with author, June 9, 1998.

190. Frances Lym (also known as Lavern Frances Lym or Lynn) would revert back to Francisca Flores sometime in the 1950s. As Ralph and Sylvia Cuarón recalled, Varela had been an older veteran of the party and a social worker by trade. At one point during this period, Varela attempted to cure Dorothy Healey of her chain-smoking habit. He failed.

191. Ralph Cuarón, February 24, 1999.

CHAPTER 2

1. I will use "Augustino" as the spelling for Salcido's name. Other spellings have included "Augustin," "Augustine," "Austine."

2. Edward J. Escobar, *Race, Police, and the Making of a Political Identity: Mexican Americans and the Los Angeles Police Department, 1900–1945* (Berkeley: University of California Press, 1999), 15–16, 288–89.

3. "Joseph Scott, 81, Honored by Civic, Business Leaders," *Los Angeles Examiner*, July 21, 1948.

4. Guy Endore, *Justice for Salcido* (Los Angeles: Civil Rights Congress of Los Angeles, 1948), box 74, p. 3, Dorothy Healey Collection, California State University, Long Beach, University Library, Special Collections/University Archives (hereafter cited as Healey Collection).

5. Albert Camarillo, *Chicanos in California: A History of Mexican Americans in California* (San Francisco: Boyd and Fraser, 1984), 68.

6. See George Sánchez, *Becoming Mexican American: Ethnicity, Culture, and Identity in Chicano Los Angeles, 1900–1945* (New York: Oxford University Press, 1993), chap. 11.

7. Howard Zinn, *A People's History of the United States*, 20th anniversary ed. (New York: HarperCollins, 1999), 407–8.

8. Ronald Takaki, *Double Victory: A Multicultural History of America in World War II* (Boston: Little, Brown and Company, 2001), 6.

9. U.S. Selective Service System, *Selective Service and Victory: The 4th Report of the Director of Selective Service, 1844–1945*, with a supplement for 1946–1947 (Washington, D.C.: U.S. Government Printing Office, 1948), 187–90.

10. Lorena Oropeza, *¡Raza Sí! ¡Guerra No! Chicano Protest and Patriotism During the Viet Nam War Era* (Berkeley: University of California Press, 2005), 36.

11. Henry A. J. Ramos, *The American GI Forum: In Pursuit of the Dream, 1948–1983* (Houston: Arte Público Press, 1998), 2.

12. See Raul Morin, *Among the Valiant: Mexican-Americans in WWII and Korea* (Los Angeles: Borden, 1963), 277; Camarillo, *Chicanos in California*, 78–83.

13. Maggie Rivas-Rodríguez, ed., *Mexican Americans and World War II* (Austin: University of Texas Press, 2005), xviii.

14. Ralph Cuarón, in discussion with author, June 18, 1998. See also Takaki, *Double Victory*, 20.

15. Bruce Nelson, *Workers on the Waterfront: Seamen, Longshoremen, and Unionism in the 1930s* (Urbana: University of Illinois Press, 1988), 29.

16. Howard Kimeldorf, *Reds or Rackets? The Making of Radical and Conservative Unions of the Waterfront* (Berkeley: University of California Press, 1988), 20–22.

17. Federal Bureau of Investigation records document that Ralph Cuarón had been a member of the Harbor Club, which they described as "the 68th Assembly District Section of the Los Angeles County CP"; contained in Sylvia Cuarón's FBI file, 100-HQ-400483.

18. Ralph Cuarón, in discussion with author, June 9, 1998.

19. Ralph Cuarón, June 9, 1998.

20. Ralph Cuarón, June 9, 1998.

21. Sylvia Cuarón FBI file, 100-HQ-400483.

22. Ralph Cuarón, June 18, 1998.

23. Ralph Cuarón, June 18, 1998.

24. Rodolfo Acuña, *Occupied America: A History of Chicanos*, 3rd ed. (New York: HarperCollins, 1988), 289. See also F. Arturo Rosales, *Chicano! The History of the Mexican American Civil Rights Movement* (Houston: Arte Publico Press, 1996), 96–97; Sánchez, *Becoming Mexican American*, chap. 12; Camarillo, *Chicanos in California*, 78–83. See also Martha Menchaca, *The Mexican Outsiders: A Community History of Marginalization and Discrimination in California* (Austin: University of Texas Press, 1995), chap. 5.

25. Menchaca, *Mexican Outsiders*, 103–8. See Morin, *Among the Valiant*, 278. Morin also writes that many Mexican Americans made conscious efforts to break with the "old days." Thus, long-established "edicts, taboos, restrictions, traditions, and

customs" were now openly questioned. "We acquired new ways in everyday doings. New thoughts and dreams entered our minds."

26. Benjamin Márquez, *LULAC: The Evolution of a Mexican American Political Organization* (Austin: University of Texas Press, 1993), 1.

27. Cynthia E. Orozco, *No Mexicans, Women, or Dogs Allowed: The Rise of the Mexican American Civil Rights Movement* (Austin: University of Texas Press, 2009), 2.

28. Márquez, *LULAC*, 17.

29. David G. Gutiérrez, *Walls and Mirrors: Mexican Americans, Mexican Immigrants, and the Politics of Ethnicity* (Berkeley: University of California Press, 1995), 76.

30. Orosco, *No Mexicans*, 2.

31. Márquez, *LULAC*, 42–45, 56.

32. Gutiérrez, *Walls and Mirrors*, 74–87.

33. Márquez, *LULAC*, 51–55.

34. Vicki Ruiz, "South by Southwest: Mexican Americans and Segregated Schooling, 1900–1950," *OAH Magazine of History* 15 (Winter 2001). See also, Márquez, *LULAC*, 53–54; Rosales, *Chicano!*, 104–5; Jacqueline Jones et al., *Created Equal: A Social and Political History of the United States*, vol. 2, *From 1865* (New York: Longman, 2003), 808, 844–46; Acuña, *Occupied America*, 3rd ed., 289.

35. Ramos, *American GI Forum*, 27–31.

36. Shana Beth Bernstein, "Building Bridges at Home in a Time of Global Conflict: Interracial Cooperation and the Fight for Civil Rights in Los Angeles, 1933–1953" (PhD diss., Stanford University, 2003).

37. U.S. Census of Population, *Special Report: Persons of Spanish Surname*, prepared under the supervision of Howard G. Brunsman, Chief Population and Housing Division (Washington, D.C.: U.S. Department of Commerce, Bureau of the Census, 1953), Healey Collection.

38. Eric Raymond Avila, "Reinventing Los Angeles: Popular Culture in the Age of White Flight, 1940–1965" (PhD diss., University of California, Berkeley, 1997), 20.

39. Avila, "Reinventing Los Angeles," 19.

40. Thomas Borstelmann, *The Cold War and the Color Line: American Race Relations in the Global Arena* (Cambridge: Harvard University Press, 2001), 53–54.

41. Beatrice Griffith, "Viva Roybal—Viva America," in *Major Problems in Mexican American History*, ed. Zaragosa Vargas (Boston: Houghton Mifflin, 1999), 342–46.

42. Bernstein, "Building Bridges at Home," 219–82.

43. Maria Linda Apodaca, "They Kept the Home Fires Burning: Mexican-American Women and Social Change" (PhD diss., University of California, Irvine, 1994), 72–75.

44. Helen Taylor, untitled, *Daily People's World*, undated, box 3, folder 26, Civil Rights Congress Collection, Southern California Library (hereafter cited as CRC Collection, SCL).

45. Apodaca, "They Kept the Home Fires Burning," 57.

46. Alinsky's philosophy was based on grassroots political organizing for mass power. He believed in working within the existing economic and political systems and

working gradually for change. This change could only occur, however, when the masses formed active alliances with different groups in society to challenge existing structures and systems of power. See Saul D. Alinsky, *Reveille for Radicals* (Chicago: University of Chicago Press, 1946); and *Rules for Radicals: A Pragmatic Primer for Realistic Radicals* (1971; repr., New York: Random House, 1989).

47. Acuña, *Occupied America*, 3rd ed., 284–87; Griffith, "Viva Roybal," 342–46; Apodaca, "They Kept the Home Fires Burning," 75–77.

48. Gutiérrez, *Walls and Mirrors*, 86–95, 118.

49. Gutiérrez, *Walls and Mirrors*, 175–77.

50. Márquez, *LULAC*, 42–45. See also Gutiérrez, *Walls and Mirrors*, 86–87, and Lorena Oropeza, *La Batalla Esta Aqui: Chicanos Oppose the War in Vietnam* (Ithaca, N.Y.: Cornell University Press, 1996), 32.

51. Márquez, *LULAC*, 46.

52. Ralph Cuarón, in discussion with author, January 22, 1999.

53. *It's You They're After*, Civil Rights Congress (Los Angeles: Published by the CRC, 1949), 15, Carey McWilliams Archives, Special Collections, University Research Library, University of California, Los Angeles (hereafter cited as Carey McWilliams Archives). "Henry Steinberg was one of the ten who served two separate jail sentences as a result of the [1948] Grand Jury investigation, the second on a conviction of criminal contempt for refusing to answer a similar series of questions. His second conviction kept him in the county jail for fifteen days. *Steinberg was imprisoned for the second time while running for Office Number Four of the Los Angeles Board of Education. He ran as a Communist, made speeches at meetings and over the radio as a Communist. The election was held while he was still in jail, and he received almost 35,000 votes in Los Angeles*" (emphasis in original). See also Dorothy Healey and Maurice Isserman, *Dorothy Healey Remembers: A Life in the American Communist Party* (New York: Oxford University Press, 1990), 135–36.

54. Ramos, *American GI Forum*, 51.

55. Luis Leobardo Arroyo, "Industrial Unionism and the Los Angeles Furniture Industry, 1918–1954" (PhD diss., University of California, Los Angeles, 1979), 129–30.

56. Acuña, *Occupied America*, 3rd ed., 230; Sánchez, *Becoming Mexican American*, 240–41; Mario T. García, *Memories of Chicano History: The Life and Narrative of Bert Corona* (Berkeley: University of California Press, 1994), 113.

57. Maurice Isserman, *Which Side Were You On? The American Communist Party During the Second World War* (1983; repr., Urbana: University of Illinois Press, 1993), 7.

58. See Elaine Tyler May, *Homeward Bound: American Families in the Cold War Era* (New York: Basic Books, 1988), and Lyn Spigel, *Make Room for TV: Television and the Family Ideal in Postwar America* (Chicago: University of Chicago Press, 1992).

59. Gerald Horne, *Communist Front? The Civil Rights Congress, 1946–1956* (Rutherford, N.J.: Fairleigh Dickinson University Press, 1988), 22.

60. *Civil Rights Congress Tells the Story*, pamphlet (Los Angeles: Printed by the Civil Rights Congress, undated). Courtesy of Celia Rodríguez. See also CRC Collection, SCL.

61. Horne, *Communist Front?*, 22.
62. Horne, *Communist Front?*, 17.
63. Horne, *Communist Front?*, 22.
64. Horne, *Communist Front?*, 330.
65. *Civil Rights Congress Tells the Story*, 1.
66. David P. Gardner, *The California Oath Controversy* (Berkeley: University of California Press, 1967), 9. See also Horne, *Communist Front?*, 335–36. In 1951, the CRC chapters in the Los Angeles area included Hollywood, Santa Monica, San Pedro, Long Beach, Tubman, Eastside, Central Avenue, East Hollywood, Echo Park, West Jefferson, and the San Fernando Valley. See also *Civil Rights Tells the Story*, 1–4. In Southern California alone, 464 dues-paying members were strewn across eleven subchapters. By 1952, the CRC could claim from forty to seventy chapters across the country. It was not long before the Un-American Activities Committee turned its omnipotent gaze toward the fledgling CRC. Indeed, as early as 1947 the CRC received the dubious designation of "communist front." See also California Legislature, *Report of Joint Fact-Finding Committee on Un-American Activities*, 57th Legislative Session (Sacramento, Calif., 1947); *Fourth Report of the Senate Fact-Finding Committee on Un-American Activities: Communist Front Organizations* (Sacramento: The Senate, 1948), 201–8.
67. Jack B. Tenney, *Red Fascism: Boring from Within . . . By the Subversive Forces of Communism* (Los Angeles: Federal Printing Company, 1947), xi. See also Horne, *Communist Front?*, 17.
68. Tenney, *Red Fascism*, xi.
69. Kevin Allen Leonard, "The Changing Face of Racism: Japanese Americans and Politics in California, 1943–1946" (master's thesis, University of California, 1988), 119.
70. Leonard, "Changing Face," 112–24. See also J. Edgar Hoover, *Masters of Deceit: The Story of Communism in America* (New York: Henry Holt, 1958), chap. 18.
71. Borstelmann, *Cold War and the Color Line*, 64–66.
72. Escobar, *Race, Police*, 11.
73. Escobar, *Race, Police*, 12.
74. See Robert Trojanowicz and Bonnie Bucqueroux, *Community Policing: A Contemporary Perspective* (Cincinnati, Ohio: Anderson, 1990), 57–58.
75. Escobar, *Race, Police*, 17.
76. Horne, *Communist Front?*, 16. As one former CRC leader stated, these acts were a "conscious policy . . . to keep the Blacks in a state of subjugation."
77. Horne, *Communist Front?*, 330.
78. Horne, *Communist Front?*, 338. See also Gerald Horne, *Paul Robeson: The Artist as Revolutionary* (London: Pluto Press, 2016), 61, 122. Horne discusses Patterson's broader cultural influences in the arts and music scene in Los Angeles.
79. Horne, *Communist Front?*, 332.
80. *Civil Rights Congress Tells the Story*, 4.
81. *Civil Rights Congress Tells the Story*, 3–4. "Emil Freed, long active as a fighter for civil rights both in and outside the ranks of the labor movement, joined the staff of

CRC early in 1950. He had been just released from jail after having served a year's sentence resulting from the mass arrests in the Hollywood Studio Strike in 1946. Mrs. [Marguerite] Robinson, herself, in the short period of two years has become not only a leader of the CRC but a recognized leader of the Negro people in this city. Her militancy in the fight for the rights of all minority peoples, her understanding of the relationship of these rights to the fight for the rights of labor has amply qualified her as Executive Director of CRC. Her particular contribution has been in the field of extradition and her work has been materially responsible for the lifting of extradition from the defense of a single individual to the national question of extradition as a positive action against the Jimcrow South and its northern confederates."

82. Michael Denning, *The Cultural Front: The Laboring of American Culture in the Twentieth Century* (London: Verso, 1997), 13. The ILD was formed in 1925 to defend civil liberties and struggle against lynching and labor repression. Denning writes: "The 'mass' or 'labor' defense developed by the International Labor Defense (ILD) combined legal action with a mass protest campaign, building popular support for jailed unionists, political prisoners, immigrant radicals facing deportation, and black defendants facing racist trials."

83. Escobar, *Race, Police*, 227, 279; Horne, *Communist Front?*, 330.

84. *Civil Rights Congress Tells the Story*, 3.

85. *Civil Rights Congress Tells the Story*, 3.

86. Ralph and Sylvia Cuarón, in discussion with author, February 24, 1999.

87. Robin D. G. Kelley, *Race Rebels: Culture, Politics, and the Black Working Class* (New York: Free Press, 1994), 110. However, the party's role as the vanguard had not always proved advantageous. For example, in the case of the CP-sponsored League of Struggle for Negro Rights and its publication the *Liberator* that demand for control (for a rigid adherence to the party line) eventually led to the organization's premature demise. See also Isserman, *Which Side Were You On?*, 22–25. See also Robbie Lieberman, *The Strangest Dream: Communism, Anticommunism, and the U.S. Peace Movement, 1945–1963* (Syracuse, N.Y.: Syracuse University Press, 2000), 15, 21–23. Here, Lieberman presents a compelling examination of how the CPUSA participated in the demise of several organizations (e.g., American League Against War and Fascism and the American Student Union) involved in the peace movement of the 1930s (though, certainly, not intentionally).

88. Ralph and Sylvia Cuarón, February 24, 1999.

89. Ralph and Sylvia Cuarón, February 24, 1999.

90. Ralph and Sylvia Cuarón, February 24, 1999.

91. Ralph and Sylvia Cuarón, February 24, 1999. Ralph Cuarón, June 9, 1998. See also Horne, *Communist Front?*, 316, 347.

92. Ralph and Sylvia Cuarón, February 24, 1999. Ralph Cuarón, June 9, 1998.

93. Ralph and Sylvia Cuarón, February 24, 1999. Ralph Cuarón, June 9, 1998.

94. Ralph and Sylvia Cuarón, February 24, 1999. Ralph Cuarón, June 9, 1998.

95. Ralph and Sylvia Cuarón, February 24, 1999. Ralph Cuarón, June 9, 1998.

96. Ramón Moran Welch to "Dear Friends," March 1, 1947, CRC Collection, SCL.

97. William R. Bidner and Leroy Parra to "Dear Friend," June 17, 1947, CRC Collection, SCL; "Is Too Young to Die," undated, box 3, file 27, CRC Collection, SCL. The second individual implicated in the shooting was identified as officer "Kaiser" in the documents. The CRC also implicated Officer Keyes, describing him as "notorious in the Mexican community, trigger happy, a bully," in paralyzing Joaquin Lopez with a shot to the head on January 10, 1946.

98. American League Against War and Fascism, *California's Brown Book* (Los Angeles: Published by the American League Against War and Fascism, Los Angeles Committee, 1934), Healey Collection. Gallagher had been an early advocate for LAPD reform and from time to time paid dearly for his outspoken activism. For example, in 1934, Red Squad agents beat Gallagher, two war veterans, and the director of the American Civil Liberties Union during a Los Angeles City Council meeting. The beating was triggered by Gallagher's demand that the Red Squad be prosecuted for its wanton violence and destruction of private property.

99. Press release, undated; letter, June 17, 1947, box 13, folder 5, CRC Collection, SCL.

100. Rodolfo F. Acuña, *A Community Under Siege: A Chronicle of Chicanos East of the Los Angeles River, 1945–1975* (Los Angeles: Chicano Studies Research Center, Publications, University of California, 1984), 26. According to Acuña, "an interesting link existed between white liberals and Mexican American political activists in Boyle Heights. This was a period when Jews and whites fled the Heights and [the] Mexican population increased. The Jewish community had many people who were concerned with human rights and saw the lack of access by Mexicans to protective institutions as undemocratic."

101. In 1947, the AVC represented over five thousand veterans of World War II in the county of Los Angeles. The AVC came under investigation by state senator Jack B. Tenney's Joint Fact-Finding Committee on Un-American Activities in 1947 for alleged "Communist influence" (California Legislature, *Report of Joint Fact-Finding Committee on Un-American Activities*, 231–33).

102. Supporter list, undated, box 13, folder 5, CRC Collection, SCL; "Proposed Officers and Executive Board of the Mexican-American Civil Rights Congress," undated, box 13, folder 5, CRC Collection, SCL.

103. "Mexican Group Holds Dance," *Eastside Sun*, August 1947.

104. Ralph Cuarón et al., "Emergency Meeting Announcement," September 26, 1947, box 13, folder 5, CRC Collection, SCL. Cuarón was the treasurer, Belvedere Chapter–AVC, and Castro was business representative–UFWA.

105. William R. Bidner to "Dear Friends," October 22, box 13, folder 5, CRC Collection, SCL; George Bodle, Chairman, AVC, Los Angeles Area Council to Assistant Chief of Police Joseph Reed, October 23, 1947, box 13, folder 5, CRC Collection; Krugar Clark, Pres. UFWA Local 576, CIO, to Chief Joseph Reed, October 24, 1947, box 13, folder 5, CRC Collection; George Bodle to Police Chief Joseph Reed, December 2, 1947, box 13, folder 5, CRC Collection; George Bodle to Police Chief Joseph Reed, December 2, 1947, box 13, folder 5, CRC Collection. See also Luis

Leobardo Arroyo, "Chicano Participation in Organized Labor: The CIO in Los Angeles, 1938–1950, An Extended Research Note," *Aztlan* xi, no. 2 (Summer 1975): 297.

106. Endore, *Justice for Salcido*, 6.

107. Endore, *Justice for Salcido*, 6.

108. Endore, *Justice for Salcido*, 11.

109. Endore, *Justice for Salcido*, 13.

110. Endore, *Justice for Salcido*, 13. See also Acuña, *Occupied America*, 3rd ed., 290–91.

111. Endore, *Justice for Salcido*, 15.

112. Bidner to Daniel G. Marshall, Catholic Interracial Committee, March 16, 1948, box 3, folder 28, CRC Collection, SCL. The attachment titled "Delegation to Dist. Atty. Simpson on Salcido Case-3-19-48" included the following additional names: Arnold Shimberg and Bessie McDonald (AYD); George Herman (IUMMSW Local 700); Max Berlow (IWO); Celia Frimkess (PCA); Minna K. Berlow (JPFO); Nell Higman (Home Protective Association); Dorothy Andrews, F. Massarik, and Nina Klowden (L.A. Youth Council); Irving Sarnoff (AYD-Earl Robinson); Carrie Carroll (L.A. CIO Women's Auxiliary); Nena Gutierrez; and Ben Rinaldo (AVC).

113. Endore, *Justice for Salcido*, 15. Endore described the escalating police repression throughout the Eastside as "Operation Strong-Arm." "Soon the whole district was aware that the police were bearing down. And residents understood this to mean: keep your nose clean, brother, if you know what's good for you." Assistant District Attorney Simpson also refused to meet with a "delegation of 50 representative citizens on . . . Tuesday, March 22," press release, undated, box 3, folder 29, CRC Collection, SCL.

114. Los Angeles CIO Council, *Resolution on the Slaying of Augustino Salcido and Police Terrorism Against Mexican Americans*, March 19, 1948, box 3, folder 28, CRC Collection, SCL; Endore, *Justice for Salcido*, 15–17; "Rally to Hear Cop Slaying Witnesses," *Daily People's World,* March 31, 1948; "Background in Augustino Shooting," March 24, 1948, box 3, folder 27, CRC Collection. "Since the shooting, Gallegos has been picked up by the police twice and booked on suspicion of drunkenness. The second time, he was picked up on Monday, March 15, after the inquest. No charges were filed, but while at the police station, he was roughed up by the police and told to get out of town. . . . Oscar del Campo was picked up by the police, first booked on a charge of suspicion of drunkenness, then the charge was changed to suspicion of robbery, and finally to a charge of vagrancy. Del Campo asserts that he was told to get out of town or the same thing would happen to him as happened to Salcido. . . . The Salcido family was picked up by the police twice after the shooting, taken to headquarters, questioned, detained, then released. No charges were filed." Oscar del Campo, "Affidavit," March 27, 1948, box 3, folder 28, CRC Collection.

115. Endore, *Justice for Salcido*, 16.

116. Sylvia Cuarón FBI file, 100-HQ-400483.

117. *Civil Rights Congress Tells the Story*, 9. The "Pull Over" was one of several methods of harassment used to intimidate minority groups on a community-wide basis. The case of Mike Ortiz demonstrates the point. "On a Saturday night Mike Ortiz was driving to Montebello to visit relatives. A car, whose driver was in civilian clothes, started following him a few blocks east of Atlantic. After several blocks he crowded Ortiz to the curb, shouting, 'Pull over, you dirty Mexican!' Ortiz kept going, finally stopped to find out why he was being followed. The man flashed a badge and demanded to know what Ortiz had been drinking. Then he called other police since he was off duty. The other police arrived, and asked in abusive language where the dope was. Ortiz denied having any dope or having had anything to drink. They parked Ortiz' car in a garage, although he protested at the expense, and took him to the station at Ford and Whittier. When he objected to being classified as a Mexican on their records, saying he was an American, they struck him. He was held in the station until the next morning, then taken to the County Jail. Sunday night his wife was able to bail him out. He was charged with drunken and reckless driving."

118. Ralph Cuarón, in discussion with author, May 12, 1998.

119. Sylvia's mother's family name was Spivak.

120. Sylvia Cuarón, in discussion with author, September 16, 2004.

121. Located on Fifty-Eighth Street and Sixth Avenue in Manhattan.

122. "Moi Solotaroff. A concert, puppet production, and auction of paintings for the sale of war bonds." On behalf of the New York State War Savings Staff, U.S. Treasury, The Group Collective Playbill (New York: Barbizon-Plaza Theatre, 1943). Courtesy of Sylvia Cuarón.

123. Now renamed César Chávez Avenue.

124. Sylvia Cuarón FBI file, 100-HQ-400483.

125. Sylvia Cuarón, September 16, 2004.

126. Sylvia Cuarón, in discussion with author, July 17, 2001. She worked in the maintenance department, which was under the direction of Ralph McMullen, who in turn reported to Howard L. Holtzendorff, the executive director of the Housing Authority.

127. Sylvia Cuarón, July 17, 2001. In looking back at the weekend "seminar," or retreat, Sylvia now believes that the CP may have sponsored the event, or at least participated in this "weekend away from work." She recalled that Frank Wilkinson and Leticia Innes were also present at the retreat.

128. Sylvia Cuarón, July 17, 2001. Joe Esquith had been the center's director for many years and had supported numerous progressive causes. Esquith would later be hounded by state senator Jack Tenney of the California Senate Fact-Finding Committee on Un-American Activities.

129. Sylvia Cuarón, July 17, 2001.

130. Rodolfo Acuña, *Occupied America: A History of Chicanos*, 4th ed. (New York: Longman, 2000), 282–83.

131. Connelly to Grillo, April 1, 1948, box 3, folder 28, CRC Collection, SCL.

132. Dolores Hayden, *Power of Place: Urban Landscapes as Public History* (Cambridge: MIT Press, 1995), 192; Acuña, *Occupied America*, 4th ed., 282–83.
133. "The Verdict: Murder," *Daily People's World*, April 10, 1948, undated press release, box 3, folder 29, CRC Collection, SCL.
134. "Verdict: Murder." The citizen jury included others such as attorney Frank Pestana; Ben Rinaldo, American Veterans Committee state chairman; José Chávez; Oscar Castro; Peter Lord, Progressive Citizens of America, Forty-Fourth Assembly District; Jack Berman; Leon Clifton; Dr. H. Claude Hudson; Ben Rothman; and Arnold Schimberg, American Veterans Committee.
135. Celia Rodríguez, in discussion with author, February 17, 1999.
136. Ralph Cuarón, May 12, 1998.
137. "Accuser of Police Arrested," *Herald-Express*, April 6, 1948; "Accuser of Officer in Slaying Charges Arrest Is Frame-up," *Daily News*, April 7, 1948.
138. "Accuser of Police Arrested."
139. "Red Squabble Overshadows Officer Case," *Daily News*, July 13, 1945.
140. "Red Charges Fly in Tiff with Judge in Police Slaying Quiz," *Herald-Express*, April 12, 1948.
141. "Red Charges Fly."
142. Endore, *Justice for Salcido*, 19.
143. "Red Charge Spurs Bench, Bar Row at Slaying Trial," *Daily News*, April 13, 1948.
144. Endore, *Justice for Salcido*, 19.
145. "Judge and Lawyer Row in Courtroom Hearing," *Los Angeles Times*, April 13, 1948, p. 1.
146. Endore, *Justice for Salcido*, 21. Nonetheless, the conduct in the court by the defense raised the concern of many observers, including the judge. "I don't like the spirit of Fascism that is sweeping America. It seems to me that the war hysteria has got everybody sort of crazy in this country, and the first thing they think about is to pull a gun and shoot somebody." See also "Judge Accused of Aiding Reds in Trial of Officer," *Daily News*, April 12, 1948, 1.
147. Copy of editorial, "Case of Justice Stanley Moffatt," *Los Angeles Times*, April 14, 1948, box 3, folder 28, CRC Collection, SCL.
148. "Case of Justice Stanley Moffatt."
149. "Case of Justice Stanley Moffatt."
150. Bidner and Shore to "Gentlemen," Los Angeles City Council, April 15, 1948, box 3, folder 28, CRC Collection, SCL.
151. "Council Echoes L.A. Times, Joins Attack on Moffatt," *Daily People's World*, April 14, 1948. The motion was introduced by Councilman Lloyd Davies and seconded by Councilman Ed Davenport.
152. Bidner and Shore to "Gentlemen."
153. Bidner to Los Angeles City Council, April 15, 1948, box 3, folder 28, CRC Collection, SCL. *People's Daily World*, April 14, 1948. The *People's Daily World* reported that Davies "eagerly championed" the complaint made by the *Times* and in turn accused Judge Moffatt of allowing his court to be used as "a sounding board for

publicity" in the case. Accordingly, "Councilman Ed Davenport 'gladly' seconded the motion, declaring 'it's a travesty on justice when they can drag one of our city police officers to appear before a judge that Leo Gallagher, a known Communist, suggested.'"

154. "L.A. Council to Get Plea on Salcido," *Daily People's World*, April 19, 1948.

155. Parra and Bidner to "Dear Friend," April 13, 1948, box 8, folder 36, CRC Collection, SCL. On April 13, Leroy Parra, MA-CRC chair, and Bidner announced an emergency meeting at the home of Frances Lym to reorganize and plan an "immediate program for action to raise the whole fight around the Salcido case to a much higher level."

156. "L.A. Cop Free on Technicality: CIO Joins in Protest," *Labor Herald*, July 20, 1948.

157. U.S. Senator Glen H. Taylor of Idaho ran for vice president on the Wallace ticket.

158. "New Party Flaws Keyes Acquittal," *Daily People's World*, July 14, 1948.

159. "Statement of Amigos de Wallace on Keyes Decision," Amigos de Wallace, July 13, 1948, box 3, folder 26, CRC Collection, SCL.

160. Endore, *Justice for Salcido*, 31.

161. Lena Horne had a long career as a popular singer, actor, and civil rights activist. Dr. Pauling was a Nobel Prize-winning chemist and head of the Crellin Laboratory of Chemistry at the California Institute of Technology.

162. "Keyes Case Rally Monday," *Daily People's World*, July 17, 1948, p. 3. The council represented a membership of over two thousand in Southern California, "composed of university professors, scientists, authors, artists and professional people." Other supporters included: Norman Corwin; Paul Draper; Dr. Arthur Galston, physicist; and Dr. Douglas Drury, a member of the county hospital medical board.

163. "L.A. Cop Free on Technicality," *Labor Herald*, July 20, 1948. In the afternoon of that day, Mollie Mason, executive board member of the CIO United Office & Professional Workers union, participated in the memorial ceremony at the site of Salcido's death. The inclusion of this union was yet another important victory. Some of the UO&PW members worked at the Jewish Welfare Federation building where Salcido died.

164. "'Call to Arms' on Killer Cops," *Daily People's World*, July 21, 1948. As the *Daily People's World* reported, "It was a furiously-mad audience—an audience that came to find out the most powerful ways to bring police killer William Keyes to justice and to kick him and his kind off the police force."

165. "'Call to Arms' on Killer Cops."

166. "'Call to Arms' on Killer Cops."

167. "L.A. Cop Free on Technicality"; Endore, *Justice for Salcido*, 31.

168. "Gallegos Threatened, 'Leave Town or You'll Die,' He Says Police Told Him," *Daily People's World*, October 11, 1948. The arresting officer was Raymond E. Varela, "a close associate of Officers Molino and Medina."

169. Lieberman, *Strangest Dream*, 35.

170. "Convention Bulletin: Excerpts from Major Reports Delivered to Los Angeles County Convention, July 10–11, 1948," Communist Party Collection, Southern

California Library for Social Studies and Research, file 1948, 4 (hereafter cited as Communist Party Collection, SCL).

171. "Convention Bulletin."

172. "Convention Bulletin."

173. Horne, *Communist Front?*, 99–100. See also Endore, *Justice for Salcido*, 23. Far from being nonpartisan, Endore wrote, *The News* (the Police and Firemen's Protective League's regular publication) red-baited every organization and individual that supported the pro-Salcido campaign, accusing them of representing "the backbone of the present Communist party line program." A linchpin in this apparent treachery, he wrote, was the "Henry Wallace Third party movement."

174. Edward E. Palmer, ed., *The Communist Problem in America: A Book of Readings* (New York: Thomas Y. Crowell, 1951), 281–89. Why, then, did the IPP appeal to some Americans? "The majority of the new Progressives," the article ascertained, "are clearly young people who are very idealistic and shocked by the poverty, insecurity, poor health and war atmosphere in the United States and the rest of the world." Their decision to join the IPP, the article continued, revealed "vast ignorance and immaturity in the realm of economics and politics." In typical fashion, the article argued that "naiveté or stupidity or both" characterized the interest given to the IPP by intellectuals and artists. See also Liebermann, *Strangest Dream*, 47.

175. Ralph Cuarón, June 9, 1998. See also Ellen Schrecker, *The Age of McCarthyism: A Brief History with Documents* (Boston: Bedford Books, 1994), 17–18. Schrecker concurs with this assessment when she states: "The notion that individual Communists were under Moscow's control had less basis in reality. True, some party members did display a Stalinist rigidity, following every zig and zag of the party line with unquestioning devotion. And many Communists did behave in what could be seen as a conspiratorial fashion, especially when they tried to conceal their political affiliation. Nonetheless, most party members were neither so rigid nor so secretive. They did not see themselves as soldiers in Stalin's army, but as American radicals committed to a program of social and political change that would eventually produce what they hoped would be a better society."

176. Henry A. Wallace, *Toward World Peace* (New York: Reynal & Hitchcock, 1948). Einstein's remark appeared on the dust jacket of the book.

CHAPTER 3

1. Thomas Borstelmann, *The Cold War and the Color Line: American Race Relations in the Global Arena* (Cambridge: Harvard University Press, 2001), 49.

2. Borstelmann, *Cold War*, 45–48.

3. Dorothy Healey and Maurice Isserman, *Dorothy Healey Remembers: A Life in the American Communist Party* (New York: Oxford University Press, 1990), 109.

4. *It's You They're After*, pamphlet (Los Angeles: Printed by the Civil Rights Congress, 1949), Carey McWilliams Archives, Special Collections, University Research Library, University of California, Los Angeles.

5. Robbie Lieberman, *The Strangest Dream: Communism, Anticommunism, and the U.S. Peace Movement, 1945–1963* (Syracuse, N.Y.: Syracuse University Press, 2000), 35.

6. Healey and Isserman, *Dorothy Healey Remembers*, 107–8.

7. Nelson Lichtenstein, *Labor's War at Home: The CIO in World War II* (Cambridge: Cambridge University Press, 1982), 234.

8. Ellen Schrecker, *The Age of McCarthyism: A Brief History with Documents* (Boston: Bedford Books, 1994), 50–52; James J. Lorence, *The Suppression of* Salt of the Earth: *How Hollywood, Big Labor, and Politicians Blacklisted a Movie in Cold War America* (Albuquerque: University of New Mexico Press, 1999), 24–25.

9. Lichtenstein, *Labor's War at Home*, 236–37.

10. Helen Taylor, *Daily People's World*, undated, Civil Rights Congress Collection, Southern California Library for Social Studies and Research (hereafter cited as CRC Collection, SCL).

11. Taylor, *Daily People's World*.

12. John C. Culver and John Hayde, *American Dreamer: The Life and Times of Henry A. Wallace* (New York: W. W. Norton, 2000), 275–86, 341.

13. Culver and Hayde, *American Dreamer*, 345–48, 369–73.

14. Roosevelt died in April.

15. Henry A. Wallace, *Sixty Million Jobs* (New York: Simon & Schuster, 1945), 14.

16. Charles Kramer, *Henry A. Wallace, 1888–1965, Sermon of the Month, First Unitarian Church of Los Angeles*, March 1966, Independent Progressive Party Collection, Southern California Library for Social Studies and Research (hereafter cited as IPP Collection, SCL), 4–7.

17. Graham White and John Maze, *Henry A. Wallace: His Search for a New World Order* (Chapel Hill: University of North Carolina Press, 1995), 158.

18. Kramer, *Henry A. Wallace, 1888–1965*, 7.

19. White and Maze, *Henry A. Wallace*, 242–43.

20. White and Maze, *Henry A. Wallace*, 242–43.

21. Culver and Hayde, *American Dreamer*, 452.

22. William Schneiderman, *California Political Perspectives and the 1948 Elections*, 1947, folder 1947, Communist Party Collection, SCL.

23. Schneiderman, *California Political Perspectives*, 3. The role of progressives, including Communists, was to help build, in Schneiderman's words, a "coalition for a people's party led by labor in alliance with all other progressive forces, to advance the people's struggle against the monopolies and Fascist trends."

24. Culver and Hayde, *American Dreamer*, 463. As the authors explain: "And the successful petition drive in California ended once and for all the efforts of Wallace supporters operating within the Democratic Party. Liberal members of Congress such as Helen Gahagan Douglas and Chet Holifield were obliged to renounce the third party if they hoped to have Democratic backing. James Roosevelt, the state party chairman, was thrown into a high-profile power struggle with the former national party treasurer Ed Pauley, which ultimately resulted in Roosevelt's reluctant endorsement of Truman's policies."

25. *A Third Party? Why? How? When?*, Educational Department, California and San Francisco Communist Party, July 1947, folder 1947, Communist Party Collection, SCL.

26. *A Third Party?*, 5.

27. Lichtenstein, *Labor's War at Home*, 236.

28. *A Third Party?*, 5.

29. . . . *Of the People*, Organizing Committee, Independent Progressive Party, folder number one, 1948, 5, IPP Collection, SCL.

30. Ralph Cuarón, in discussion with author, January 29, 1999.

31. . . . *Of the People*, 5–13.

32. California Legislature, *Fourth Report of the Senate Fact-Finding Committee on Un-American Activities: Communist Front Organizations* (Sacramento: The Senate, 1948), 146. Bryson was identified as a "Communist" and the IPP as a front organization for the CPUSA by the Tenney Committee.

33. . . . *Of the People*, 5–13. In a speech Bryson delivered later in September, he enumerated the reasons why the new party was poised at a historic crossroads. Not only had "our two party system . . . become a one party system. That one party is the party of monopoly and reaction." The IPP leadership was very concerned over the growing trend of monopoly power in the United States and its negative effects on the nation's democratic institutions. The following quotation by FDR provides some indication of how this issue had reached the attention of those at the highest levels of power and was used by the IPP to support their claims: "Liberty in a democracy is not safe if the people tolerate the growth of private power to a point where it becomes stronger than their democratic state itself. That, in essence, is fascism—ownership of government by an individual, by a group, or by another controlling private power. Among us today a concentration of private power without equal in history is growing."

34. . . . *Of the People*, 20–21.

35. Eric Avila, *Popular Culture in the Age of White Flight: Fear and Fantasy in Suburban Los Angeles* (Berkeley: University of California Press, 2004), 20.

36. Avila, *Popular Culture*, 41.

37. Sherna Berger Gluck, *Rosie the Riveter Revisited: Women, the War, and Social Change* (Boston: Twayne, 1987), 3–18, 259–70; Elizabeth R. Escobedo, *From Coveralls to Zoot Suits: The Lives of Mexican Women on the World War II Home Front* (Chapel Hill: University of North Carolina Press, 2015).

38. . . . *Of the People*, 14. See also Clete Daniel, *Chicano Workers and the Politics of Fairness: The FEPC in the Southwest, 1941–1945* (Austin: University of Texas Press, 1991). Bryson's marriage to folk singer Abigail Alvarez certainly expressed a very personal desire and commitment to bridge a cultural divide: Edward Mosk Manuscript Collection, box 3, SCL (hereafter cited as Edward Mosk Manuscript Collection).

39. Luis Leobardo Arroyo, "Industrial Unionism and the Los Angeles Furniture Industry, 1918–1954" (PhD diss., University of California, Los Angeles, 1979), 176–81.

40. "Independent Progressive Party Is Launched This Week in the Eastside," *Eastside Sun*, November 14, 1947. Members of the executive board of the provisional committee to head the mobilization of petition circulars included "Zoe Goldsmith, area coordinator for the new party; Sam Sussman; Edward Bronson; W. T. Hicks; Fannie Hittel; Charles Schfartz, Leo Potegal, Al Furth; Joe Mauss; Celia Frimkess; David Helfman and Rosemary Haskell."

41. John H. Burma, *Spanish-Speaking Groups in the United States* (Durham, N.C.: Duke University Press, 1954), 112–13.

42. Burma, *Spanish-Speaking Groups*, 113.

43. George Sánchez, *Becoming Mexican American: Ethnicity, Culture, and Identity in Chicano Los Angeles, 1900–1945* (New York: Oxford University Press, 1993), 72–83.

44. Antonio Ríos-Bustamante and Pedro Castillo, *An Illustrated History of Mexican Los Angeles, 1781–1985* (Los Angeles: University of California, Chicano Studies Research Center Publications, 1986), 163; Rodolfo Acuña, *Occupied America: A History of Chicanos*, 3rd ed. (New York: HarperCollins, 1988), 275–83, 313–16; Arturo Rosales, *Chicano! The History of the Mexican American Civil Rights Movement* (Houston: Arte Público Press, University of Houston, 1996), 102–5.

45. Ralph Cuarón, in discussion with author, May 12, 1998. Sylvia had not worked for the Menorah Center (located at 961 N. Alma Avenue) as Ralph stated in our interview. However, the Menorah Center and the Soto/Michigan Center often worked closely together on a number of issues and social/cultural activities.

46. Shana Beth Bernstein, "Building Bridges at Home in a Time of Global Conflict: Interracial Cooperation and the Fight for Civil Rights in Los Angeles, 1933–1954" (PhD diss., Stanford University, 2003), 225–26, 270–71.

47. Sylvia Cuarón, in discussion with author, May 12, 1998.

48. U.S. Congressional Hearings, House Un-American Activities Committee, 1955, 84th Cong. (1956), Appendix to Hearings, 7236, 7237, 7239, 7243.

49. "Holds Meeting," *Eastside Sun*, October 24, 1947. The newly elected members to the executive board included: Jack Berman, executive secretary; Eunice Rosenfield, corresponding and recording secretary; Leo Potegal, treasurer; Sam Sussman, education and legislative chairman; Sam Glassberg, precinct chairman; Jeanette Stein, membership chairman; Henry Radin, Max Hittleman, and Norman Brown, members at large. In recognition of her "outstanding work with youth groups," the Fortieth Assembly District chapter of the Progressive Citizens of America invited her to speak before its membership in October.

50. Ralph Cuarón, May 12, 1998. U.S. Congressional Hearings, House Un-American Activities Committee, 1955, 84th Cong. (1956), Appendix to Hearings, 8041. The *Daily Worker*, dated September 28, 1949, announces the return of American delegates to the Second World Youth Congress in Budapest, Hungary.

51. "IPP Announces Support for Candidate," *Eastside Sun*, March 18, 1948. According to Berman, "They need a man who not only understands the problems of all the people but who for the first time in the history of Los Angeles will give a voice to the thousands of Mexican American residents of this area."

52. "Jose Ramon Chavez Woos IPP Support," *Eastside Sun*, March 26, 1948.

53. Mario T. García, *Memories of Chicano History: The Life and Narrative of Bert Corona* (Berkeley: University of California Press, 1994), 161–62.

54. "Hablara en Castellano el Domingo en El Estadio del Lincoln Park en L.A.," *El Expectador*, May 15, 1948, El Expectador Collection (M0255), Department of Special Collections, Green Library, Stanford University (hereafter cited as El Expectador Collection).

55. Acuña, *Occupied America*, 3rd ed., 239, 285; Mario T. García, *Mexican Americans: Leadership, Ideology, and Identity, 1930–1960* (New Haven, Conn.: Yale University Press, 1989), 84–112. See also Sánchez, *Becoming Mexican American*, 260–61.

56. "Henry Wallace Habla a Los Mexicanos en L.A.: Su Discurso Sera el Domingo 16 en el Estadio del Lincoln Park," *El Expectador*, May 17, 1948, El Expectador Collection.

57. Julia and George Mount, in discussion with author, March 26, 1999.

58. Zaragosa Vargas, "In the Years of Darkness and Torment: The Early Mexican American Struggle for Civil Rights, 1945–1963," *New Mexico Historical Review* 76, no. 4 (2001): 399–400.

59. Ralph Cuarón, in discussion with author, January 29, 1999.

60. Taylor, *Daily People's World*, CRC Collection, SCL. As the *Daily People's World* further observed: "The effect of the May 16 Wallace meeting was electric. For the first time, organizations and individuals traditionally middle class are shedding their fears and marching with the workers." See also "Apoyan A Wallace Desde Mexico," *El Expectador*, May 15, 1948, El Expectador Collection; Maze and White, *Henry A. Wallace*, 250–51. Similar crowds greeted Wallace across the country, and his popularity also reached beyond the nation's boundaries. In Mexico, for example, noted artists and activists such as David Alfaro Siqueiros and Diego Rivera helped form the Sociedad Amigos de Wallace (Friends of Wallace Society), which spread from Mexico City to the states of Monterrey, Morelia, and Oaxaca. The explicit mission of these societies was to support Wallace and the Progressive Party's call to combat imperialism and to bring peace to the world.

61. "Candidate Makes Appeal to Mexican-Americans," *Los Angeles Times*, May 17, 1948, 2.

62. "Candidate Makes Appeal," 2.

63. Ralph Cuarón, January 29, 1999.

64. Edward Mosk Manuscript Collection. Abigail Alvarez rallied the crowd with "A Corrido for Wallace and Taylor." Taylor, *Daily People's World*, CRC Collection, SCL; García, *Memories of Chicano History*, 120.

65. Josefina Fierro, oral history interview by Albert Camarillo (M0811), 1995, Department of Special Collections, Green Library, Stanford University.

66. Curtis D. MacDougall, *Gideon's Army*, vol. 1, *The Components of the Decision* (New York: Marzani & Munsell, 1965), 750.

67. The *Los Angeles Times* was not alone in vilifying Wallace. Newspapers throughout the country, large and small, maintained a steady barrage of attacks that kept

Wallace on the defense much of the campaign. According to biographers Culver and Hayde, attacks from the liberal camp, from such prominent sources as the *Washington Post, New York Times,* and the *Chicago Daily News,* were "most vexing" for the campaign (466–70). See Avila, *Reinventing Los Angeles.*

68. Chester G. Hanson, "Third-Party Candidate Picks Up $46,000 Here," *Los Angeles Times,* May 18, 1948, A1.

69. "Henry Shows Us How to Do It," *Los Angeles Times,* May 18, 1948, A4.

70. "The Stalin-Wallace Letters," and "Another Poke at Hollywood's Popularity," *Los Angeles Times,* May 19, 1948, A4.

71. "Wallace Believed Likely to Quit Before Election," *Los Angeles Times,* May 30, 1948, 7.

72. MacDougall, *Gideon's Army,* vol. 1, 751.

73. "Chavez Still Very Much in Evidence," *Eastside Sun,* June 11, 1948. See also Rodolfo F. Acuña, *A Community Under Siege: A Chronicle of Chicanos East of the Los Angeles River, 1945–1975* (Los Angeles: Chicano Studies Research Center, Publications, University of California, 1984), 28. In fact, the success of the Chávez campaign was so surprising that it left many political pundits embarrassed by their early pronouncements of victory for the incumbent.

74. "Chavez Still Very Much in Evidence."

75. "Chavez, Berman Receive High IPP Offices," *Eastside Sun,* July 23, 1948. The *Eastside Sun* identified Cuarón as taking "an active part in the meeting." A number of other prominent community members were also elected to distinguished positions, including Jack Berman, member of the county Central Committee and its executive committee; Edward Mosk (an attorney and wartime officer in the Office of Strategic Services in the Mediterranean) as first chairman; Charlotta A. Bass, publisher of the *California Eagle,* as first vice chairman.

76. Taylor, *Daily People's World,* CRC Collection.

77. Culver and Hayde, *American Dreamer,* 484.

78. "El Grito de Dolores," IPP Collection. Edward Mosk became chair of the IPP and Norman Smith its treasurer.

79. "Wallace Appears at Gilmore Stadium in . . . Political Rally," *Eastside Sun,* October 1, 1948.

80. Sylvia Cuarón, in discussion with author, July 17, 2002.

81. "Henry A. Wallace Hablara Ante el Monumento Patrio," *El Expectador,* October 1, 1948, El Expectador Collection.

82. Julia and George Mount, March 26, 1999.

83. "Wallace Addresses Eastside Adherents," *Eastside Sun,* October 15, 1948. López officiated the rally.

84. MacDougall, *Gideon's Army,* vol. 1, 756–70.

85. MacDougall, *Gideon's Army,* vol. 1, 745–75; White and Maze, *Henry A. Wallace,* 264–70.

86. White and Maze, *Henry A. Wallace,* 276–77.

87. Healey and Isserman, *Dorothy Healey Remembers,* 110–11.

88. "Results of 1948 Election Campaign: Preliminary Report by the Executive Committee of the Los Angeles County Control Committee," November 11, 1948, Edward Mosk Manuscript Collection; see also Eugene Dennis, "The Main Lessons of the 1948 Elections," *Political Affairs*, December 1948, 1047–54. Dennis maintained that the CP had not miscalculated the election, nor had it shared in "the utopian dreams of some" that Wallace would prevail. The support of "a new people's antimonopoly, anti-war party" by the party was imperative. The party helped produce a substantial "democratic and peace coalition around concrete issues" and helped elect a number of pro-labor and progressive congressional representatives. Indeed, he concluded, "without the Progressive Party in the field the results of this election would have been a complete reactionary sweep."

89. *Results of 1948 Election Campaign: Preliminary Report by the Executive Committee of the Los Angeles County Control Committee*, November 11, 1948, Edward Mosk Manuscript Collection.

90. Carey McWilliams, *North from Mexico: The Spanish-Speaking People of the United States* (New York: Greenwood Press, 1968), 283.

91. *Resolution on Mexican Work*, folder 1956, Communist Party Collection.

92. *Resolution on Party Work Among the Mexican People*, August 31, 1948, file 1948, Communist Party Collection.

93. Ralph Cuarón, in discussion with author, June 9, 1998.

94. García, *Mexican Americans*, 199–227, and Mario T. García, "Mexican American Labor and the Left: The Asociación Nacional México-Americana, 1949–1954," in *Beyond 1848: Readings in the Modern Chicano Historical Experience*, ed. Michael R. Ornelas (Dubuque, Iowa: Kendall/Hunt, 1993), 221; See also Enrique M. Buelna, "Asociación Nacional México-Americana (ANMA) (1949–1954)," in *Latinas in the United States: A Historical Encyclopedia*, vol. 2, ed. Vicki L. Ruiz and Virginia Sánchez Korrol (Bloomington: Indiana University Press, 2006), 67–68.

95. García, *Memories of Chicano History*, 170.

96. Virginia Ruiz to "Dear Friends," August 16, 1950, folder 1950, Communist Party Collection.

97. "Association Will Hold Founding Convention Today," *Eastside Sun*, October 20, 1949.

98. "Over a Hundred Delegates for Mexican-American National Association," *Eastside Sun*, October 27, 1949.

99. García, "Mexican American Labor," 231. Mario T. García explains that ANMA had more well-established contacts with "left-oriented" groups and less so with Mexican American civic organizations. The list of "progressive collectives" supporting ANMA included the IPP, the Civil Rights Congress, the Jewish Peoples Fraternal Order, the International Workers Order, and soon the Los Angeles Committee for Protection of Foreign Born.

100. "Over a Hundred Delegates."

101. *Preliminary Call: To a National Founding Convention*, August 16, 1950, folder 1950, Communist Party Collection.

102. *Preliminary Call.* Translation: "Para La Proteccion De Los Derechos Civiles, Economicos y Politicos y Para El Fomento de la Educacion, La Cultura y El Progreso Del Pueblo Mexico-Americano de los Estados Unidos."

103. *Preliminary Call.* The invitation continued:

> We see all this, and at the same time we declare our unshakable hope in the future and in the eventual and complete vindication of our people in this region.
>
> Bitter experience has taught us valuable lessons. We note every day how our people have begun to mature politically, socially and economically, constantly striving to improve their standard of living; forging leaders in every field who are loyal, capable, respected and honored; producing musicians, artists, business men and professionals; and taking their place in civic and political life, as an integral part of the community.
>
> Statistics speak eloquently.

104. Virginia Ruiz to "Dear Friends," August 16, 1950, folder 1950, Communist Party Collection; Ralph Cuarón, in discussion with author, May 5, 1998; García, "Mexican American Labor," 221.

105. *Toward the Unity of the Mexican People in the United States,* October 14, 1950, pamphlet files, Communist Party Collection.

106. Acuña, *Occupied America,* 3rd ed., 321.

107. García, "Mexican American Labor," 222, 227–28.

108. García, "Mexican American Labor," 228.

109. Ralph Cuarón, in discussion with author, June 18, 1998.

110. Ralph Cuarón, May 19, 1998. The strike carried out by Mine-Mill Local 890, which lasted from October 1950 to January 1951 was immortalized in the film *Salt of the Earth* in 1953.

111. Herbert Biberman had been a film director and one-time member in the Communist Party. He had also been active in various popular front organizations. He testified before HUAC in 1947 and served six months in prison for contempt of Congress. Michael Wilson had been a screenwriter and involved in progressive politics. In 1953, he was branded an unfriendly witness by HUAC and blacklisted in the film industry. See Lorence, *Suppression of* Salt of the Earth, 47–53.

112. Sylvia Cuarón, in discussion with author, August 17, 2001. Mike Wilson wrote the story for *Salt of the Earth,* Paul Jarrico was the producer, and Herbert J. Biberman the director. Biberman was one of the famed Hollywood Ten screenwriters and directors who had refused to cooperate with HUAC in 1947. As Victor Navasky explains, Biberman and his wife, Gale Sondergaard, had been members in the CP (80).

113. Herbert Biberman, *Salt of the Earth: The Story of a Film* (Boston: Beacon Press, 1965), 43. Biberman's original intention in putting together the Independent Productions Company was to provide blacklisted workers in the film industry with employment so that they might continue to work within their professions and remain creative in their crafts. See also Glenn Frankel, *High Noon: The Hollywood Blacklist and the Making of an American Classic* (New York: Bloomsbury, 2017). This

book chronicles the struggles of writers and producers, like Carl Foreman, affected by HUAC and anti-Communism and their efforts to use film as an allegory about the Red Scare and the blacklist.

114. Sylvia Cuarón, August 17, 2001. Sylvia and Mita (Margarita) their daughter, who was a year old at the time, were also cast as extras in the same scene but are not visible like Ralph. Chris Ruiz is next to Ralph Cuarón in the scene. See Ellen R. Baker, "*Salt of the Earth*: Women, the Mine, Mill and Smelter Workers' Union, and the Hollywood Blacklist in Grant County, New Mexico, 1941–1953" (PhD diss., University of Wisconsin, Madison, 1999), 270–88.

115. Schrecker, *Age of McCarthyism*, 13.

116. Schrecker, *Age of McCarthyism*, 10. See also Avila, *Popular Culture in the Age of White Flight*, chap. 2. See also *Civil Rights Congress Tells the Story*, 40. The Civil Rights Congress in Los Angeles spoke of the power that film had to make people aware of important issues and to become critical thinkers.

> The group of writers and film makers now known around the world as the Hollywood Ten were subpoenaed in 1947 by the J. Parnell Thomas House Un-American Activities Committee. Mr. Thomas was carrying on one of the periodic investigations of Hollywood amidst a flurry of big headlines. But there was something behind the headlines. There was the fact the films were evolving in a way not altogether comfortable for some powerful American interests; the moving pictures which had become talking pictures were now developing into thinking pictures. They dealt with integrity and dramatic power with poverty, race relations, peace, labor rights, and democracy as a way of life. They were reaching 85,000,000 Americans a week, and tens of millions of other people abroad. The optic nerve is the shortcut to the brain; the pictures were putting ideas into peoples' heads. It had to be stopped.

117 Deborah Silverton Rosenfelt and Michael Wilson, *Salt of the Earth* (Old Westbury, N.Y.: Feminist Press, 1978), 108–9.

118. Lorence, *Suppression of* Salt of the Earth, 1–8. See also Gerald Horne, *Class Struggle in Hollywood, 1930–1950: Moguls, Mobsters, Stars, Reds, and Trade Unionists* (Austin: University of Texas Press, 2001).

119. Schrecker, *Age of McCarthyism*, 57–58. See also George Lipsitz, *Rainbow at Midnight: Labor and Culture in the 1940s* (Urbana: University of Illinois Press, 1994), chap. 12.

120. Elaine Tyler May, *Homeward Bound: American Families in the Cold War Era* (New York: Basic Books, 1988), 66–69.

121. Baker, "Salt of the Earth," 276.

122. Lary May, *Screening Out the Past: The Birth of Mass Culture and the Motion Picture Industry* (New York: Oxford University Press, 1980), 218–20.

123. Baker, "*Salt of the Earth*," 276; Ellen R. Baker, *On Strike and on Film: Mexican American Families and Blacklisted Filmmakers in Cold War America* (Chapel Hill: University of North Carolina Press, 2007).

124. Lorence, *Suppression of* Salt of the Earth, 28.
125. James J. Lorence, *Palomino: Clinton Jencks and Mexican-American Unionism in the American Southwest* (Urbana: University of Illinois Press, 2013).
126. Lorence, *Suppression of* Salt of the Earth, 26–28.
127. Ralph Cuarón, U.S. Department of Justice, Federal Bureau of Investigation, FOIPA No. 0987822–000, June 22, 1956.
128. Lorence, *Suppression of* Salt of the Earth, 56–62.
129. Biberman, *Salt of the Earth*, 298. See also Lorence, *Suppression of* Salt of the Earth, 171–77.
130. Victor Navasky, *Naming Names* (New York: Viking, 1980), 78. See also Schrecker, *Age of McCarthyism*, 76–86.
131. Lorence, *Suppression of* Salt of the Earth, 36.
132. Biberman, *Salt of the Earth*.
133. Biberman, *Salt of the Earth*, 9.
134. Juan Chacón, "We Didn't Have to Act . . . ," *March of Labor*, June 1954, vol. 6, no. 5, Clinton Jencks Papers (MSS-137), box 1, folder 14, Chicano Studies Research Collection, Arizona State University.
135. "Attacks Can't Stop Strike Film," *Labor Herald*, March 23, 1953, folder 59, Robert W. Kenny Collection, SCL.
136. "Attacks Can't Stop Strike Film."
137. "Attacks Can't Stop Strike Film."
138. Navasky, *Naming Names*, 85.
139. See Lipsitz, *Rainbow at Midnight*, 292–94.
140. García, *Mexican Americans*, 223–24.
141. Ralph Cuarón, in discussion with author, June 14, 1999.
142. Vicki L. Ruiz, *Cannery Women, Cannery Lives: Mexican Women, Unionization, and the California Food Processing Industry, 1930–1950* (Albuquerque: University of New Mexico Press, 1987), chap. 6. Here, Ruiz explores the often fierce struggle that ensued between UCAPAWA/FTA, a CIO affiliate, and the AFL's International Brotherhood of Teamsters. See also Schrecker, *Age of McCarthyism*, 50–53, 61; Lipsitz, *Rainbow at Midnight*, 335–46.
143. Arroyo, "Industrial Unionism," 232–33.
144. Arroyo, "Industrial Unionism," 234–35.
145. Arroyo, "Industrial Unionism," 258.
146. Ralph Cuarón, January 22, 1999.
147. Arroyo, "Industrial Unionism," 239.
148. Ralph Cuarón, January 22, 1999; June 9, 1999.
149. Ralph Cuarón, June 14, 1999.
150. Ralph Cuarón, June 14, 1999.
151. Ralph Cuarón, June 14, 1999.
152. Ralph Cuarón, June 14, 1999.
153. Ralph Cuarón, June 14, 1999.
154. Ralph Cuarón, June 14, 1999.

155.   May, *Homeward Bound*, 3–15. See also Lynn Spigel, *Make Room for TV: Television and the Family Ideal in Postwar America* (Chicago: University of Chicago Press, 1992).

156.   Sylvia Cuarón, in discussion with author, June 14, 1999.

CHAPTER 4

1.   See Karl Marx and Friedrich Engels, *Ireland and the Irish Question* (New York: International Publishers, 1972); V. I. Lenin, *National Liberation, Socialism, and Imperialism* (New York: International Publishers, 1968), and *Critical Remarks on the National Question: The Right of Nations to Self-Determination* (Moscow: Progress Publishers, 1971); Joseph Stalin, *Marxism and the National Question: Selected Writings and Speeches* (New York: International Publishers, 1942), and *Marxism and the National and Colonial Question*, ed. A. Fineberg (New York: International Publishers, 1936).

2.   Benjamin Davis, "Summary Remarks on the Discussion of the Resolution on Negro Rights," *Political Affairs* 26, no. 1 (January 1947): 59.

3.   Clarence E. Walker, *Deromanticizing Black History: Critical Essays and Reappraisals* (Knoxville: University of Tennessee Press, 1991), xi–xxvi, 1–33.

4.   Walker, *Deromanticizing Black History*, 13–15.

5.   William Z. Foster, "On the Question of Negro Self-Determination," *Political Affairs* 26, no. 1 (January 1947): 54–58.

6.   Dorothy Healey and Maurice Isserman, *Dorothy Healey Remembers: A Life in the American Communist Party* (New York: Oxford University Press, 1990), 70.

7.   Paul Buhle and Edmund B. Sullivan, *Images of American Radicalism* (Hanover, Mass.: Christopher Publishing House, 1998), 266.

8.   Douglas Monroy, "Anarquismo y Comunismo: Mexican Radicalism and the Communist Party in Los Angeles During the 1930s," *Labor History* 24 (Winter 1983): 56.

9.   *The Marx-Engels Reader*, ed. Robert C. Tucker, 2nd ed. (New York: W.W. Norton, 1978), 472–500. See also *V.I. Lenin, Essential Works of Lenin: "What Is To Be Done?" and Other Writings*, ed. Henry M. Christman (New York: Dover, 1987), 298; and James M. Blaut, *The National Question: Decolonizing the Theory of Nationalism* (London: Zed Books, 1987), 142–56.

10.   V. I. Lenin, *Critical Remarks on the National Question: The Right of Nations to Self-Determination*, 5th printing, Scientific Socialism Series (Moscow: Progress Publishers, 1971), 21–23, 51–52. See Victor Serge, *From Lenin to Stalin* (New York: Pathfinder Press, 2000). See also Blaut, *National Question*, 23.

11.   V. I. Lenin, *Critical Remarks*, 66.

12.   V. I. Lenin, *Critical Remarks*, 22–23.

13.   V. I. Lenin, *Critical Remarks*, 56, 80. The role of the working class was not to promote nationalism; the goal was to bring unity. If, on the other hand, mass national movements already existed, then the working class was bound to support the progressive elements within them.

14. *The National Question*, Educational Department of the California Communist Party, February 1947, CPUSA Collection, folder 1947, SCL.

15. J. Amter, *Project for Resolution on Negro Question*, 1924, CPUSA Collection, delo 360, Library of Congress, Washington, D.C.

16. *American Negro Situation*, 1924, CPUSA Collection, delo 360, Library of Congress.

17. Robin D. G. Kelley, *Hammer and Hoe: Alabama Communists During the Great Depression* (1990; repr., Chapel Hill: University of North Carolina Press, 2015), 13–14.

18. Dolsen to C. E. Ruthenberg, Workers Party of America, January 8, 1925, delo 360, CPUSA Collection, Library of Congress.

19. Levin to "To the C. E. C. of W. P.," undated, delo 360, CPUSA Collection, Library of Congress.

20. Indeed, Levine even went as far as to suggest that the Central Executive Committee assist the district in forming a "sub-committee to meet in Los Angeles" if the "seat of the D.E.C. Committee is retained in San Francisco (which perhaps would not be wise)." The CP finally divided California into a northern and southern district around 1957. Dorothy Healey, *Tradition's Chains Have Bound Us*, interviewed by Joel Gardener, vol. 2 (Los Angeles: University of California, 1982), 501.

21. Gerald Horne, *Black Liberation/Red Scare: Ben Davis and the Communist Party* (Newark, N.J.: University of Delaware Press, 1994), 9. The Communist International was the "umbrella grouping of world-wide Communist parties based in Moscow."

22. Kelley, *Hammer and Hoe*, 13–33, 92–116.

23. Robert Thompson, "Basic Aspects of the Negro People's Struggle," *Political Affairs* 26, no. 1 (February 1947): 164. See also Kelley, *Hammer and Hoe*, 13.

24. Quoted in Benjamin Davis, "Summary Remarks on the Discussion of the Resolution on Negro Rights," *Political Affairs* 26, no. 1 (January 1947): 59.

25. Benjamin Davis, "The Negro People's Liberation Movement," *Political Affairs* 27, no. 9 (September 1948): 880.

26. Horne, *Black Liberation/Red Scare*, 67.

27. Horne, *Black Liberation/Red Scare*, 68.

28. Emma Tenayuca and Homer Brooks, "The Mexican Question in the Southwest," *The Communist* 18 (March 1939): 262.

29. Tenayuca and Brooks, "Mexican Question."

30. Zaragosa Vargas, "Tejana Radical: Emma Tenayuca and the San Antonio Labor Movement During the Great Depression," *Pacific Historical Review* 66, no. 4 (November 1997): 553–80. See also David G. Gutiérrez, *Walls and Mirrors: Mexican Americans, Mexican Immigrants, and the Politics of Ethnicity* (Berkeley: University of California Press, 1995), 107–10. See also John Weber, *From South Texas to the Nation: The Exploitation of Mexican Labor in the Twentieth Century* (Chapel Hill: University of North Carolina Press, 2015).

31. Weber, *From South Texas to the Nation*, 263.

32. Weber, *From South Texas to the Nation*, 265–66.

33. Weber, *From South Texas to the Nation*, 265–66.

34. Weber, *From South Texas to the Nation*, 262.

35. Monroy, "Anarquismo y Comunismo," 43–46.

36. Vargas, "Tejana Radical," 553.

37. Monroy, "Anarquismo y Comunismo," 74–75.

38. See Norma Barzman, *The Red and the Black List: The Intimate Memoir of a Holly-wood Expatriate* (New York: Thunder's Mouth Press, 2003), 62–63.

39. Browder was formally expelled from the Communist Party USA on February 14, 1946. Norma Barzman reveals how party rank and file were torn by these abrupt changes in CP policy and how they perceived the "Eastern hierarchy," 64–65.

40. See also Horne, *Black Liberation/Red Scare*, 74.

41. Horne, *Black Liberation/Red Scare*, 129.

42. *Resolution on Mexican Work*, 1956, folder 1956, CPUSA Collection, SCL.

43. Antonio Ríos-Bustamante and Pedro Castillo, *An Illustrated History of Mexican Los Angeles, 1781–1985* (Los Angeles: University of California, Chicano Studies Research Center Publications, 1986), 173.

44. *Report on Mexicans in the U.S.A.*, undated, folder 1946, CPUSA Collection, SCL, 6. See also *The Mexican Question in the United States*, file 64–35, Dorothy Healey Collection, California State University, Long Beach, University Library, Special Collections/University Archives (hereafter cited as Healey Collection). In this analysis of the Browder period, prepared approximately in 1950, the authors echo the evaluation of the Mexican Commission.

"Under the impact of Browderism, with the treatment of the Mexican question as a national group question, there was no special approach and special attention to the Mexican comrades in our Party. Mexican comrades were placed in English-speaking branches with no regard for their right to speak Spanish and excluded from participation in the Party because of their lack of knowledge of English. It is only recently that Mexican branches have been re-established and the beginnings of a special approach been taken.

Under such circumstances the Party could not but decline in its Mexican membership. For Mexican people joining the Party expecting to find understanding of their special problems and seeking ways to fight, found in many respects the same attitude as encountered outside of the Party. There was a complete failure to develop Mexican leadership in the Party. Up until recently there was not one full-time Mexican Party functionary in the entire Party, the only one to our knowledge now being in Colorado. The disastrous effects of this can be seen in the disappearance of the FTA organization in the Southwest because of its failure to develop a special approach on the Mexican question."

45. *Report on Mexicans in the U.S.A.*

46. Rodolfo Acuña, *Occupied America: A History of Chicanos*, 3rd ed. (New York: HarperCollins, 1988), 272; U.S. Congressional Hearings, House Un-American Activities Committee, 1955, 84th Cong. (1956), Appendix to Hearings, 7279. Rose Chernin is quoted in "Exhibit No. 102E" from an annual report, "Report for 1955–

1956," as stating: "There is still a severe impact on the Mexican-American community. Two weeks ago Jose Castelum [*sic*], who has lived here since he was ten years old, and has U.S. born wife and children, was arrested for deportation for political reasons."

47. Ralph Cuarón, May 12, 1998, conducted by the author. Blaut, *National Question*, 165.

48. "Southern California Party Building Conference," June 14–15, 1947, file 1947, CPUSA Collection, SCL.

49. "Southern California Party Building Conference."

50. "Southern California Party Building Conference."

51. U.S. Congressional Hearings, House Un-American Activities Committee, 1955, 84th Congress (1956), Appendix to Hearings, 7737.

52. Isabel González, *Step-Children of a Nation: The Status of Mexican-Americans* (New York: American Committee for Protection of Foreign Born, 1947), Pamphlet Files, SCL.

53. Luisa Moreno, "Caravans of Sorrow: Noncitizen Americans of the Southwest," in *Between Two Worlds: Mexican Immigrants in the United States*, ed. David G. Gutiérrez (Wilmington, Del.: Scholarly Resources, 1996), 119–23. See also Aviva Chomsky, *Undocumented: How Immigration Became Illegal* (Boston: Beacon Press, 2014).

54. Natalia Molina, *How Race Is Made in America: Immigration, Citizenship, and the Historical Power of Racial Scripts* (Berkeley: University of California Press, 2014), 7.

55. MacDougall, *Gideon's Army*, vol. 1, 773–75.

56. González, *Step-Children of a Nation*, 3–13.

57. González, *Step-Children of a Nation*, 3–13.

58. Ralph Cuarón, in discussion with author, June 9, 1998. Not only did this national leadership appear to dictate a significant number of policy decisions, they also seemed to act as the filters and disseminators of all official party doctrine. According to Sylvia: "The West had the vast number of Latino[s] whereas the East had the vast number of Jewish and Black people. So, there was not [an] understanding of the coming issue of a minority in the West that was vastly becoming an entity in itself. The West needed its own leadership, and the leadership had to come from that minority group which was the Mexican. . . . It was a question of elitism. And here was a young Mexican, an upstart [Cuarón], who was saying, 'Wait a minute, we understand that there is a Negro question that needs to be taken into consideration and rallied to, but there is also in the West a Mexican American element that is crying for its identity."

59. Ralph Cuarón, in discussion with author, January 22, 1999.

60. Monroy, "Anarquismo y Comunismo," 54.

61. It is very likely that Frank López authored this article. The author pointed out that the Mexican Commission and the County Committee of the CP were not successfully coordinating their activities such that meaningful discussions and exchanges of information were taking place.

62. *Pre-Convention Discussion Bulletin–No. 2*, June 25, 1948, box 1945–1957, CPUSA Collection, SCL.

63. *Convention Bulletin: Excerpts from Major Reports Delivered to Los Angeles County Convention, July 10–11, 1948*, file 1948, CPUSA Collection, SCL.

64. *Convention Bulletin.*

65. Cuarón had a strained relationship with Ben Dobbs dating back to 1947. In that year, Cuarón was sent by the party to attend a conference in New York to oppose military conscription. After his return, Dobbs castigated him for having taken a detour to Denver, Colorado, where he met with Art Berry and Patricia Blau, high-ranking CP members, to discuss issues relating to the national question and how this affected Mexican Americans. Cuarón also recalled that Dorothy Healey was not very happy with his meeting with the Communists of the Rocky Mountain region.

66. *Convention Bulletin.*

67. *State Convention Report*, August 21, 1948, box 1945–1957, CPUSA Collection, SCL.

68. *Political Affairs*, the theoretical organ of the Communist Party USA, was founded in 1944 after the closure of its predecessor, *The Communist*, which was founded in 1924.

69. Pettis Perry, "National Group Work in California," *Political Affairs* 27, no. 8 (August 1948): 749–56.

70. White and Maze, *Henry A. Wallace*, 204. Again, the attraction to Wallace among people of color was not difficult to understand. Wallace had been on record supporting the idea of racial equality across all sectors of American life. For example, at a Democratic Party convention in 1943 he brazenly bucked tradition by broaching the race question. "The future belongs to those who go down the line unswervingly for the liberal principles of both political democracy and economic democracy regardless of race, color, or religion. In a political, educational, and economic sense there must be no inferior races. The poll tax must go. Equal educational opportunities must come. The future must bring equal wages for equal work regardless of sex or race."

71. Wallace was officially nominated as the official presidential candidate for the IPP at this convention.

72. Ralph Cuarón, January 22, 1999.

73. *Resolution on Party Work Among the Mexican People*, August 3, 1948, file 1948, CPUSA Collection, SCL. Also see "The Mexican Americans—Their Plight and Struggles," *Political Affairs* 28, no. 5 (May 1949): 71–80.

74. *Resolution on the Conditions of the Mexican People*, August 3, 1948, file 1948, CPUSA Collection, SCL.

75. Kenneth C. Burt, "Freedom Fiesta," *Labor's Heritage*, Summer 1996, 16.

76. Sylvia Cuarón, in discussion with author, July 17, 2002.

77. Ralph Cuarón, in discussion with author, May 5, 1998.

78. Sylvia Cuarón, July 17, 2002.

79. Sylvia Cuarón, July 17, 2002.

80. Jack B. Tenney, *Red Fascism: Boring from Within . . . By the Subversive Forces of Communism* (Los Angeles: Federal Printing Company, 1947), 522–24. See also Kelley, *Hammer and Hoe*, 79; Perez v. Sharp, 32 Cal. 2d 711 (1948).

81. Dara Orenstein, "Void for Vagueness: Mexicans and the Collapse of Miscegenation Law in California," *Pacific Historical Review* 74, no. 3 (2005): 406. See also Vicki L. Ruiz and Virginia Sánchez Korrol, "Pérez v. Sharp," in *Latinas in the United States: A Historical Encyclopedia*, ed. Ruiz and Sánchez Korrol (Bloomington: Indiana University Press, 2006), 573.

82. Orenstein, "Void for Vagueness," 371, 395.

83. Frank G. Mittelbach and Joan W. Moore, "Ethnic Endogamy: The Case of Mexican Americans," in *Mexican-Americans in the United States: A Reader*, ed. John H. Burma (Cambridge, Mass.: Schenkman, 1970), 235–48. Some forty-five years later, Moore recounts, with some trepidation, the "assimilative potential" and economic integration she expected for Mexican Americans have, sadly, not come to pass. Despite the large demographic presence of Mexican Americans, they remain a marginalized majority-minority. See also Edward E. Telles and Vilma Ortiz, *Generations of Exclusion: Mexican-Americans, Assimilation, and Race* (New York: Russell Sage Foundation, 2008).

84. Sylvia Cuarón, July 17, 2002.

85. Sylvia Cuarón, July 17, 2002.

86. Sylvia Cuarón (by phone), in discussion with author, September 11, 2003; Ralph and Sylvia Cuarón, in discussion with author, January 22, 1999.

87. Sylvia Cuarón, September 11, 2003; Ralph and Sylvia Cuarón, January 22, 1999. Irene, Ralph's younger sister and the mother of the newborn initiate, felt pressured to comply with the wishes of the Church.

88. *The Mexican Question in the United States*, 1962, box 64–45, Healey Collection.

89. Healey and Isserman, *Dorothy Healey Remembers*, 125.

90. Healey and Isserman, *Dorothy Healey Remembers*, 126–27.

91. Horne, *Black Liberation/Red Scare*, 203.

92. Horne, *Black Liberation/Red Scare*, 129.

93. Sylvia Cuarón, July 17, 2002. Sylvia Cuarón FBI File, 100-HQ-400483. This file discusses another incident in 1955 in which Sylvia was charged by the Los Angeles County Communist Party "with an alleged act of white chauvinism arising from a wedding reception for an unknown individual. . . . It was indicated CUARON was involved in the planning of this reception and that certain Negro co-workers of [deleted text] were not invited to the reception." This action was not been intended as "a disciplinary measure but rather to assist her in achieving better understanding and leadership on the question."

94. Jeffrey Garcílazo, "The Brown Scare: McCarthyism, the Los Angeles Committee for Protection of the Foreign-Born, and Mexican-American Workers, 1950–1954," December 19, 1990, Los Angeles Committee for Protection of Foreign Born Collection, SCL.

95. Schrecker, *Age of McCarthyism*, 192.

96. *Fact Sheet on the McCarran Immigration Act*, undated, box 1, file 5, Los Angeles Committee for Protection of Foreign Born Collection, 1950s–1960s, SCL.

97. *Fact Sheet on the McCarran Immigration Act*.

98. Juan Ramón García, *Operation Wetback: The Mass Deportation of Mexican Undocumented Workers in 1954* (Westport, Conn.: Greenwood Press, 1980), 198. See also Acuña, *Occupied America*, 3rd ed., 259–60.

99. Mario T. García, *Mexican Americans: Leadership, Ideology, and Identity, 1930–1960* (New Haven, Conn.: Yale University Press, 1989), 98–100.

100. Vicki L. Ruiz, *Cannery Women, Cannery Lives: Mexican Women, Unionization, and the California Food Processing Industry, 1930–1950* (Albuquerque: University of New Mexico Press, 1987), 113–16.

101. *Civil Rights Congress Tells the Story*, 58–60.

102. Dorothy Healey, in discussion with author, January 22, 1999. With organizations such as ANMA under relentless investigation and harassment by federal and states authorities, radical and progressive activists inside and out of the Mexican American community undertook to devise an alternative strategy to assist the most vulnerable members among the working class and the immigrant communities. The irony, unfortunately, would be that the most vocal leaders and activists, regardless of political affiliation, often became the targets of harassment, arrest, and, in some cases, deportation.

103. Jeffrey M. Garcílazo, "McCarthyism, Mexican Americans, and the Los Angeles Committee for Protection of the Foreign-Born, 1950–1954," *Western Historical Quarterly* 32, no. 3 (2001): 273–95. According to Garcílazo, "Some of the charter member organizations were the CRC, the IPP, ANMA, and the First Unitarian Church. Among the labor unions active in the Committee were the International Union of Mine, Mill and Smelter Workers . . . , International Longshoremen's and Warehousemen's Union . . . , Steelworkers, local 1414, and the Furniture Workers local 576."

104. Garcílazo, "McCarthyism, Mexican Americans," 5. This assessment was also laid out in a report she authored in May 1951 titled "The Question of Mexican Nationals in the Southwest" and another titled "The Role of the United States Immigration and Naturalization Service in Relation to the Mexican People." See box 10, file 2, LACPFB Collection, SCL.

105. Ralph Cuarón, May 5, 1998; Garcílazo, "McCarthyism, Mexican Americans," 5.

106. See Healey and Isserman, *Dorothy Healey Remembers*, chap. 8.

107. *Decision*, published by the California Emergency Defense Committee and the Civil Rights Congress, undated, box 6, file 5, CRC Collection, SCL; "The Story of a Courageous Woman," undated, published pamphlet by the Rose Chernin Defense Committee, box 6, file 4, CRC Collection, SCL. Chernin was arrested in July 1951 by the FBI along with Dorothy Healey, William Schneiderman, Albert Jason Lima, Oleta O'Connor Yates, Carl Rude Lambert, Philip "Slim" Connelly, Al Richmond, Ernest Otto Fox, Henry Steinberg, Loretta Starvus Stack, Berna-

dette Doyle (later dropped from the case due to ill health), Frank Spector, Frank Carlson, and Ben Dobbs. Chernin remained in jail until December 1951.

108. *Associated Farmers of Orange County*, undated, box 2, file 24, LACPFB Collection, SCL.

109. *Associated Farmers of Orange County*.

110. See Rodolfo F. Acuña, *Corridors of Migration: The Odyssey of Mexican Laborers, 1600–1933* (Tucson: University of Arizona Press, 2007), 281–82. Two other associated organizations were the Orange County Defense Committee and the Orange County Publicity Committee.

111. *Associated Farmers of Orange County*.

112. Garcílazo, "McCarthyism, Mexican Americans," 5–6.

113. The Eastside branch was located at 3656 East Third Street. Ralph and Sylvia Cuarón recalled that Yañez had been a member of the Communist Party. Yañez testified before the U.S. House Committee on Un-American Activities in 1956 under the name of Josephine Yañez Van Leuven and was questioned about her involvement with the LACPFB. She refused to answer any questions about her work and political activities by citing her right to do so under the First and Fifth Amendments of the Constitution of the United States.

114. Ralph Cuarón, in discussion with author, January 29, 1999; Healey and Isserman, *Dorothy Healey Remembers*, 70.

115. See LACPFB Collection, SCL. By 1953, the LACPFB could boast an impressive array of support. For example, in April 1953 *The Torch* reported that "hundreds of organizations, of all shades of political opinion, have gone on record opposing the McCarran-Walter Act. . . . LABOR—C.I.O., A.F. of L., U.A.W., Amalgamated Clothing Workers, I.L.G.W.U., U.E., I.L.W.U., International Association of Machinists (AFL). Church—National Council of Churches of Christ, National Catholic Welfare Assn., National Lutheran Council, Union of American Hebrew Congregations, American Friends' Service Committee, National Council of Catholic Workmen, Protestant Council of the City of New York (Brooklyn Div.). VETERAN—Jewish War Veterans, American Veterans Committee, Polish Legion of American Veterans. NATIONALITY GROUPS: Anti-Defamation League of B'nai B'rith, American Jewish Committee, National Council of Jewish Women, Order of the Sons of Italy of America, American Jewish Congress, Czechoslovak National Council, Lithuanian American Council, Chinese American Citizens National Assn., Ukrainian American Congress, Hungarian American Club. EDUCATION AND PROFESSIONAL—American Bar Assn., American Civil Liberties Union, NAACP, YMCA, American Academy of Arts and Sciences. MISCELANEOUS[*sic*]—Americans for Democratic Action, N.Y. Post, N.Y. Times, American Labor Party, Liberal Party, Mutual Benefit Life Insurance Company, Society of Friends." See also *Report: Los Angeles Committee for Protection of Foreign Born*, undated, U.S. Congressional Hearings, House Un-American Activities Committee, 1955, 84th Cong. (1956), Appendix to Hearings, 8001–8005.

116. Sylvia worked for the Mund Boilers company, located on North Soto Street, from 1949 to 1952. The company produced large boilers used on merchant shipping. She ended her employment after giving birth to Mita on June 14, 1952.

117. "Lawyer to Explain Mexican Immigration," *Eastside Sun*, April 16, 1953.

118. *The Torch*, April 1953, box 1, file 39, LACPFB Collection, SCL. In April of that year, the LACPFB reported that of the eighty-three individuals it was defending, fifteen were "Mexican American." See also, Garcílazo, "McCarthyism, Mexican Americans," 1–18.

119. *The Torch*, March 1953, box 1, file 39, LACPFB Collection, SCL; "Foreign-Born Committee Sets Parley February 28," *Daily People's World*, February 2, 1954, U.S. Congressional Hearings, House Un-American Activities Committee, 1955, 84th Cong. (1956), Appendix to Hearings, 7863; "Foreign Born Rights Rally Set Feb 7," *Labor Herald*, January 23, 1953.

120. "Northwest Smith Act Defendants," April 4, 1953, U.S. Congressional Hearings, House Un-American Activities Committee, 1955, 84th Cong. (1956), Appendix to Hearings, exhibit no. 441, 7865.

121. *Associated Farmers of Orange County*, undated, box 2, file 24, LACPFB Collection, SCL.

122. *The Torch*, April 1954, box 1, file 39, LACPFB Collection, SCL. As one event announcement at the time proudly affirmed, "This is the annual all-day picnic and entertainment that is outstanding in Los Angeles."

123. Garcílazo, "McCarthyism, Mexican Americans," 6–7.

124. "The Meaning of Cinco de Mayo," *The Torch*, April 1954, box 1, file 39, LACPFB Collection, SCL.

125. "Dear Friend," July 15, 1954, LACPFB, U.S. Congressional Hearings, House Un-American Activities Committee, 1955, 84th Cong. (1956), Appendix to Hearings, exhibit no. 434, 7859; "Meaning of Cinco de Mayo."

126. Acuña, *Occupied America*, 3rd ed., 267.

127. Matt Garcia, *A World of Its Own: Race, Labor, and Citrus in the Making of Greater Los Angeles, 1900–1970* (Chapel Hill: University of North Carolina Press), 174–88. See Gutiérrez, *Walls and Mirrors*, 153. Consequently, by the early 1950s, the view of another group of Mexican Americans began to gain more attention. As Gutiérrez explains, "From their perspective the growing controversy over legal and illegal Mexican immigrants was diverting attention from the true source of Mexican Americans' depressed position—the persistence of discriminatory policies and practices that allowed the exploitation of Mexican Americans and other ethnic minorities in American society to continue." See also García, *Operation Wetback*, 28–31. García discusses the litany of groups and organizations that carried out an active campaign to stop the Bracero Program and to end the practice of importing agricultural workers from abroad. The rationale for their opposition to this policy ranged from the concern over exploitation to concerns that braceros lowered the working conditions and wages of domestic workers.

128. Mae M. Ngai, *Impossible Subjects: Illegal Aliens and the Making of Modern America* (Princeton, N.J.: Princeton University Press, 2004), 132, 149–52, 158–61.

129. *Torchlight*, "Operation Terror," July 1954, box 1, file 39, LACPFB Collection, SCL.

130. *Torchlight*, "Operation Terror." *Torchlight* reported that thousands of Mexican nationals were being held at the Elysian Park Recreation Center, a temporary holding facility during Operation Wetback. "To them the park was not a park. It was a prison—a concentration camp—a herding place for banishment."

131. García, *Operation Wetback*, 115.

132. García, *Operation Wetback*, chap. 4.

133. Ngai, *Impossible Subjects*, 149–52. The term "wetback" remains a derogatory and racial slur used to describe undocumented Mexican migrants as well as Mexican Americans. The term is sometimes used to cast disparaging remarks against all Latino groups residing in the United States—immigrant and citizen alike. See also Alfonso Gonzales, *Reform Without Justice: Latino Migrant Politics and the Homeland Security State* (Oxford: Oxford University Press, 2014), 1–15. Gonzales discusses the current anti-immigrant debates, the increasing criminalization of immigrants (Mexicans in particular) under the growth of the homeland security state, and the movements by immigrants to fight back and influence immigration reform. The struggle is rife with problems, however, as the underpinnings for such mass movement of people is rarely addressed. Meanwhile, the legitimation of "state violence against women and entire Latinos families" goes unabated.

134. García, *Operation Wetback*, 175–76, 201.

135. Enrique Buelna Echeverria, in discussion with author, August 8, 2003. Enrique Buelna Echeverria is the author's father. He immigrated to the United States in 1956 and purchased his first home in Los Angeles three years later. In 1963, he married my mother, Lilia Meza Otáñez, whose family lived in Tijuana, Mexico. They have lived in the same home for nearly fifty years, located in the city's southwest area. For more information regarding pressures placed on Mexico due to the massive deportation drive, see Ngai, *Impossible Subjects*, 156.

136. García, *Operation Wetback*, chap. 7, 216; Acuña, *Occupied America*, 3rd ed., 266–68.

137. Buelna Echeverria, August 8, 2003. Buelna and other officers routinely escorted these travelers to ensure their safe passage. Unfortunately, these deportees often became targets of would-be assailants hoping to rob them of their meager government ration. See also Kelly Lytle Hernandez, *Migra! A History of the U.S. Border Patrol* (Berkeley: University of California Press, 2010), 127–37.

138. Hernandez, *Migra!*, 157.

139. Hernandez, *Migra!*, 8–9.

140. Hernandez, *Migra!*, 45–54, 162–63, 224–25.

141. Patricia Morgan, *Shame of a Nation: A Documented Story of Police-State Terror Against Mexican-Americans in the U.S.A.* (Los Angeles: Los Angeles Committee for Protection of Foreign Born, 1954), 3–5.

142. Morgan, *Shame of a Nation*, 38.

143. *Resolution on Mexican Work*, submitted by the Emiliano Zapata Conference, Eastern Division, Los Angeles, CPUSA Collection, SCL.

144. Isabel González, "Resolution on Mexican Activity," *The Party Forum*, October 2, 1956, vol. 1, no. 5, CPUSA Collection, SCL.

145. *Resolution on Mexican Work*. "Both the National and local levels of Party organization have the responsibility to establish the channels so that an effective program of Mexican work can be developed and carried through. We must combat all Anglo-chauvinistic influence within our ranks which might deter the attainment of this objective. Therefore, to give proper consideration to the development of Mexican work, we should:

> 1. Plan an educational program which would include constant publica[tion] of discussion material on Mexican work.
> 2. Give great[e]r emphasis to the development of Mexican cadre.
> 3. Publish material for mass distribution in English and Spanish for use in Mexican concentration areas.
> 4. Document facts and do research so that facts and figures may be furnished to prove existing conditions, which are generally accepted and acknowledged in the community, but which are not available through official statistics (number of workers in food processing, garment, steel industries; income figures in these industries; etc.)
> 5. Re-establish the Mexican Commission on a sustained basis."

146. Healey and Isserman, *Dorothy Healey Remembers*, 153.

147. Sylvia Cuarón, in discussion with author, January 22, 1999. "There was a rift. Do you or don't you? Are you still [in the Party] or . . . ? So things were really never the same again. About that time, I don't recall any meetings anymore. Attending meetings as we used to in the very beginning. And doing the various activities like precinct walking, leaflet distribution and selling of the *People's World*. That seems to have come to a halt. . . . Then we became very involved with finishing raising our family."

148. Ralph Cuarón, January 22, 1999.

149. Healey and Isserman, *Dorothy Healey Remembers*, 164.

150. *Resolution on Mexican Work*; *District Draft Resolution*, submitted by the Mexican-American Comm., Los Angeles, box 22, file 33, CRC Collection, SCL; *Situation, Problems, and Possibilities in the Mexican-American Community*, submitted by the Mexican Caucus, undated, CPUSA Collection, SCL; *Report on Mexican-Americans*, Second Southern California District Convention, undated, CPUSA Collection, SCL; *The Mexican Question in the United States*, 1962, box 64–45, Healey Collection; *District Draft Resolution*, submitted by the Mexican-American Comm., 1966 Convention, Mexican-American file, Healey Collection; *Resolution: Mexican-American People*, 1968, Healey Collection.

151. Ralph Cuarón, U.S. Department of Justice, Federal Bureau of Investigation, FOIPA No. 0987822–000, May 3, 1957.

152. Ralph Cuarón, U.S. Department of Justice.

153. Located at 1251 South Saint Andrews Place, Los Angeles.

154. Ralph Cuarón, U.S. Department of Justice.

155. Ralph Cuarón, U.S. Department of Justice.

156. Lenin, *Critical Remarks on the National Question*, 99. For Cuarón, Lenin's work held more relevance now than ever before. "The socialist revolution," Lenin once stated, "is not a single act, it is not one battle on one front, but a whole epoch of acute class conflicts, a long series of battles on all fronts."

157. Sylvia Cuarón, January 22, 1999.

CHAPTER 5

1. John R. Chávez, *Eastside Landmark: A History of the East Los Angeles Community Union, 1968–1993* (Stanford, Calif.: Stanford University Press, 1998), 15–16. As Chávez explains: "Despite its relatively benign appearance, East LA in the sixties faced serious difficulties according to almost every socioeconomic indicator. . . . Because of the absence of densely populated, high-rise apartment buildings, East LA did not look as poor as it actually was, but close inspection revealed that in some neighborhoods deteriorating or dilapidated structures made up as much as 60 percent of the housing." See also Gilbert G. Gonzalez, "Factors Relating to Property Ownership of Chicanos in Lincoln Heights," *Aztlan* 2, no. 2 (Fall 1971): 107–30.

2. Jerry Gonzalez, "A Place in the Sun: Mexican Americans, Race, and the Suburbanization of Los Angeles, 1940–1980" (PhD diss., University of Southern California), 64–101.

3. *The Mexican American: A New Focus on Opportunity, Before the Inter-Agency Committee on Mexican American Affairs*, Testimony Presented at the Cabinet Committee Hearings on Mexican American Affairs, El Paso, Texas, October 26–28, 1967, v, SCL. President Lyndon B. Johnson established the agency on June 9, 1967. Vicente T. Ximenez, commissioner of the Equal Employment Opportunity Commission, chaired the committee. The members of the committee included Orville L. Freeman, secretary of agriculture; W. Willard Wirtz, secretary of labor; John W. Gardner, secretary of health, education, and welfare; Robert C. Weaver, secretary of housing and urban development; and Sargent Shriver, director of the Office of Economic Opportunity.

4. *Mexican American: A New Focus*, 167–69.

5. *Mexican American: A New Focus*. Monitors for the Cabinet Committee Hearings included a number of prominent Mexican Americans: Tom E. Robles, area director for the Equal Employment Opportunity Commission; Louis Tellez, national chair of the American GI Forum; Roberto Ornelas, national president of LULAC; Mario Vazquez, United Council; Alberto Piñon, president of the Community Service Organization; and Roy J. Elizondo, president of the Political Association of Spanish-Speaking Organizations.

6. Dana Cuff, *The Provisional City: Los Angeles Stories of Architecture and Urbanism* (Cambridge, Mass.: MIT Press, 2000), 47.

7. See Jorge Mariscal, "The Chicano Movement: Does Anyone Care About What Happened 45 Years Ago," foreword to *The Chicano Movement: Perspectives from the Twenty-First Century*, ed. Mario T. Garcia (New York: Routledge, 2014). Historian Jorge Mariscal writes a very thoughtful, yet critical, analysis of the Chicano Movement, Chicano studies, and the challenges posed by neoliberalism and globalization. In it, he posits that as elite research universities move further and further away from the California Master Plan, with their increasing reliance on outside funding, recruitment of foreign students, online education, and an emphasis on education as a commodity—as a "private good" rather than a "public responsibility"—these institutions find no reason to tolerate courses that challenge their power—and the status quo. As these institutions privilege elitism, and the upper class, over the poor and working class, our history is marginalized, decontextualized and placed out of reach to our students. Hence, when theory is privileged above hands-on, direct engagement with communities, disconnect ensues. "Education for the market," writes Mariscal, "does not permit education that empowers the working class." The Movimiento of over forty years ago demanded that universities serve their communities and that they establish "a pedagogy that empowers our youth." Ralph Cuarón, the inveterate organic intellectual, was at the forefront of these very challenges and strove to pursue an educational framework that elevated the working class as a means of breaking down that very elitism.

8. Thomas P. Carter, *Mexican Americans in School: A History of Educational Neglect* (New York: College Entrance Examination Board, 1970), 204.

9. Carter, *Mexican Americans in School*, 147.

10. F. Arturo Rosales, *Chicano! The History of the Mexican American Civil Rights Movement* (Houston: Arte Público Press, University of Houston, 1996), 174–95.

11. Carlos Muñoz, *Youth, Identity, Power: The Chicano Movement* (London: Verso, 1989), 64.

12. Mike Davis, *City of Quartz: Excavating the Future in Los Angeles* (New York: Vintage Books, 1990), 3–11.

13. Robert V. Hine, *California Utopian Colonies* (San Marino, Calif.: Huntington Library, 1953), 5.

14. E. J. Dionne Jr., *Why Americans Hate Politics* (New York: Simon & Schuster, 1991), 329–30. See David Montejano, *Quixote's Soldiers: A Local History of the Chicano Movement, 1966–1981* (Austin: University of Texas Press, 2010). Montejano examines the Chicano Movement in San Antonio, Texas, and draws many parallels to the struggles of similar Chicano communities across the country. Militancy, youth activism, and new identities helped fuel a movement for change that helped alter and usher in a new political order in this southwestern city.

15. Sylvia Cuarón, in discussion with author, June 7, 2002.

16. County of Los Angeles v. Cuaron and Carreon, 602.9 Municipal Court of East Los Angeles Judicial District, County of Los Angeles (1969). Althea Alexander,

supervisor of Plaza Community Center, also explained Ralph's long relationship with the organization. "Mr. Cuaron has been very responsive and responsible in relationship to almost anything we had asked him to do. He has, for instance, been a volunteer a number of occasions with groups of young people which is my specific area of responsibility, that is the group work program, and he has been responsible, and we have asked for people to relate to other community people of various issues and generally we have found him . . . although at times we had basic disagreements . . . we have found him most helpful" (360).

17. Modernity, as this relates to housing, invariably meant that technology would bring efficiency and scientific rationality to human habitation. As Dana Cuff explains, "Technology would inevitably breed cooperative living, 'good mass produced meals, in great apartment complexes where all the services were done for us'" (Cuff, *Provisional City*, 164).

18. Constantinos A. Doxiadis, *Architecture in Transition* (New York: Oxford University Press, 1963), 96.

19. Doxiadis, *Architecture in Transition*, 96.

20. Doxiadis, *Architecture in Transition*, 96–99.

21. Doxiadis, *Architecture in Transition*, 96–99.

22. Sylvia Cuarón, June 7, 2002.

23. Sylvia Cuarón, June 7, 2002.

24. *Mexican-American Study Project, Progress Report* (Division of Research, Graduate School of Business Administration, University of California, Los Angeles, June 1966), Carey McWilliams Papers, Special Collections, University Research Library, UCLA. Under the section titled "Broken Families on the East and South Sides," the report identified this issue as one that had been largely ignored within the Mexican American community. Though the figures for "broken families," that is, those families "represented by those with a female head of household," were significantly less for Chicanos (17.2 percent) than for African Americans (25.5 percent) in 1965, this area deserved "attention in light of the conventional notion of the strength of the family in the Mexican-American group."

25. Harry Gamboa, in discussion with author, June 10, 2002.

26. Steve Valencia and Mita Cuarón, in discussion with author, January 6, 2018.

27. Steve Valencia and Mita Cuarón, January 6, 2018.

28. Harry Gamboa, June 10, 2002.

29. Harry Gamboa, June 10, 2002.

30. Harry Gamboa, June 10, 2002.

31. Thomas Byrne Edsall and Mary D. Edsall, *Chain Reaction: The Impact of Race, Rights, and Taxes on American Politics* (New York: W. W. Norton, 1992), 48.

32. See Gonzalez, "A Place in the Sun," 64–101.

33. George Lipsitz, *The Possessive Investment in Whiteness: How White People Profit from Identity Politics* (Philadelphia, Penn.: Temple University Press, 2006) vii–xx, 24–47.

34. Robert Bauman, *Race and the War on Poverty: From Watts to East L.A.* (Norman: University of Oklahoma Press, 2014), 5–8. See also Bauman, "The Neighborhood

Adult Participation Project: Black-Brown Strife in the War on Poverty in Los Angeles," in *The Struggle in Black and Brown: African American and Mexican American Relations During the Civil Rights Era*, ed. Brian D. Behnken (Lincoln: University of Nebraska Press, 2012), 104–24.

35. *Mexican-American Study Project*, 7.

36. *Mexican-American Study Project*, 7.

37. Muñoz, *Youth, Identity, Power*, 51.

38. Ernesto B. Vigil, *The Crusade for Justice: Chicano Militancy and the Government's War on Dissent* (Madison: University of Wisconsin Press, 1999), 19–30. See also Rosales, *Chicano!*, 179–84.

39. Vigil, *Crusade for Justice*, 57.

40. Rosales, *Chicano!*, 179–81, 228. See also Rudy V. Busto, *King Tiger: The Religious Vision of Reies López Tijerina* (Albuquerque: University of New Mexico Press, 2005), 68, 211n49.

41. Muñoz, *Youth, Identity, Power*, 56–57.

42. County of Los Angeles v. Cuaron and Carreon, 502. Vincent Villagran, a specialist in the Office of Urban Affairs and Community Relations, recalled Cuarón initiating "an evening adult class for community persons interested in housing and some of the problems existing."

43. Several photographs belonging to the family show Ralph, Mita, John, and a number of unidentified youth busily working on the scale model. The model was constructed using small, slender pieces of wood that Ralph produced using the equipment from his various carpentry jobs.

44. Harry Gamboa, June 10, 2002.

45. "A Poor Housing Protest from East Los Angeles," *Los Angeles Herald-Examiner*. Image courtesy of Cuarón family. John Ortiz has his back in the photo and the young woman kneeling before the coffin is unidentified.

46. Harry Gamboa, June 10, 2002.

47. Steve Valencia, in discussion with author, January 6, 2018.

48. Jack B. Tenney, *Red Fascism: Boring from Within . . . By the Subversive Forces of Communism* (Los Angeles: Federal Printing Company, 1947), 233. Raul Morin and Frances Flores to Councilman Edward R. Roybal, March 3, 1960, Edward Ross Roybal Papers, Department of Special Collections, Young Research Library, University of California, Los Angeles. In 1960, Lym held the title of acting secretary within the Mexican American Citizens Committee of Los Angeles.

49. Naomi H. Quiñones, "Flores, Francisca (1913–1996)," in *Latinas in the United States: A Historical Encyclopedia*, ed. Vicki L. Ruiz and Virginia Sanchez Korrol (Bloomington: Indiana University Press, 2006), 264–65.

50. Anne Shore and Frances Lym to "Dear Friends," August 12, 1948, Civil Rights Congress Collection, SCL.

51. Harry Gamboa, June 10, 2002.

52. Steve Valencia, January 6, 2018.

53.   *Carta Editorial,* August 1, 1964, vol. 2, no. 5, and *Carta Editorial,* March 22, 1966, vol. 3, no. 11, box 54, file 8, Ernesto Galarza Papers, Special Collections and University Archives, Stanford University. For a more complete biographical description of Francisca Flores, see Quiñones, "Flores, Francisca (1913–1996)," 264–65.

54.   Vicki L. Ruiz, *From Out of the Shadows: Mexican Women in Twentieth-Century America* (New York: Oxford University Press, 1998), xiii–xvii. See also Dionne E. Espinoza, "Pedagogies of Nationalism and Gender: Cultural Resistance in Selected Representational Practices of Chicana/o Movement Activists, 1967–1972" (PhD diss., Cornell University, 1996).

55.   Dolores Delgado Bernal, "Grassroots Leadership Reconceptualized: Chicana Oral Histories and the 1968 East Los Angeles School Blowouts," *Frontiers: A Journal of Women Studies* 19, no. 2 (1998): 113–42.

56.   Alma M. Garcia, ed., *Chicana Feminist Thought: The Basic Historical Writings* (New York: Rutledge, 1997), 5.

57.   Bernal, "Grassroots Leadership Reconceptualized." In their interviews with Bernal, Rachel Ochoa Cervera and Rosalinda Méndez González relay how important these conferences were to their development as leaders and to making them aware of the broader issues affecting Mexican Americans.

58.   Gerald Paul Rosen, "Political Ideology and the Chicano Movement: A Study of the Political Ideology of Activists in the Chicano Movement" (PhD diss., University of California, Los Angeles, 1972); Marguerite V. Marin, *Social Protest in an Urban Barrio: A Study of the Chicano Movement, 1966–1974* (Lanham, Md.: University Press of America, 1991), 71–84. See also Rosales, *Chicano!,* 186.

59.   Mario T. García and Sal Castro, *Blowout: Sal Castro and the Chicano Struggle for Educational Justice* (Greensboro: University of North Carolina Press, 2011), 88.

60.   García and Castro, *Blowout,* 94, 110–128.

61.   García and Castro, *Blowout,* 138–40. See also 307–24.

62.   Ernesto Chávez, *"¡Mi Raza Primero!" Nationalism, Identity, and Insurgency in the Chicano Movement in Los Angeles, 1966–1978* (Berkeley: University of California Press, 2002), 44–45. Here, Chávez describes how the Piranya Coffee House had also become a place "where prominent civil rights leaders expressed their views to an ever-increasing number of Chicano youth. Among those making appearances were César Chávez, Reies López Tijerina of New Mexico's Alianza Federal de Mercedes, and African-American leaders Hubert "Rap" Brown and Stokely Carmichael of the Student Non-Violent Coordinating Committee and Ron Karenga of United Slaves (US)." The coffee house also hosted meetings to encourage students to go to college, to meet college and university recruiters, and to be informed of issues presented by local community groups.

63.   Muñoz, *Youth, Identity, Power,* 59.

64.   Rosen, "Political Ideology and the Chicano Movement," 72–74.

65.   Marin, *Social Protest in an Urban Barrio,* 76–77.

66.   Bernal, "Grassroots Leadership Reconceptualized," 8.

67. Carlos Montes, in discussion with author, July 16, 2002. Montes could not recall in any detail who if anyone had initiated the walkouts. However, prior to the school actions, the idea of the walkout as a protest strategy "was slowly spread by word of mouth, fliers, and newspapers."

68. Rosales, *Chicano!*, xvii–xviii.

69. County of Los Angeles v. Cuaron and Carreon, 587. Jack Jones, "Federal Policy Hit: Mexican-Americans Want Own Kind of New Homes," *Los Angeles Times*, April 24, 1968, sec A, 6.

70. County of Los Angeles v. Cuaron and Carreon, 522. In response to a question from defense attorney F. Fernandez Solis as to whether Kenneth Ortiz had accompanied Ralph Cuarón to Washington D.C., Ortiz responded, "Yes, January 1968, I went as a youth representative to Washington, D.C. representing the youth council. This is primarily of a housing organization." Asked if he had had the opportunity to discuss educational problems with officials in Washington, Ortiz responded in the affirmative. "Yes, I attended several meetings in Washington, D.C. at the Department of Health, Education and Welfare, and we spoke to several officials in Washington, D.C. on problems specifically of Garfield, because that was the school that I went to, and I actually didn't know about the others."

71. County of Los Angeles v. Cuaron and Carreon, 356.

72. *Mexican American: A New Focus.* The hearing participants represented various states, including Illinois, Texas, California, New Mexico, Arizona, New York, and Colorado. Among the leaders were Dionicio Morales, executive director, Mexican American Opportunity Foundation; Hector Abeytia, state director, Manpower Opportunities Project; Dr. Miguel Montes, California State Board of Education; Priscilla S. Mares, education director, Latin American Education Foundation; Augustine A. Flores, former national chair, American GI Forum; and Judge Alfred J. Hernández, immediate past president of LULAC.

73. *Mexican American: A New Focus*, 147, 169.

74. *Mexican American: A New Focus*, 145–58.

75. County of Los Angeles v. Cuaron and Carreon, 513–14.

76. County of Los Angeles v. Cuaron and Carreon, 577–78.

77. Carter, *Mexican Americans in School*, 66.

78. County of Los Angeles v. Cuaron and Carreon, 499–500.

79. County of Los Angeles v. Cuaron and Carreon, 285–87.

80. Mita Cuarón, in discussion with author, April 13, 2002.

81. County of Los Angeles v. Cuaron and Carreon, 366–67.

82. Rosales, *Chicano!*, 184–90; Ruiz, *From Out of the Shadows*, 102–4.

83. Rosales, *Chicano!*, 185.

84. County of Los Angeles v. Cuaron and Carreon, 454. In 1969, Eva Esparza was a student at California State University, Los Angeles.

85. The United Presbyterian Church served seven Head Start projects in the East Los Angeles area. Their headquarters was located at 1120 South McDowell Avenue.

86. County of Los Angeles v. Cuaron and Carreon, 290–92.

87. County of Los Angeles v. Cuaron and Carreon, 506.

88. County of Los Angeles v. Cuaron and Carreon, 457.

89. County of Los Angeles v. Cuaron and Carreon, 623.

90. Mita Cuarón, in discussion with author, January 6, 2018. See also García and Castro, *Blowout*, 177–78.

91. Mita Cuarón, January 6, 2018.

92. County of Los Angeles v. Cuaron and Carreon, 459.

93. County of Los Angeles v. Cuaron and Carreon, 589.

94. County of Los Angeles v. Cuaron and Carreon, 374.

95. County of Los Angeles v. Cuaron and Carreon, 548–75.

96. County of Los Angeles v. Cuaron and Carreon, 587–94.

97. Sylvia Cuarón, in discussion with author, June 12, 2002.

98. Jones, "Federal Policy Hit," A6.

99. County of Los Angeles v. Cuaron and Carreon, 281.

100. County of Los Angeles v. Cuaron and Carreon, 730–47.

101. County of Los Angeles v. Cuaron and Carreon, 745–46. Deputy district attorney Reuben Ortega continued his commentary on the issue of law enforcement during his closing argument.

102. County of Los Angeles v. Cuaron and Carreon, 527, 744–45.

103. Mita Cuarón, in discussion with author, June 22, 2002.

104. County of Los Angeles v. Cuaron and Carreon, 283. During his opening statements, defense attorney F. Fernandez Solis made the following observations:

> Because of the disruptive activity throughout the high schools of this area at that particular time and the concern of administrators such as [Reginald] Murphy, the Board of Education, and other people who are close to the picture about putting out the fire before sitting down and discussing this problem, they felt that the presence of Mr. Cuaron was not a presence they could tolerate at the moment.

105. Bernal, "Grassroots Leadership Reconceptualized," 6.

106. Chávez, *Mi Raza Primero!*, 42–48.

107. Muñoz, *Youth, Identity, Power*, 68; Rosales, *Chicano!*, 192–94.

108. Jack Jones, "Federal Policy Hit," A6.

109. Bauman, *Race and the War on Poverty*, 90–109.

110. Chávez, *Eastside Landmark*, 26–28.

111. Sylvia Cuarón, June 12, 2002. Ralph and Sylvia often used the word "student" to describe a mentor/mentee relationship they developed with a number of young people who came into their lives. The relationship and trust between Ralph and Torres was close. On one occasion, Torres asked the Cuaróns to temporarily house Walter Reuther's nephew and his wife. According to Sylvia, "Torres came to us one day. . . . Would we please keep an eye on Eric Reuther in East Los Ange-

les . . . Eric Reuther and his wife Barbara. They're new to the community; they're new to activities in the barrio. Well, we took them in and there was a vacant apartment and they stayed there for several months, rent-free and we fed them as well."

112. Jones, "Federal Policy Hit," A6.

113. Sylvia Cuarón, 12 June 2002.

114. Jones, "Federal Policy Hit," A6.

115. Chávez, *Eastside Landmark*, 62.

116. Jones, "Federal Policy Hit," A6.

117. Jones, "Federal Policy Hit," A6. According to the *Los Angeles Times*, "He [Ralph Cuarón] called on legislators and agencies and made contact with groups from other parts of the country who feel they, too, cannot convince officialdom that mortar and bricks are not enough."

118. Chávez, *Eastside Landmark*, 62.

119. Chávez, *Eastside Landmark*, 61.

120. Steve Valencia, January 6, 2018.

121. Albert Valencia, in discussion with author, February 23, 2018.

122. Muñoz, *Youth, Identity, Power*, 47.

123. Sylvia Cuarón, June 12, 2002.

124. Sylvia Cuarón, June 12, 2002.

125. Sylvia Cuarón, June 12, 2002.

126. "East L.A.'s First Community-Built Apartments Open," *Los Angeles Times*, July 17, 1971.

127. Abraham Hoffman, "Jewish Student Militancy in the Great Depression: The Roosevelt High School Blowouts of 1931," *Los Angeles Westerners Corral*, no. 121 (March 1976): 7.

128. Hoffman, "Jewish Student Militancy." As Hoffman explains: "Unlike the Chicanos of the late 1960s, the Jewish militants failed to garner much community support. Their protests for the most part were brushed aside, and later events—the creation of the House Un-American Activities Committee, the Stalinist purges of the mid-1930s, and the New Deal offered by the Roosevelt Administration—suggested reform rather than revolution as the cure for the ills of the Depression. Pressures from the Chicano community after the blowouts of 1968, on the other hand, have succeeded in moving the Los Angeles Board of Education, however slowly, towards an understanding of the needs of minority students."

129. David Forgacs, *A Gramsci Reader: Selected Writings, 1916–1935* (London: Lawrence & Wishart, 1988), 313; Lynne Lawner, *Antonio Gramsci: Letters from Prison* (New York: Harper & Row, 1973).

130. Jacqueline Leavitt, *Defining Cultural Differences in Space: Public Housing as a Microcosm* (College Park, Md.: University of Maryland, Urban Studies and Planning Program, 1994), 13.

131. Davis, *City of Quartz*, 223–24. See also Leavitt, *Defining Cultural Differences in Space*, 42–44.

CONCLUSION

1. California Legislature, *Report of Joint Fact-Finding Committee on Un-American Activities* (Sacramento: The Senate, 1947), 46.
2. California Legislature, *Report of Joint Fact-Finding Committee*, 45–46.
3. California Legislature, *Report of Joint Fact-Finding Committee*, 46–47.
4. California Legislature, *Report of Joint Fact-Finding Committee*, 45.
5. Rosales, *Chicano!*, 194.
6. Cynthia H. Cho and Anna Gorman, "The Immigrant Debate," *Los Angeles Times*, March 28, 2006, A1.
7. "The Producer: Moctesuma Esparza—Hollywood Producer and Owner of a Budding Chain of Theaters—Is Still a Crusading Activist," *Monterey County Weekly*, April 6, 2006, http://www.montereycountyweekly.com/news/local_news /moctesuma-esparza-hollywood-producer-and-owner-of-a-budding-chain/article _10b43a06-6f4d-55ac-90ab-90d2cbdd8d07.html.
8. Arizona State Senate Bill 1070 (Support Our Law Enforcement and Safe Neighborhoods Act) passed in 2010.
9. Susan Domagalski Fleming, "A Teacher Put to the Test: Curtis Acosta '94 and Ethnic Studies in Arizona," *The Scene*, Willamette University (2011); Jing Fong, "When This Teacher's Ethnic Studies Classes Were Banned, His Students Took the District to Court—and Won," posted to *Yes! Magazine*, April 25, 2014, http://www .yesmagazine.org/issues/education-uprising/interview-with-curtis-acosta; Roque Planas, "Arizona's Mexican-American Studies Ban Questioned by Appeals Judges," posted to *Huffington Post*, January 1, 2015 (10:16pm EST), http://www.huffington post.com/2015/07/07/arizona-mexican-american-studies_n_7748102.html; Naureen Khan, "Five Years After SB 1070, Arizona Immigrants Defy Climate of Intimidation," *Al Jazeera America*, March 23, 2015, http://america.aljazeera.com/articles /2015/3/23/five-years-after-sb-1070-arizona-immigrants-defy-law.html; Maria Ines Taracena, "9th Circuit Upholds Most of Anti Mexican-American Studies Law But Discrimination Issue Is Going to Trial," *Tucson Weekly*, posted July 7, 2015 (3:34 pm), http://www.tucsonweekly.com/TheRange/archives/2015/07/07/9th -circuit-upholds-most-of-anti-mexican-american-studies-law-but-discrimination -issues-are-going-to-trial; "U.S. Judge Dismisses Challenge of Arizona's SB 1070 Immigration Law," *Los Angeles Times*, September 6, 2015, http://www.latimes.com /nation/immigration/la-na-nn-arizona-immigration-law-20150905-story.html.
10. Linda Chavez, "Focus on U.S. history, Not Ethnic Studies," *Dallas Morning News*, May 14, 2010, http://www.dallasnews.com/opinion/latest-columns/20100514-Linda -Chavez-Focus-on-U-6265.ece.
11. Stephanie Siek, "The Dismantling of Mexican-American Studies in Tucson," CNN, January 22, 2012, http://inamerica.blogs.cnn.com/2012/01/22/how-tucson-schools -changed-after-mexican-american-studies-ban/.
12. California Legislature, *Fourth Report*, 23. "Behind a propaganda barrage of progress, reform and liberal slogans, the Communists steadily pursue a formal, dogmatic,

organized program of infiltration into, and creation of, mass organizations, because they are studious, fanatical and single-minded in their service to Soviet foreign policy and the preparation for revolution in the country where they live."

13.   Howard Zinn, *You Can't Be Neutral on a Moving Train: A Personal History of Our Times* (Boston: Beacon Press, 1994), 4.

EPILOGUE

1.   Kingston Homes Inc. was a subsidiary of Key West Mobile Homes Inc.

2.   Ralph Cuarón, U.S. Department of Justice, Federal Bureau of Investigation, FOIPA No. 0987822–000, June 26, 1971. "On February 3, 1971, a regular meeting of the SBRCCP [San Bernardino-Riverside County Communist Party] was held with CUARON in attendance. CUARON was introduced as a commander, and he advised that he had been in the CPUSA before but had dropped out. He was described as the chairman of a new club being formed at Riverside, California. Also, CUARON advised that he was continuing Marxist classes at the San Jacinto Mountains. . . . CUARON urged the cooperation of the SBRCCP to help build a school at this ranch."

3.   Ralph Cuarón, U.S. Department of Justice.

4.   Steve Valencia, in discussion with author, January 6, 2018.

5.   Carol Weissert, "Carpenter Union Families Picket in this Strike," *Daily Enterprise*, October 27, 1971, B7–8. Ralph Cuarón, U.S. Department of Justice.

6.   Weissert, "Carpenter Union Families."

7.   Weissert, "Carpenter Union Families."

8.   Weissert, "Carpenter Union Families."

9.   Sylvia Cuarón, in discussion with author, March 27, 2000.

10.   Jim Smith, in discussion with author, July 24, 2002. See also Ralph Cuarón, U.S. Department of Justice.

11.   Smith, July 24, 2002.

12.   Edna Bonacich, "Working with the Labor Movement: A Personal Journey in Organic Public Sociology," *The American Sociologist* 36 (Fall/Winter 2005): 107.

13.   American Federation of State, County and Municipal Employees, Service Local 3246, "Certificate of Appreciation," original in possession of Sylvia Cuarón.

14.   Mita Cuarón, "In Memory: Ralph Cuarón, 1923–2002," eulogy of Ralph Cuarón, distributed to those present at his wake, author's copy.

INDEX

ABOUT THE AUTHOR

Enrique M. Buelna is a professor in the History Department at Cabrillo College in Santa Cruz, California. His research interests include working-class history, civil rights, social movements, immigration, race, class, and oral history.